✠

THE SAINT AND THE COUNT

THE SAINT AND THE COUNT

✠

A Case Study for Reading Like a Historian

LEAH SHOPKOW

UNIVERSITY OF TORONTO PRESS

Toronto Buffalo London

© University of Toronto Press 2021
Toronto Buffalo London
utorontopress.com
Printed in Canada

ISBN 978-1-4875-0843-2 (cl.)   ISBN 978-1-4875-3823-1 (EPUB)
ISBN 978-1-4875-2586-6 (pbk.)   ISBN 978-1-4875-3822-4 (PDF)

Library and Archives Canada Cataloguing in Publication

Title: The saint and the count / Leah Shopkow.
Names: Shopkow, Leah, author.
Description: Includes bibliographical references and index.
Identifiers: Canadiana (print) 20200411527 | Canadiana (ebook) 20200411683 |
    ISBN 9781487525866 (softcover) | ISBN 9781487508432 (hardcover) |
    ISBN 9781487538231 (EPUB) | ISBN 9781487538224 (PDF)
Subjects: LCSH: France – History – Capetians, 987–1328 – Biography – Sources. |
    LCSH: France – History – Capetians, 987–1328 – Historiography. | LCSH: France –
    History – Capetians, 987–1328 – Biography. | LCSH: France – History – Capetians,
    987–1328. | LCSH: Christian hagiography. | LCSH: Historiography. | LCSH: Vitalis,
    of Savigny, Saint, –1122. | LCSH: Etienne, de Fougères, Bishop of Rennes, –1178.
Classification: LCC DC82.A2 S56 2021 | DDC 944/.021092–dc23

We welcome comments and suggestions regarding any aspect of our publications – please feel free to contact us at news@utorontopress.com or visit us at utorontopress.com.

Every effort has been made to contact copyright holders; in the event of an error or omission, please notify the publisher.

University of Toronto Press acknowledges the financial assistance to its publishing program of the Canada Council for the Arts and the Ontario Arts Council, an agency of the Government of Ontario.

 Canada Council **Conseil des Arts**
for the Arts **du Canada**

 **ONTARIO ARTS COUNCIL**
CONSEIL DES ARTS DE L'ONTARIO
an Ontario government agency
un organisme du gouvernement de l'Ontario

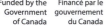 Funded by the   Financé par le
Government   gouvernement
of Canada   du Canada

Canada

CONTENTS

✠

PREFACE

✠

This book is intended to be a **"worked example"** of how an historian analyzes a primary source text. In the sciences, teachers and students are familiar with the concept of the worked example, where a teacher goes through a problem in front of the students, asking the questions that he or she would ask at each juncture and doing the steps. The worked example is analogous to the "think aloud" practiced by cognitive psychologists, where a person is given something to work on, perhaps a text to read, and is asked to say aloud what he or she is thinking while doing so. Sam Wineburg, to whom those of us interested in teaching and learning in history owe so much, has used this technique to great effect. The website whose construction he directed with the late Roy Rosenzweig, "Historical Thinking Matters" (http://historicalthinkingmatters.org/), offers examples of professional historians doing just that, and it also offers case studies of topics from American history.

There is great value in these kinds of shorter exercises, but there is also value, I believe (or else I wouldn't be writing this book!), in a longer and more sustained examination of how an historian approaches a text, because it addresses the fundamental challenges posed to novices by historical work in general and primary sources in particular. First, to the novice, the surface of primary sources is often "slippery." Unless there is something very odd in a text, primary sources may not offer obvious places to dig in. Students often take them to be illustrations of a past we already know and understand rather than clues to a past that historians are always constructing, using these sources as constituent elements. Second, primary sources may use unfamiliar vocabulary, may use familiar words to mean quite unfamiliar things, or may talk about familiar things in unfamiliar ways. Primary sources are like new neighbors: It can take us some time to get beyond the surface pleasantries and disagreements, commonalities and differences, to explore who those people really are. Finally, we bring ourselves to the past. As Thomas Aquinas puts it, that which is known is known according to the capacity of the knower. Our knowing is shaped in the present, so to get a better understanding of the past, we have to change our capacity as knowers, which is difficult. We have to become aware of our **positionality** (our view of the world as it has been shaped by our own **historical context**, our individual experiences, and our personalities), and we have to become aware of the positionalities of the texts we are reading. This is a slow process, but one well worth doing, and it has many applications beyond history.

This is a different sort of book than perhaps you have encountered before, a hybrid between a scholarly monograph (a single-subject scholarly book aimed primarily at other scholars) and a methods book. I learned new things I wanted to share as I was writing it, and I've observed normal scholarly conventions like citation. But I have also thought about the intellectual moves I was making and have tried to make them as visible as possible, since I know through my work in teaching and learning in history that intellectual moves are often invisible. I have always liked the analogy of figure skating to explain the problem. The name of the sport comes from the patterns that skaters left on the ice, and originally judges based a large part of their score on these patterns, not on how the skater looked while making them. The technique that produced clean figures, however, was often not pretty to look at.[1] A scholarly book to a reader not attuned to scholarly methods is like patterns on the ice: The patterns are obvious, but how they came to be is not. Of course, scholarly books do contain clues to their genesis. We leave footnotes at the bottom of the page (or worse, WORSE!, endnotes at the back of a book where they can be ignored) that show what moves we've made. Yet even so, this can be very hard for novices to grasp, as Laura Westhoff has shown in her illuminating article on historiographic mapping with students.[2] Novice readers of history assume that all historians are doing is reporting factual information, when we are actually arguing, analyzing, constructing, and, very importantly, drawing on the work of other scholars. For that reason, I've brought the names of many of the scholars I've consulted into the body of the text (as I've just done here), as well as naming them in the notes, to make it clearer where I'm having conversations with others or drawing on their work. However, there is additional information in the notes that you'll miss if you skip over them. Reading a scholarly work can be like listening on two different levels to a conversation: hearing what is said on the surface, while scanning for what is below the surface as well.

In addition, I have tried to write in as clear and engaging a manner as someone trained in academese can manage. I am certain that any idea can be expressed in jargon-free language. Sometimes **terms of art** (vocabulary specific to a discipline

---

1 Ellyn Kestnbaum, *Culture on Ice: Figure Skating & Cultural Meaning* (Middletown, CT: Wesleyan University Press, 2003), 60, 81f.

2 Laura M. Westhoff, "Historiographic Mapping: Toward a Signature Pedagogy for the Methods Course," *Journal of American History* 98, no. 4 (March 2012): 1114–26.

and used in precise ways) are very helpful, but the first time I use them, I offer a definition (again as I have done here). Because many terms will not be familiar to novice readers, I have also provided a glossary. Words in the glossary appear in boldface in the text the first time they appear in a chapter, often with an explanation at first use in the book. Within the glossary definitions, dependent words are also set in boldface. I hope any academic readers will not be put off, but I am writing for an audience that will include some novices.

I had a tremendous amount of fun writing this book. I hope you, the reader, will have at least some fun reading it.

Although the stereotype of historians is that we work alone in dusty archives (and many of us do, at least some of the time), any book is a community effort. I would like first to thank Natalie Fingerhut, my editor at the University of Toronto Press, who had faith in this somewhat unusual approach and whose suggestions have improved the book. The readers for the press also had invaluable suggestions, even when they didn't like what they were reading, and that is the very best kind of friend an author can have. Martin Boyne, who edited the copy, rode herd on my wicked ways with commas, gently improved the prose without cramping my style, and generally caught errors and omissions. Any reader who uses the glossary owes a debt of thanks (as do I) to my younger daughter, Linnea, who read the manuscript to make sure that even someone mostly interested in plant biology would find it comprehensible. My wonderful older daughter Maya offered boundless encouragement. They, along with Dirk, Sara, and Cerisa, all listened to me drone on about medieval people and events as though they lived and happened yesterday, mostly with interest. And finally, to the SoTL gang (you know who you are and special thanks Lendol!), it's great to have a place where everybody knows your name.

ABBREVIATIONS

✠

AASS	*Acta Sanctorum quotquot toto orbe coluntur, vel a Catholicis Scriptoribus celebrantur*, 68 vols. (1643–1940).
Bernard	Geoffrey Grossus, *The Life of Blessed Bernard of Tiron*, trans. Ruth Harwood Cline (Washington, DC: Catholic University of America Press, 2005).
De s. Guilielmo	*De s. Guilielmo Firmato, Moritonii in Normannia*. In *AASS III Aprilis*, 334–41. [*The Life of St. Firmat*]
GC	*Gallia christiana, in provincias ecclesiasticas distribute*, 16 vols., 2nd ed. (Paris: V. Palme, 1739–1880).
LM	Etienne de Fougères (Stephen of Fougères), *Le livre des manières*, ed. R. Anthony Lodge (Geneva: Droz, 1979).
ODNB	*Oxford Dictionary of National Biography*, online edition (Oxford; New York: Oxford University Press, 2004–).
Orderic	Orderic Vitalis, *The Ecclesiastical History of Orderic Vitalis*, 6 vols., ed. and trans. Marjorie Chibnall (Oxford: Clarendon, 1969–80).
Pigeon (1)	Émile-Aubert Pigeon, "Vie de Saint Firmat, patron de Mortain," *Mémoirs de la Société Académique du Cotentin* 13 (1897): 57–80.
Pigeon (2)	Émile-Aubert Pigeon, "Vie de Saint Firmat, patron de Mortain (suite)," *Mémoirs de la Société Académique du Cotentin* 14 (1898): 32–59.
PL	*Patrologia cursus completus, Series Latina*, 221 vols. in 222, ed. J.-P. Migne (Paris, 1844–1904).
RT	Robert of Torigni, *Le chronique de Robert de Torigni, abbé de Mont Saint-Michel*, 2 vols., ed. Léopold Delisle (Rouen: A. Le Brument, 1872–3).
Sauvage	E.P. Sauvage, ed., *Vitae BB. Vitalis et Gaufridi primi et secundi abbatum Saviniacensium in Normannia*, in *Analecta Bollandiana* 1 (1882): 354–410. [*The Life of St. Vitalis*]

Venarde   Bruce L. Venarde, *Robert of Arbrissel: A Medieval Religious Life* (Washington, DC: Catholic University of America Press, 2003).

Vital   Jaap van Moolenbroek, *Vital l'ermite, prédicateur itinérant, fondateur de l'abbaye normande de Savigny*, trans. Anne-Marie Nambot (Assen/Maastricht, Netherlands: Van Gorcum, 1990).

MAPS AND FIGURES

✠

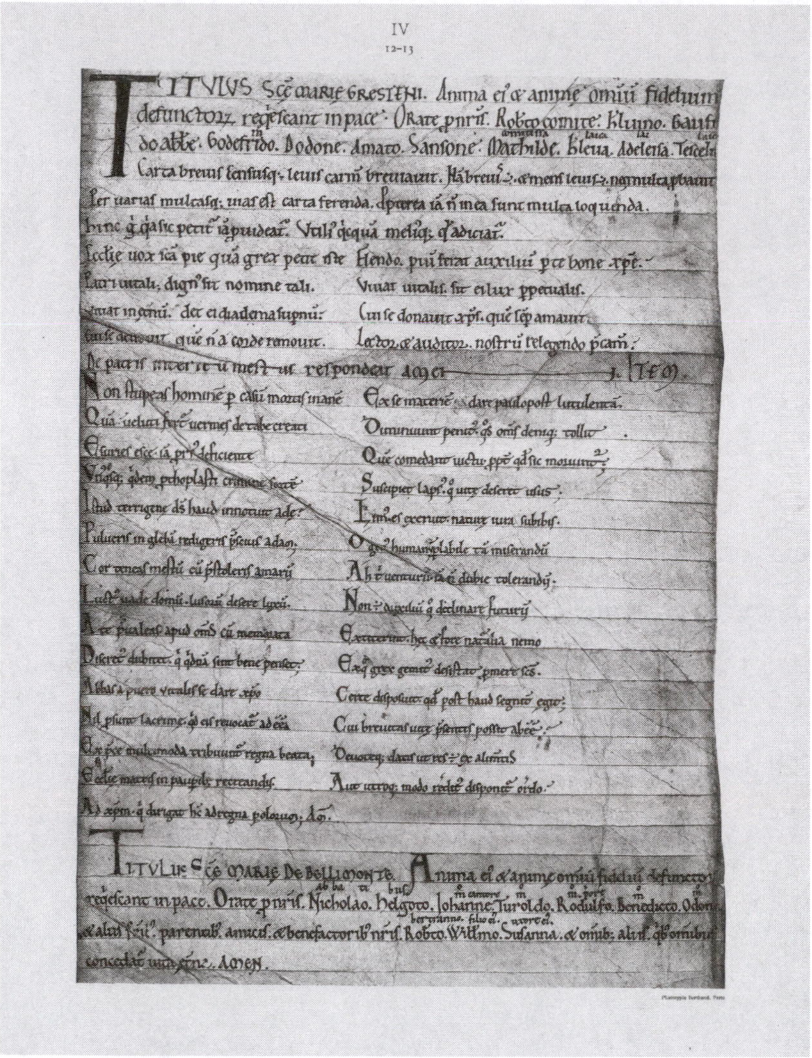

FIGURE I: *Titulus of St. Mary of Grestain.* (*Léopold Delisle, Rouleau mortuaire du B. Vital [Mortuary Roll of St. Vitalis] [Paris, 1909], Table IV.*)

The text reads as follows: "His soul and the souls of all the dead faithful, may they rest in peace. Pray for ours: Count Robert; Herluin and abbot Geoffrey; the monk Godfrey; Dodo; Aimé; Samson, Countess Matilda; Herleva, a laywoman; Alice, a laywoman; Tesceline, a laywoman."

Among those for whom Grestain requested prayers were Robert of Mortain and his first wife, Matilda. However, Robert's father (Herluin) and mother (Herleva) are also included. Herluin founded Grestain and ended his life as a monk there, so he was doubly important to the monastery. Herleva was also buried there (or at least a plaque at the site claims that she was). Presumably the other individuals mentioned were donors to the monastery. This notice, which includes two poems, is far more elaborate than the entry for Grestain in another mortuary roll created in 1114 for Matilda, the abbess of Holy Trinity in Caen, William the Conqueror's daughter, where Herleva is left off, although she was Matilda's grandmother.

INTRODUCTION

✠

"We Should Not Pass Over in Silence"

6. But we should not pass a matter over in silence that he told one of his disciples, because of that man's authority. One time, he found the countess weeping and troubled by great sobbing and sorrow. He quickly asked the reason for her sorrow and learned from her own mouth that the count did not respect her and had presumed to beat her. The venerable man was moved by her pain and said that he was angry that the count had presumed to do such things to her and that the bond between himself and the count would have to be broken, unless the count agreed to refrain from visiting such injuries upon the lady.

7. So then it happened that Vitalis left Mortain and did not let the count know about his departure. But when it was announced to the count, the count followed him without delay and once the count had given him a pledge that he would make satisfaction [for his misdeed], the count got him to return. But the reason he left remained hidden and only those two knew it. When they returned and secretly entered the chapel, the count, who begged for compassion, began to implore the venerable man not to hesitate to whip him as much as he wished. The prince took off his clothes and stood nude before the reverend man who stood over him and struck him with bitter blows. But as the prince humbly begged Vitalis to have mercy on him, the venerable man chastised him as much as he wanted to with the descending switches.

Oh, he was a man endowed with the greatest liberty! Oh, he was a man outstanding for his great authority! The apostolic statement which says, *where the spirit of God is, there is liberty* (2 Cor. 3:17) is really true. He was truly free, this man to whom the countess did not fear to disclose her pain and at whose hands the count himself did not blush to humbly submit himself to be beaten! (I: 6–7)

This story appears early in the biography of St. Vitalis of Savigny, who died in 1122. Vitalis was a hermit who, around 1112, founded a **monastery** at Savigny, which after his death became the mother-house of a short-lived **monastic order**. His reputation was very widespread at the time of his death, so when he died, the monks of Savigny travelled to many monasteries in northern France and England to collect written tributes. As each house wrote its contribution, these prayers, poems, and names of individuals who hoped to be prayed for by the monks of Savigny were attached to a **mortuary roll** that has survived. (I'll say more about the mortuary roll in the first chapter.) In the end, they collected over two hundred surviving tributes. Some were probably lost, because the roll is missing both the beginning and the end; it has also probably been taken apart and reassembled, as the entries do not follow a logical geographic order.[1]

The people in the story died well before Vitalis did. The count of Mortain in this story was Robert, the half-brother of William the Conqueror (r. 1066–87). Robert died in 1095, and the monastery of Grestain, in lower Normandy, specifically requested prayers for his soul from the monks of Savigny, underlining the connection between the count and the saint. (This is the notice from the mortuary roll that appears in Figure 1.) The countess is not named in the biography (this is the only place in the biography where she appears), but Robert was married twice, first before 1066 to Matilda, from the Montgomery family, and then afterward by 1088 to Almodis, probably the daughter of a count of Toulouse. Matilda is specifically named in the prayers requested by Grestain because she was buried there, as was Robert himself.[2]

It may not matter which of Robert's wives was intended in the story, however, because the author of the biography was writing many decades after Robert's death and therefore after the incident chronicled in the text. The author, Stephen of Fougères, was a local man (Fougères is just over 40 km from Mortain by modern roads, with Savigny lying almost midway between the two), but he travelled far from home.[3] He had been a **chancery** clerk for King Henry II of England (r. 1154–89) and a royal chaplain, before being appointed the bishop of Rennes in Brittany in 1168. We don't know exactly when he wrote his account of Vitalis's life, but the scholarly consensus is sometime between 1174 and 1178, when Stephen died. So this story took place at least eighty years before Stephen wrote about it and possibly a decade or so before that, if it actually happened at all.

---

1 Jean Dufour and Jean Favier, *Recueil des rouleaux des morts (VIIIe siècle vers 1536)*, vol. 1 (VIIIe siècle–1180) (Paris: Bocard, 2005), 519.

2 Brian Golding, "Robert, count of Mortain (d. 1095)," *ODNB*, http://www.oxforddnb.com/view /article/19339.

3 When I give distances by modern roads, I have used Google Maps. Modern roads are often laid over medieval ones, but even where they aren't, modern roads can give us an idea of the distance between places, if not the greater difficulty medieval people would have had in going from one place to another.

This story and the text that contains it can stand for many of the issues that historians and general readers have with **hagiography**. To many people, hagiographies (biographies and accounts of the lives and miracles of saints) stand in opposition to historical facts. They contain stories of miracles and visions, which modern readers tend not to believe in and which they may explain as coincidences, hallucinations, or fabrications. I overheard some students of mine discussing a hagiographic text and one student indignantly announced that he thought the author had made the whole thing up. Even where the events themselves can be explained by science or where a story doesn't appear particularly miraculous, as above, and thus can be accepted as potentially factual, readers are very much aware that the authors are making a case for the holiness of a given individual, that the stories we see may be partial (both in the sense of telling only part of the story and in the sense of being biased in favor of the subject). We may see these medieval texts as being akin to Parson Weems's hagiographic treatment of George Washington, with its fanciful inventions about hatchets and cherry trees. Finally, we may be suspicious when there is such a long gap between the date of the story and the date of the story's composition. How likely was it that stories passed along orally would retain their integrity or truthfulness?

None of these questions would really matter if we were prepared to reject these tales of the saints as serious historical sources, if we wanted to read them only as fanciful narratives intended for credulous medieval people who cannot be expected to have been as smart as we are. But one of the arguments of this book is that hagiographic texts can be extremely useful as historical sources if we know how to use them and for what. We need, however, to understand how they came to be written, how they were positioned, and how medieval people understood them. Medieval people viewed the world differently in many ways from how we see it (and we don't all see it the same way either), because they came from a much different society. Not all possible conceptions were open to them, because of how they were positioned. The concept of **positionality** – the idea that our understanding is shaped by the environments in which we develop – will come up again and again in this book, and the implications of that understanding will be explored at some length.

At the same time, we need to put aside the notion that medieval people were totally different from us. As far as credulity is concerned, medieval writers themselves were aware, at least from the twelfth century onward, of the need to impress a sometimes skeptical audience. Stephen of Fougères himself recognized the possibility that readers would scoff at his narrative. And our current moment suggests that even in this day and age, our **motivated reasoning** (reasoning mobilized to support prior beliefs rather than to inquire after the factual situation) sometimes leads people to believe six impossible things before breakfast. So learning to read medieval saints' lives, or any historical sources for that matter, means struggling to free ourselves from our own positionality, the lens through which we view the past. This is also true if we want to better understand contemporaries from a different culture, so this is a competency with important applications in the world we live in.

In the chapters that follow, I will be exploring some of the opportunities that hagiography offers the historian as a source, while also exploring some of the challenges it presents. I will be using the *Life of St. Vitalis* by Stephen of Fougères as my test case and **worked example**, because any time we want to use a source for historical purposes, we need to treat it in its specificities, while at the same time, theory and methods make more sense when you can see how they are applied. The *Life of St. Vitalis* has several advantages for these purposes: We have some independent documentation about the saint to compare to the biography, and we also know who the author of the biography was and something about his life (which is not always true for medieval authors).

There are many things to be learned from Stephen's life of Vitalis. However, this book cannot and will not explore all the possibilities presented by this text. That is why I have provided a complete translation of Stephen's work at the end of the book, so you can do your own explorations. And readers who are ready to leap into this kind of interpretive work will find a translation of Stephen's other holy biography, the life of St. Firmat, to play with as well.

and used in precise ways) are very helpful, but the first time I use them, I offer a definition (again as I have done here). Because many terms will not be familiar to novice readers, I have also provided a glossary. Words in the glossary appear in boldface in the text the first time they appear in a chapter, often with an explanation at first use in the book. Within the glossary definitions, dependent words are also set in boldface. I hope any academic readers will not be put off, but I am writing for an audience that will include some novices.

I had a tremendous amount of fun writing this book. I hope you, the reader, will have at least some fun reading it.

Although the stereotype of historians is that we work alone in dusty archives (and many of us do, at least some of the time), any book is a community effort. I would like first to thank Natalie Fingerhut, my editor at the University of Toronto Press, who had faith in this somewhat unusual approach and whose suggestions have improved the book. The readers for the press also had invaluable suggestions, even when they didn't like what they were reading, and that is the very best kind of friend an author can have. Martin Boyne, who edited the copy, rode herd on my wicked ways with commas, gently improved the prose without cramping my style, and generally caught errors and omissions. Any reader who uses the glossary owes a debt of thanks (as do I) to my younger daughter, Linnea, who read the manuscript to make sure that even someone mostly interested in plant biology would find it comprehensible. My wonderful older daughter Maya offered boundless encouragement. They, along with Dirk, Sara, and Cerisa, all listened to me drone on about medieval people and events as though they lived and happened yesterday, mostly with interest. And finally, to the SoTL gang (you know who you are and special thanks Lendol!), it's great to have a place where everybody knows your name.

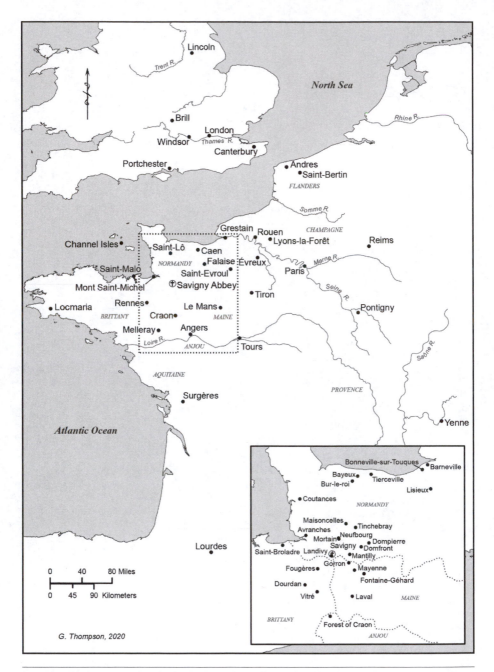

MAP I: *Places mentioned in this book. (Map drawn by Gordie Thompson.)*

✠

CHAPTER ONE

"In the province of Bayeux":
St. Vitalis in the Historical
and Hagiographic Record

In the province of Bayeux, one may find a certain village that the inhabitants call Tierceville. A man named Renfred lived in this town; he was married to a woman named Rohaid.[1] They strove hard and diligently to serve God; they did not turn a deaf ear to his commands, but devoutly carried them out (cf. Mic. 7:16; Ps. 37:14). Indeed, they were vigilant in supporting the poor and needy and they gave them alms, for as it is written, *Give alms and lo all things will be clean for you* (Luke 11:41). They also sheltered them at night, which does not have last place among the works of mercy. The apostle [that is, St. Paul] says about this action that *they have pleased God through this, for they have taken angels into their dwelling* (cf. Heb. 13:2). They worshipped God very eagerly, making the payments sanctioned by canon law [that is, **tithes**] without any pretext or delay, and they carried on living through their righteous labors. While they were persisting in these things and in these sorts of holy works, they had a son, at whose birth they had much reason for joy, and they quite properly took the most attentive care in raising him. When he was washed in the holy font of baptism this baby was named Vitalis. (I: 1)

This opening to the *Life of St. Vitalis* is completely unremarkable as an opening to a saint's life. It names the saint's parents, devout people who deserve a fine child and thus receive one. To the medieval reader this opening would call to mind a number of biblical precedents: Sara and Abraham, the parents of Isaac (Gen. 17:15–21); Hannah and Elkanah, the parents of the prophet Samuel (1 Sam.); and Zechariah and Elizabeth, the parents of John the Baptist (Luke 1:5–11). There are certainly elements of these earlier holy stories that Stephen

---

1 *Reigfredus* and *Rohardem* [*Rohardis* in the subject case]. The mortuary roll entries give different forms for the names, *Rainfredus* and *Roha* (Dufour and Favier, *Rouleaux des morts*, 524).

of Fougères, the author, did not invoke (these marriages were all childless for a long time), but his telling created a general atmosphere of holiness around his subject nonetheless.

Understanding how a medieval text might be composed and understood

The way in which contemporary readers would have made connections of this kind is foreign to modern ideas about how to narrate the story of the past, which raises an important question for us. How do we understand something written for people who lived in a completely different culture from our own? One thing we do is think about what experiences those people had that we don't typically have. In the circle of **monks** for which this work was written and in which it was read, the words of many parts of the Bible, heard over and over again as **liturgical** readings (readings as part of church services), readings at meals, texts for sermons, and personal reading, were deeply familiar. This was also true for regular church-goers up through the nineteenth century, but weekly church attendance and regular Bible reading are no longer the practice of the majority of western Christians. So while some modern people know the Bible very well, many modern Christians don't have that degree of familiarity with it. Furthermore, we live in a more cosmopolitan world in which many modern readers are not Christians at all. So one of our tasks as modern readers of old texts is to ask questions about the conventions the readers or hearers (because these kinds of texts might well have been read aloud) would be familiar with.

I was able to say that this opening to this biography is typical because I've read a lot of saints' lives. In addition, I am familiar from my scholarly training with how medieval writers framed what they wrote. So when I read a saint's life, I'm always thinking about how the biography draws on the Bible and earlier saints' lives and looking for echoes and sometimes outright copying. However, when I read a **primary source** of a type that I'm not familiar with, I have to ask what is typical about it and what is unique to this source. The only way to answer these questions is to read other examples of this type. I'll say more about that in the third chapter.

I mentioned above how steeped in the language and stories of the Bible medieval people were. Those who learned to read Latin at all learned to do so from the Bible, at least initially. In addition, those who received any training in interpreting the Bible were taught to see the events and individuals in Jewish scripture not just as historical figures but also as pointing to events and people in Christian scripture (this is a notion called *figura*, a concept explored by the great medievalist

Erich Auerbach).[2] This means that sometimes when an author quoted the Bible, he or she was providing a moral lesson or pointing to a parallel situation, but not always. So I always check the biblical citations to determine whether they were chosen because the biblical context inspired the quotation or only because the words were applicable.

In the case of the first citation in the passage above, the biblical context is Jesus reprimanding the Pharisees for caring more about the ritual observance of cleanliness (washing before a meal) than spiritual purity (giving alms to the needy). While Stephen may be saying in a roundabout way that it was okay for a charitable and pious married couple to have sex (which might be considered unclean), my suspicion is that the quotation was triggered in his mind by the word "alms," so he inserted a passage referring to the importance of alms from the Bible, and cleanliness came along for the ride. This kind of adaptation of biblical words to a different situation is common among medieval writers, who sometimes put the words of the Bible to vulgar and bawdy use.[3]

The second quotation is more situational and represents an adaptation of Paul's letter to the Hebrews, which opens with an exhortation to carry out acts of mercy. Here the whole context supports the use of the quotation, as it presents Vitalis's parents as fulfilling the command Paul sets out in his letter to the Hebrews. Stephen has added the phrase about pleasing God, however, to set up the notion of reward. It is just possible that the connection between the recipients of the two biblical messages – both groups of Jews – may have influenced Stephen to put them in the passage together. Medieval memory training encouraged readers to create these kinds of links between texts.[4] While the twelfth century was a period of increasing anti-Jewish polemic, and clearly this kind of linkage could play a role in sermon construction, I won't explore the issue of medieval anti-Semitism in this book.

I've shown here how even a simple narrative passage in a medieval text – this is not limited to saints' lives but may be the case with any narrative – could resonate with meaning for a medieval reader, making connections and creating

---

2 Erich Auerbach, "Figura," in *Scenes from the Drama of European Literature*, 11–78 (Minneapolis: Minnesota Archival Editions, 1984).

3 For instance, one might think about biblical parodies, of which there were quite a few. See Martha Bayliss, *Parody in the Middle Ages: The Latin Tradition* (Ann Arbor: University of Michigan Press, 1996), chap. 5 ("Humorous Centos") on that score. Centos took lines from other works and stitched them together to create new meanings. The most famous of the biblical parodies is probably *The Gospel According to the Mark of Silver* (136ff.).

4 On memory construction, see Mary Carruthers, *The Book of Memory: A Study of Memory in Medieval Culture* (Cambridge: Cambridge University Press, 1990), particularly 44ff., where she discusses the *catena*, the linking of material in memory.

undercurrents that modern readers may simply miss. It would be a mistake, however, to assume that all medieval readers "got" all or any of these connections any more than we necessarily "get" the visual references in movies to other movies. What they undoubtedly "got," however, was Stephen's underlying purpose, which under all the layers I've described above was to convince an audience that the man he was celebrating was indeed a saint. That the message was dressed in the rhetoric of its day and reflected the understandings and practices of its readers and authors was simply a function of its author's **positionality**.

That this was so means that Stephen's biography of Vitalis is a picture of the saint, filtered through Stephen's eyes and organized according to what he thought was important. Stephen was telling a particular story about a past individual for his own purposes and for a particular audience: his positionality and that of his audience shaped that story. He was making a case, not only for Vitalis's holiness but also for a particular kind of holiness, and he was speaking to *his* contemporaries, *not Vitalis*'s, about things they cared about. In the chapters that follow, I'll write at some length about what he thought it was important to say. But this raises the question of what Vitalis's life was *really* like, what Stephen chose and what he thought less important, and even what he or his informants may have invented. If we want to understand this, we have to know what other evidence may be out there against which to measure Stephen's account. Fortunately, there are other sources, for Stephen's was not the only source of information about Vitalis. Before I turn to those sources, however, I want make some observations about the issues that primary sources present to historians.

The challenges posed by primary sources

Primary sources are the only objects that remain to us from the past, although they never tell us everything we want to know. Stephen's narrative is in some senses a primary source, as it is the only full account of Vitalis's life. But Stephen was writing more than half a century after Vitalis's death and never met him (if he had, he would almost certainly have said so). He was instead gathering stories people told him about Vitalis and working from Vitalis's mortuary roll. One of my colleagues, Eric Robinson, who is a classicist, for that reason refers to many sources from the past as "**ancient sources**" rather than "primary sources," since many classical sources are not contemporary with the events they describe. If these kinds of sources are all that we have to work with, we work with them. Still, we need to be very much aware of ways in which they are removed from the events they chronicle.

But even if Stephen's life of Vitalis isn't exactly a primary source for the life of Vitalis (but only an "ancient" source), we *do* have sources written by contemporaries against which to gauge Stephen's narrative, although unfortunately we have nothing composed by Vitalis himself.[5] There are two sorts of sources: **documentary sources** and **narrative sources**. The documentary sources were not intended to provide us with information about Vitalis but to record transactions such as gifts of land and legal settlements. In contrast, the narrative sources, including Stephen's biography, were indeed intended to tell us about the saint, but naturally tell us only the parts that fit into whatever larger story the author was trying to tell.

In other words, both types of evidence exhibit **bias**. When scholars say that evidence has bias, non-professional readers often assume that this involves some sort of cheating or conscious misrepresentation. However, when scholars use this expression (and not only historians do; social scientists and scientists also talk about bias in data), they generally mean that all forms of evidence and evidence gathering have limitations that affect our understanding. Of course, some medieval writers must have lied deliberately or misrepresented evidence, but we often have no way to know when that happened or why they might have done so. And once we've concluded that a narrative writer is lying, everything that person has written becomes suspect, so we have to treat the work more as a type of literary fiction than as a factual account.

But it is more common for our evidence to be unrepresentative because of patterns of survival. For instance, we know much more about the lives of medieval elites than about less privileged individuals, because elites (the top 30 per cent or so of the population) figure much more heavily in the documents than the rest. Furthermore, many documents from the Middle Ages have simply not survived. Science is remedying some of the gaps in our knowledge through archaeology and scientific analysis, but it cannot fill in all the holes. To find out about these more ordinary people, we often have to read sources "**against the grain**," that is, for the things the author or creator does not intend to tell us but does anyway. Furthermore, we also have much less evidence about most individuals in the twelfth century, even some famous or important ones, than we have about even quite ordinary people in the twentieth, much less the obsessively tracked twenty-first.

So, with this in mind, I want to turn to the sources apart from Stephen's biography that we have for the life of Vitalis. In doing this, I have been very dependent on the work of Jaap van Moolenbroek, who has identified every scrap of evidence about Vitalis and discussed each at length; I have also looked at some (but not all) of the primary sources he discusses. As an historian I rely on the work of other

---

5 As a famous preacher and educated man, he would probably have composed many sermons. On Vitalis's preaching, see below, p. 27.

historians, but I also go back to the original sources sometimes, because I may interpret them differently, think that another historian has made an error, or see something other historians appear to have overlooked. As a result, I may end up drawing on different evidence or arriving at different conclusions using the same sources. You should also remember that I too am selecting what I report. There's a lot that I won't mention, because Moolenbroek's purposes and mine are not the same. Again, our positionalities play a role in what we write.

Documentary sources about Vitalis of Savigny

The earliest piece of documentary evidence about Vitalis is a request for prayers for his family that appears in a fragment of a **mortuary roll** probably composed for Robert, abbot of Saint-Etienne in Caen, who died in 1107.[6] Mortuary rolls were made when significant figures (usually, but not exclusively, church officials) died, by the communities to which those people belonged. The community would write a circular letter, which would acquaint the recipients with the person and community for whom prayers were being requested. Clerics would then travel from place to place with the letter, collecting subscriptions from the institutions they visited. These might be formulaic; a number of **formularies** (collections of samples for people to imitate or simply copy) have survived from various institutions.[7] In contrast, they might be more individualized; a number of poems written by Baudri of Bourgueil (c. 1050–1130) for various mortuary rolls in the late eleventh century have survived as part of his collected poems, and Marbode of Rennes (c. 1035–1123) provided personalized poems as well.[8] The churches that were visited might in turn request prayers for specific individuals, whose names would be added. The fragment from Robert's roll contains prayers requested for Sainte-Trinité in Mortain and names Vitalis's parents and other relatives among those to be prayed for. Since Vitalis may have been directing the church himself, he could have requested their inclusion or the monks may have done so as a favor to him.

---

6 *Vital*, 8–11; Dufour and Favier, *Rouleaux des morts*, 365. The roll seems to have circulated in 1108.

7 For example, ninth-century models from Reichenau and Laon and some unidentified ones (Dufour and Favier, *Rouleaux des morts*, 1: 28–33); examples drawn from a tenth-century work of St. Dunstan (45–7); and an early-twelfth-century one from S. Père in Melun (240).

8 Dufour and Favier, *Rouleaux des morts*, #90 (pp. 240–2, the formulary); ##81–8, 91, 125 (pp. 227–38, 242–3, 596–7, the poems of Baudri); ##106, 120 (pp. 352, 510–11, the poems of Marbode). Marbode himself was the object of a mortuary roll, although only a copy of the circular letter has survived (#121, pp. 511–14). Dufour and Favier's project has identified 440 mortuary rolls or parts of rolls between the eighth and sixteenth centuries (p. v).

Vitalis also appears in some **charters**. The **cartulary** of Savigny (a collection of the charters of the **monastery**), compiled in the thirteenth century, contained copies of charters relating to Savigny, the monastery that Vitalis founded around 1112, including the foundation charter by which Ralph of Fougères gave Vitalis the land on which the monastery was established; the confirmation of that donation by the bishop of Avranches; an additional confirmation by Henry I of England (r. 1100–35; he was also the duke of Normandy, where Savigny was located); and a charter issued by Henry I granting Savigny alms that Vitalis had earlier given to St. Stephen's monastery at Caen.[9] (This last charter is referred to in Stephen's biography of Vitalis [I: 15].) Vitalis's brother Osbert appears as one of the witnesses to the bishop's confirmation of the donation. The foundation charter of Neufbourg (later known as Abbaye Blanche), a **convent** founded by Vitalis, is also extant, although it may be a medieval forgery.[10]

A more literary piece of surviving evidence is an undated letter to Vitalis from Bishop Marbode of Rennes in Brittany, noting that Vitalis had founded a community for women and requesting that he accept a girl into that house who would bring no property with her but who had already had some education.[11] Normally when someone entered a monastery, his or her family made a contribution to the monastery's endowment, but exceptions might be made when a candidate was particularly desirable or had pull.[12]

The most striking documentary testimony to Vitalis's significance to his contemporaries is the mortuary roll compiled by the monks of Savigny after his death

---

9   Jacqueline Buhot, "L'Abbaye normande de Savigny: Chef d'ordre et fille de Cîteaux," *Moyen Age* 46 (1936): 109–10, 111–12. For the charters issued in Vitalis's lifetime, see *Vital*, 257–80 (Buhot offers an edition as well).

10 The copy of the charter may have been misdated when it was copied, as Buhot argues ("L'Abbaye normande," 6); the grant was probably made in 1115, but it is dated 1105. Moolenbroek thinks the charter is a medieval forgery and provides a lengthy discussion of it (*Vital*, 128–39). He believes that whatever female community Vitalis established was probably not established before 1118 (p. 198).

11 Marbode of Rennes, *Epistola IV*, PL 171: 1474–5. Marbode does not name the monastery; he simply calls it a monastery for women. As Vitalis died in 1122, the letter has to date from before then, but probably no earlier than 1118.

12 Even for candidates with money, entry into a small monastery might be difficult, as most monasteries had a relatively small complement of monks and growing beyond the limits set by the endowment could present serious problems. Noble families might pressure a monastery to offer an "expectation," that is, the next available slot. Meanwhile, it was in the interests of the monastery to admit monks in cohorts roughly similar in age to facilitate educating them. That the girl in question had some education meant that the convent wouldn't have to worry as much about providing her with the necessary instruction, and she might immediately prove useful to the community. We don't know whether she was admitted.

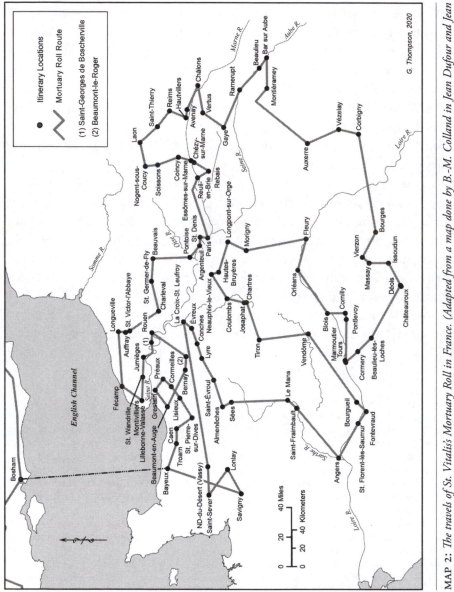

MAP 2: *The travels of St. Vitalis's Mortuary Roll in France. (Adapted from a map done by B.-M. Colland in Jean Dufour and Jean Favier,* Recueil des rouleaux des morts (VIIIe siècle–vers 1536), vol. 1 (VIIIe siècle–1180) *[Paris: Boccard, 2005]; map drawn by Gordie Thompson.)*

and preserved more or less intact, by a lucky act of scholarly larceny.[13] It is more than nine meters long (the beginning of it was lost, probably well before the seventeenth century) and contains 208 surviving *tituli* (that is, contributions from different collegiate churches and monasteries).[14] Some of the *tituli* have probably been lost as well, as a seventeenth-century edition contains one entry more than the surviving roll and there are no *tituli* from Brittany.[15] The monks of Savigny took their roll to many houses in Normandy, northern France, and England, where it was subscribed by members of monastic communities, **collegiate churches**, and cathedral **chapters** (the cathedral at Rouen promised a thousand masses for Vitalis's soul).[16]

The extraordinary circulation of this roll, which spread Vitalis's reputation far and wide, would have contributed to the creation of the short-lived **Order of Savigny**.

This represents the sum total of the documentary evidence.

Narrative sources for the life of Vitalis

In addition to the documentary sources, there are a few narrative sources, some contemporary and some from the period between Vitalis's death and Stephen's biography. In his biography of the saint, Stephen provided an extract from the circular letter, now lost, that formed the original head of the mortuary roll. It gives a portrait of Vitalis and was intended, as Stephen's biography was, to highlight Vitalis's general holiness (see II: 13–14). To this we can add what a few contemporaries wrote about Vitalis in the course of writing biographies of others or other

---

13 The following account is drawn from Béatrice Poulle, "Les sources de l'histoire de l'abbaye cistercienne de Savigny au diocèse d'Avranches," *Revue Mabillon* 68 (1996): 105–25. Since the French revolutionary currency, the *assignat*, was based on land appropriated from the Church, revolutionary committees collected monastic charters, which did not always survive the experience. Fortunately in the case of Savigny, the documents were not of interest after the land was sold, and they slumbered at Mortain until the third decade of the nineteenth century. Natalis de Wailis carried off many of the documents for the national library in Paris, including the mortuary roll; many of the remaining documents went to the departmental archives at Saint-Lô, where they were destroyed in 1944.

14 *Vital*, 14.

15 Léopold Delisle, *Rouleaux de morts du XIe au XVe siècles* (Paris: Renouard, 1866), 281. A more recent edition of the roll can be found in Dufour and Favier, *Rouleaux des morts*, #122, pp. 514–86. However, Delisle also published a facsimile of the roll: Léopold Delisle, *Rouleau mortuaire du B. Vital, abbé de Savigni* (Paris: Berthaud Frères [photographs]; Renouard [text], 1909). Dufour and Favier also print a poem by Baudri of Bourgueil about Vitalis that may originally have appeared in the roll (*Rouleaux des morts*, 518); there are no *tituli* from Brittany or the west of France, so these have been presumed lost.

16 Delisle, *Rouleaux de morts*, 291–2.

narratives. Orderic Vitalis (1075–c. 1142), an English monk who spent most of his life in Normandy, was the saint's younger contemporary. He does not say that he had met Vitalis, although it seems possible that both men were present at the council of Reims in 1119.[17] The shared name is by chance; Orderic was renamed Vitalis at age ten when he arrived in Normandy in 1085 from England, because he came to the monastery around the time of the feast of another St. Vitalis, a third-century companion of St. Maurice.[18] (I will henceforth refer to the historian only as Orderic, to avoid confusion.) Because Orderic was particularly interested in the new forms of spirituality being explored at the turn of the twelfth century, in which Vitalis of Savigny was a participant, Orderic naturally said a few things about him.[19] Orderic also mentions Vitalis when he writes about the battle of Tinchebray in 1106 as one of the men urging the warring brothers, Henry I of England and Duke Robert of Normandy, to set aside their fraternal hatreds.[20]

Vitalis is also mentioned in the biography of Bernard of Tiron (d. 1116), written around 1147;[21] Bernard was for a time a **hermit** in the woods with Vitalis. Bernard's **hagiographer**, unsurprisingly, is more interested in his subject than in a supporting player. Vitalis is not mentioned, however, in the biography of another of his fellow hermits, Robert of Arbrissel (d. 1116), perhaps because Vitalis was still alive when it was written. However, Bernard's biographer puts Vitalis alongside Robert, and Stephen also refers to the trio of Bernard, Robert, and Vitalis.[22] A very brief mention of Vitalis also appears in a chronicle written at the monastery of Saint-Maixent in Poitiers, probably in the 1120s.[23] Finally, there is an account of Vitalis's activities in a treatise that Robert of Torigni (c. 1110–86), the abbot of Mont Saint-Michel and a friend of Stephen of Fougères, wrote about the new monastic orders. Robert knew Orderic's treatise on the subject, but although Robert mentions Vitalis in this treatise, he does not include any information about the saint in his chronicle or anything about the founding of Savigny. He does, however, mention the death of Haimo, the prior of Savigny,

---

17 For St. Vitalis, see *Vital*, 26, and below II: 12; for Orderic Vitalis, see Orderic, 1: 26.

18 Orderic, 5: 555.

19 For this account, see Orderic, 4: 310–37 for the new religious movements of his day, and 330–3 for Vitalis specifically. Marjorie Chibnall, the editor of the Orderic edition, argues that this treatise was written in 1135 or 1136 (Orderic, 4: xix).

20 Orderic, 6: 87.

21 *Bernard*, xiii, for the dating.

22 *Bernard*, 54–5, 87. See Venarde for Baudri's biography and other documents related to Robert. See below, II: 13, for Stephen's reference to Bernard and Robert.

23 *Chronique de Saint-Maixent*, ed. and trans. Jean Verdon (Paris: "Les Belles Lettres," 1979), 176. The passage, under the year 1103, simply mentions that three men lived holy lives at that time, Vitalis in Normandy, someone named Roscelin in Aquitaine, and a third, Renaud, in Brittany and the Touraine.

in the chronicle.[24] The one place Vitalis appears in the main text is in Robert's **obituary** for his friend Stephen of Fougères (which is how we know that Stephen wrote Vitalis's biography).[25] Nevertheless, one manuscript of Robert's chronicle, copied at Savigny, has more information, as monks at that monastery used their copy to jot down additional material. These jottings have become known as the *Chronicle of Savigny*; this is the last of our narrative sources.[26]

These additions and omissions reflect the bias in the various pieces of narrative data. Robert of Torigni clearly knew about Vitalis, as he wrote about him in his treatise on the new orders, but Vitalis simply wasn't as important to Robert as Haimo, Robert's own contemporary and a man reputed to be particularly holy himself. Meanwhile, the monks of Savigny were adapting Robert's chronicle to their own local needs, adding things that interested them that he had omitted (and, according to the editor, Léopold Delisle, omitting things that didn't). In other words, what we have to work with is always going to be filtered through the interests and concerns of those who created the documents (which is also true of this book).

Non-existent sources, lost sources, oral sources

Non-existent sources

The surviving texts represent rather meager pickings of evidence (at least by modern standards) for a man evidently quite important to many of his contemporaries. This is not atypical for a medieval person, however. While modern people move through the world awash in written, and now digital, records generated for and about us, typical modern records, such as birth and death registries, were not kept for most of the Middle Ages. Churches and monasteries generally kept written records of their property in this period, but formal governmental records were kept in England only from the later eleventh century and only well after that in most other places. While starting in the twelfth century we have some autobiographical writings, these are very unusual and invariably written by elite people. There aren't personal diaries – cheap paper and more widespread literacy are required before more ordinary people can write about their experiences – and the letters that have survived (also produced by and for elite people) are seldom personal, since letters were seldom private. Truly private information might be conveyed only verbally and so would not be available to us.

---

24 RT, 2: 48; *Vital*, 74.
25 RT, 2: 74.
26 On the *Chronicle of Savigny*, see RT, 1: vi.

Lost sources

Of course, many of the sources that did exist have been lost. Fires were common in an age when roofs were wooden and buildings heated with flame; Guibert of Nogent (1055–1124) describes the fire that destroyed much of Laon, including its cathedral, after a riot in 1109 in which the bishop was murdered.[27] The danger is evident in a more recent event, when on April 15, 2019, the wooden roof of Notre-Dame in Paris caught fire, destroying the thirteenth-century wood, collapsing the spire, and bringing down some of the vaulting. The rest of the church was saved only by the modern technology of firefighting and the courage of the firefighters; in the Middle Ages, the building would have been completely destroyed.

Documents were particularly vulnerable to fires of this kind, as they might well be stored in the church or in the chapter house, usually adjacent to the church. William of Andres (c. 1177–1234) describes the fire in the 1140s that destroyed some of his monastery's records, and his cartulary chronicle contains some charters that are probably reconstructions (or forgeries) rather than copies.[28] Parchment (made of animal skin) could also be a tasty treat for rats. In France, the French Revolution destroyed both records and buildings. The great monastery of Saint-Bertin in Saint-Omer was used as a quarry until the first antiquarian society, supported by the novelist Victor Hugo, was formed to preserve the patrimony.[29] Since church lands were the basis of the revolutionary currency, the *assignat*, committees of public safety (arms of the revolutionary government) gathered sacks of documents to determine what lands were owned by churches, and once the land was identified, the documents often didn't survive, either because they were discarded or because the parchment was used to make cartridges for bullets (necessary for the two decades of war that followed). Many of Savigny's documents survived the French Revolution, but many others were destroyed while "safely" housed in the departmental archives at St-Lô; the town was reduced to ruins in 1944. Still, it is worth asking what was available to Stephen that is not available to us.

I've already mentioned that the circular letter that accompanied the mortuary roll on its journeys had lost its head by the seventeenth century, but Stephen had access to it, as he provided a synopsis of it (II: 13–14). In fact, it is possible that this

---

27 Guibert of Nogent, Monodies *and* On the Relics of Saints: *The Autobiography and a Manifesto of a French Monk from the Time of the Crusades*, trans. Joseph McAlhany and Jay Rubenstein (New York: Penguin, 2011), 136–41.

28 William of Andres, *Chronicle of Andres*, trans. Leah Shopkow (Washington, DC: Catholic University of America Press, 2017), 70–1; he also mentions a great fire at Charroux, Andres's motherhouse (75).

29 "Notre Histoire," Société Académique des Antiquaires de la Morinie, https://www.antiquaires delamorinie.org/historique.htm.

part of the roll disappeared *because* it had been detached and given to Stephen to use in his biography of the saint and never got returned to Savigny. Not only modern borrowers are bad at returning things! Or detached as it was, it may not have been recognized as belonging to the roll and so was lost. This is, of course, simply speculation on my part.

Aside from the material Stephen says he copied from the roll, it is not possible to say what he either borrowed silently or skipped over. He refers to "things written in the **vernacular**" about Vitalis in the beginning of the narrative and adds, after writing the story that furnishes the title of this book, that he was translating the story from a written French version (I: prologue, 7). Scholars have disagreed about how much written vernacular material Stephen actually had access to.[30] It is certainly possible that he did have a written vernacular source, for even much of monastic life was carried out in the vernacular and Stephen himself wrote in both Latin and French.[31] On the other hand, if vernacular sources existed, they were probably not systematic biographies, and Stephen could have invented the claim that he had such materials to bolster the authority of his work. As I will discuss in chapter 4, he was aware that some readers would doubt his veracity.

Oral sources

More important, in a culture still heavily dependent on the spoken word, there were the oral accounts of the saint passed along by the monks of Savigny. It is possible that someone who had personally known Vitalis was still alive when Stephen was writing, although that person would have to have been fairly old. However, at least a few of the men at Savigny when Stephen was writing would have known people who had known Vitalis personally. Prior Haimo entered the monastery shortly after Vitalis's death, for example, so he would have interacted with many people who had personally known the saint.[32] This raises an issue that scholars of the Middle Ages struggle with continuously. While medieval people did produce documents, in some times and places in great abundance, many parts of their lives

---

30 See *Vital*, 59f.

31 Michael Richter, "Kommunikationsprobleme im lateinischen Mittelalter," *Historische Zeitschrift* 222, no. 1 (February 1976): 43–80, points out that by the high Middle Ages, no one spoke Latin as a mother tongue and suggests that even within the Church, the vernacular was regularly used in non-liturgical situations, since the novices would have to learn Latin and **lay brothers** might never learn much Latin. Orderic, who had probably learned some Latin by the time he went to Normandy, says that "like Joseph in Egypt, I heard a language which I did not understand." This would have been French (Orderic, 6: 555). For Stephen's literary production, see below.

32 Lorna E.M. Walker, "Hamo of Savigny and His Companions: Failed Saints?," *Journal of Medieval History* 30 (2004): 49.

were lived aloud (this is particularly true for peasants, but not only for them) and we have no access to that oral dimension of life. This was true even for monasteries, great centers of storytelling, whose tales only occasionally leave traces in the written record.

Because Savigny has not left extensive narrative records, primarily the biographies of four exemplary figures (Vitalis among them), it is hard to know which stories about Vitalis were in circulation, but we know a lot about the kinds of stories these might have been.[33] Caesarius of Heisterbach (c. 1170–c. 1240) created a collection of *exempla* (moral narratives) based on stories he had been told by his **Cistercian** brethren. Because Cistercian houses were grouped in lineages called **filiations** and because the Cistercian rule, the *Charter of Love*, stipulated that there would be regular visitations between mother and daughter-houses within the filiations as well as a yearly meeting of the order, stories must have passed back and forth swiftly, but conversation, storytelling, complaints, and the like were part and parcel of the lives of all people who were companions for life.[34] Caesarius generally reports not just stories but also who told him particular stories.[35]

Furthermore, monasteries were centers of commemoration. For **lay people** this meant that their names would be added to the monastery's obituary and more or less elaborate services (depending on an individual's importance and contributions to the monastery) would have been said on the anniversary of the person's death. For the monastic dead, who were automatically added to the obituary, we have to imagine that some stories might have been told about more notable individuals upon their anniversaries. This may be the source of comments that sometimes appear in monastic histories, as when William of Andres comments on a long-dead brother who had only one hand but who nonetheless had planted many of the monastery's boxwood hedges and copied many of its books. That man would have died long before William joined the monastery,

---

33 These four biographies, including Stephen's biography of Vitalis, have been translated in *The Lives of the Monastic Reformers, 2: Abbot Vitalis of Savigny, Abbot Godfrey of Savigny, Peter of Avranches, Blessed Hamo*, trans. Hugh Feiss, Maureen M. O'Brien, and Ronald Pepin (Collegeville, MN: Liturgical Press for Cistercian Publications, 2014).

34 *Carta Caritatis* [*Charter of Love*] at the website of the Order of Cistercians of the Strict Observance, https://www.ocso.org/wp-content/uploads/2016/05/EN-Carta-Caritatis.pdf. This version, however, is the one confirmed in 1165; there is some argument about the evolution of the document (Janet Burton and Julie Kerr, *The Cistercians in the Middle Ages* [Woodbridge: Boydell, 2011], 29–30).

35 On Cistercian storytelling, with particular attention to Caesarius, see Brian Patrick McGuire, "Cistercian Story-Telling – A Living Tradition: Surprises in the World of Research," *Cistercian Studies Quarterly* 39, no. 3 (2004): 208–309. Savigny became a Cistercian house and was assigned to the filiation of Clairvaux. Heisterbach was also filiated to Clairvaux.

but his memory was preserved not just in the fabric of the monastery but also in monastic lore.[36]

So, for Stephen, a big portion of the information he was able to draw on would have been oral. Once he embarked on writing his biography of the saint, he would have been told stories. This makes his enterprise a different one from that of a modern historian. A modern historian would be worrying about whether these stories were "true," that is, factual. For Stephen to doubt the veracity of a story would be to throw shade on the reputation of the teller. Furthermore, what mattered more than whether something had really happened was its moral significance and what it said about Vitalis. So there was no reason for Stephen to reject a story that seemed meaningful and plausible to him.

The life of Vitalis of Savigny (my version)

For now, I'd like to end this chapter with what we know or can surmise about Vitalis's life. To figure out where to look, I will be using Stephen's narrative as a guide, although not necessarily taking what it says as fact. Earlier generations of scholars generally accepted what hagiographies said about their subjects – Claude Auvray did in his history of Savigny[37] – but modern scholars tend to be more aware of the partial nature of these kinds of records and also more skeptical about our ability to separate conventional or fictitious material from factual accounts. Therefore, while we start with the hagiographic accounts, we look for corroboration elsewhere whenever possible, which is why this chapter began with a consideration of the other sources. But where we have only a single source, we have to be extremely careful about what it can (or cannot) tell us.

I have to acknowledge, however, that what I offer is simply another account of the life of Vitalis. The purpose of my account is to present the life of Vitalis according to the modern rules of history making (and relying upon the work of other scholars, also part of our practice). It is much shorter and considerably less thorough than Moolenbroek's systematic study, because he was focused on finding out everything he could about the saint, whereas I want to offer a more summary version that can help me situate the saint and his biography in a larger

---

36 William of Andres, *Chronicle*, 80. William included a number of stories about his fellow monks, such as the monk who died after falling through the hole in the floor of the attic of the fore-church (76) or the abbot who took his monks ice-skating and was deposed for his wandering hands (84).

37 Claude Auvray, *Histoire de la congrégation de Savigny*, 3 vols., ed. Auguste Laveille (Rouen and Paris: A. Lestringant & A. Picard, 1896–8), vol. 1, which is based largely on Stephen's biography. Auvray was the prior of Savigny, writing in the seventeenth century. His work was published in the nineteenth.

historical context. This modern purpose is also different from Stephen's, which was to provide the monks of Savigny with material to enhance their active and ongoing veneration of their saintly founder. But today Vitalis has been largely forgotten, except by a few specialists in medieval religion or history. Nonetheless, his biography can be useful to us because it can help us understand human experience in a particular time and place, if we know how to make sense of it. Demonstrating how to do this – providing a **"worked example"** of doing this – is the purpose of this entire book.

Although the date of Vitalis's birth has been disputed, more recent scholars have tended to put his birth around 1060. (Note that here I'm accepting the arguments of secondary authors; we have no smoking-gun document that tells us when he was born; earlier scholars placed his birth around 1050.)[38] We can surmise from the specific mention of Vitalis's parents in the mortuary roll of Robert and also Vitalis's own mortuary roll, where prayers are requested for their souls by the church of St. Stephen's in Caen, that Vitalis's parents probably were, as Stephen reports, very pious people.[39] While we don't know from these sources exactly how many children they had, we do know that at least two of their children went into the religious life: Vitalis himself (obviously), but also his brother Osbert (because he witnessed one of the charters and because Stephen specifically says that one of Vitalis's brothers joined Savigny); his sister may have joined a convent, and another relative, perhaps, did also.[40] This is a pattern one finds in other devout families of the time. Bernard of Clairvaux (d. 1153) arrived at Cîteaux with thirty others, some of them his relatives (at least two brothers and a sister entered the

---

38 See Patrick Conyers, "Changing Habits: The Norman Abbey of Savigny and Its Congregation, 1105–1175" (PhD Dissertation, University of Iowa, 2001), 33n21.

39 Dufour and Favier, *Rouleaux des morts*, 1: 524. There is no *titulus* for the church of Mortain in this mortuary roll. I assume that the prayers requested for Vitalis's relatives by Caen were the result of the settlement of the legal case between Vitalis and the abbot of Caen over the church of Mortain (*Vital*, 266–7), by which Mortain was returned to Savigny.

40 Moolenbroek (*Vital*, 198–9) points out that many scholars have referred to a sister of Vitalis named Adeline, but he suggests that they are being misled by *Gallia christiana*, which assumed that a holy woman buried at Savigny named Adeline was both Vitalis's sister and the abbess of Vitalis's foundation at Neufbourg (Abbaye Blanche); as this argument runs, Adeline was run together with Ameline, a relative of Vitalis and an abbess, who is mentioned in the mortuary roll (but who predeceased him). However, Abbaye Blanche was a priory in Vitalis's day and so was headed by a prioress, and Moolenbroek also raises a doubt that Ameline was really related to Vitalis at all (149–50), because Vitalis's family was not noble and abbesses were almost uniformly noble by birth. However, perhaps he is being a bit too cautious. The entry in Vitalis's roll for St. Stephen in Caen (Dufour and Favier, *Rouleaux des morts*, 524) lists nine people as Vitalis's kin, including both an Ameline and an Adeline. It does not list Osbert, but as a monk of Savigny he was ensured of Savigny's prayers upon his death anyway.

monastic life), and two of Christina of Markyate's (d. c. 1155) siblings entered the monastic life as well.[41]

Stephen does not say that Vitalis's parents were noble or unusually rich, so it is likely that they were neither of those things. However, they were probably not simple peasants either, because they were able to afford to educate Vitalis. Perhaps they were the elite of their village, a community that was sufficiently affluent at the end of the twelfth century that the parishioners could afford to pay for the nave of their church to be vaulted.[42]

Here I want to raise an entirely speculative question about the name Vitalis. Stephen suggests that this name was particularly apt, as it is based on the Latin word *vita* (life). This was undoubtedly the name by which the man was known to his contemporaries, as the contemporary documents show. However, it seems possible to me that it was not the name he received when he was baptized, as Stephen says (I: 1), but a name he took upon becoming a monk. His siblings were named Osbert and Adeline, both common Norman names, and his parents' names, as well as other family names that appear in the mortuary roll entries, are also.

Changing one's name when one entered the religious life was not required, but it was not uncommon either. Christina of Markyate's baptismal name was Theodora, for instance.[43] The editor and translator of the life of Firmat has suggested that his baptismal name may have been William, even though his biographer never calls him that.[44] It is possible that Vitalis's parents *did* choose to name him after any one of a number of Sts. Vitalis, perhaps because he was baptized on that saint's day or because they envisioned a church career for their son, or for some other religious reason. But Vitalis may not be the name with which he began his life.

41 C.H. Talbot, trans., *The Life of Christina of Markyate*, rev. Samuel Fanous and Henrietta Leyser (Oxford: Oxford University Press, 2010), 61, 70; see Gillian R. Evans, *Bernard of Clairvaux*, 9, for a general statement and the rather chatty article by Thomas Merton reprinted in *Cistercian Quarterly* ("St. Bernard's Family," *Cistercian Quarterly* 40, no. 1 [2005]: 29–44).

42 Jean-Jacques Bertaux, "Contribution à l'étude de l'art roman en Normandie: L'architecture des églises paroissiales romanes de l'ancien doyenné de Creully," *Annales de Normandie* 16, no. 1 (1966): 20. The lord would generally pay for the vaulting in the choir. In this case, the lord (or at least half of the lord) was the monastery of Grestain. Normally the parishioners would pay for the nave, so naves in the deanery were mostly timber.

43 Talbot, *Life of Christina*, 3; Theodora also has religious connotations. While the biographer is quite hostile to Christina's parents and suggests that they hated her religiosity, the biography offers other hints to suggest that fear played a great role in their actions and that they were more than usually pious.

44 Pigeon (1), 60–1. The name William is preserved in traditions about the saint. Firmat (*Firmatus*) means "strengthened" or "fortified." I'd be inclined to translate it as "steadfast."

Since Stephen tells us that Vitalis came from Tierceville, his first education may well have been at the hands of the local priest; the monastery of Grestain, where Robert of Mortain was buried, held half a manor in Tierceville and got to appoint the priest.[45] We know (because he tells us so) that Orderic's education similarly began at the hands of a local priest in Shrewsbury, and we can presume something of the sort for the girl for whom Marbode requested a placement.[46]

There are some other possibilities. The school at Mortain was founded in Vitalis's adulthood, so he could not have been educated there. But Grestain had a noteworthy school that was not only endowed but was actually founded by Robert of Mortain's father.[47] Against this we have to consider that while monasteries often did educate children who would not enter monastic life, many monastic schools were intended primarily for children who would become monks.

Wherever he got his first schooling, Vitalis's education could not have ended there. To receive an appointment at Mortain, he would have to have had more than a basic education, for the canons of Mortain had the exclusive right to run a school in their region and would have required more education for their canons than was typical. A logical place for Vitalis to go for further education was Bayeux. Bayeux is around 14 km from Tierceville by modern roads, the closest major ecclesiastical center, and so not a terribly long distance even in the Middle Ages (a few hours on foot). There are reasons other than proximity, however, to consider the possibility that at least part of Vitalis's education took place at Bayeux. The bishop of Bayeux during Vitalis's youth was Odo (d. 1097), the half-brother of William the Conqueror (they shared a mother) and the full brother of Robert of Mortain. Orderic tells us that Bishop Odo sent some of his **clergy** to Liège and other places for further education.[48] Stephen says that after Vitalis's initial studies, he left his country to be educated (he does not tell us where), so if Vitalis was studying at Bayeux, he could have been one of those so sent. Taken together, the evidence from Stephen and the evidence from Orderic seem to point in the same direction, but there is nothing certain.

However, there is an additional reason to suspect some education at Bayeux. At some unspecified date, Vitalis received an appointment at the collegiate church

---

45 The inhabitants of Tierceville were able to afford to have a stone church built in the last quarter of the twelfth century, which suggests that the community had the funds to support a priest very well, which means they could have had a very competent one. For the rights of Grestain over Tierceville, see David Bates and Véronique Gazeau, "L'abbaye de Grestain et la famille d'Herluin de Conteville," *Annales de Normandie* 40, no. 1 (1990): 14, 14n27. Robert of Mortain donated the half-manor (ibid., 28).

46 Orderic, 6: 553; see above, p. 13, for Marbode's letter.

47 Moolenbroek suggests his education there as a possibility (*Vital*, 150).

48 Orderic, 4: 119.

of Mortain, which was founded by Robert of Mortain in 1082. Robert funded eight of the fifteen **prebends** at the church (one might think of a prebend as an endowment producing a salary for the holder of the prebend) and the dean (the head of the **canons**), which would have given Robert control of who was appointed. Indeed, he stipulated that no other school would be permitted in the Mortain valley, that the dean and the **cantor** (the person responsible for organizing the church singing), when they were with him, would be considered his **chaplains**, and that the canons, whenever he was at Mortain, would share his own chaplains' offerings.[49] This placed education at the center of Mortain's mission and ensured a personal relationship between the count and the canons of his collegiate church.

Given how little we know about Vitalis and his family, we have to wonder how he came to Robert's attention to receive such a plum appointment. In contrast to Stephen's suggestion that Robert requested that Vitalis be his chaplain because he already had a reputation for holiness – if Vitalis was one of the original canons, he might have been only in his mid-twenties, probably not old enough to create an impressive reputation – we might imagine something else: that Robert was looking for a chaplain and asked his brother for a recommendation, or simply that Vitalis was one of a number of men recommended by Odo to fill the prebends and that Robert came to know Vitalis that way. This would fit in with the normal way in which men might receive ecclesiastical appointments; among Odo's protégés were a large number of men who became bishops and abbots.[50]

You will note that all of these possibilities are mere conjecture, but they begin to suggest a world of personal networks. They also evoke a world in which formal education was increasingly important and might be transformative. However, we have no information, either from Stephen or from any source, about when Vitalis received his appointment as a canon at Mortain or when he became Robert's chaplain. Sources other than Stephen mention that he held these positions, but none say for how long. If Vitalis was born around 1060, he could easily have been the holder of one of the original prebends. If so, he would have served as a canon for thirteen years, which would fit Stephen's comment that Vitalis was Robert's chaplain for "a long time" (I: 5). Not all scholars agree on this point. Conyers, for instance, has argued that Vitalis was Robert's chaplain for only a few years.[51] But since Stephen's summary of the circular letter says that Vitalis was a hermit

49 *GC*, 11: 508; Brian Golding, "The Religious Patronage of Robert and William of Mortain," in *Belief and Culture in the Middle Ages: Studies Presented to Henry Mayr-Harting*, ed. Richard Gameson (Oxford: Oxford University Press, 2001), 217.

50 David Bates, "Odo, Earl of Kent," *ODNB*, https://doi.org/10.1093/ref:odnb/20543.

51 Conyers, "Changing Habits," 35.

at Dompierre for seventeen years, most scholars are agreed that he withdrew to become a hermit around the time that Robert died, in 1095.[52] If we add 17 to 1095, we get 1112 – around the time Savigny was founded, when Vitalis would have definitively ceased to be a hermit.

If Vitalis was a canon for only a few years, this would mean that he was probably already in his thirties when he became one. However, this seems unlikely to me; it simply shifts the uncertainty about how long he was a canon to a lengthy blank period before he became one. If we look at the life of his contemporary Robert of Arbrissel, we see a man who was a secular cleric and teacher for some years before going off to become a hermit, after that becoming a wandering preacher and finally, like Vitalis, the founder of a monastery.[53] Medieval thinkers were generally of the opinion that only the experienced should try the life of the hermit, which was full of difficulties and temptations.[54] I'd posit then quite a lengthy period as a canon, ending in 1095.

Of Vitalis's life as a hermit, we know almost nothing. Stephen was uninterested in it, and the biography of his contemporary Bernard of Tiron simply describes Bernard seeking Vitalis out because of his reputation and depicts Vitalis as the head of an informal community of hermits. The text says little about Vitalis's actual practice or activities or the duration of his endeavors.[55] The other narrative sources that mention Vitalis don't provide much more evidence. The sources agree that the hermits resided in the forests of Craon in the corner of France where Brittany, Normandy, Anjou, and Maine came together (see Map 1). Many of the noble families of these parts held property in more than one of these territories, including the lords of Fougères (in Brittany), who donated the land (in Normandy) where Savigny was founded. Orderic says that the saint was already leading a monastic life in the forest (the part of the mortuary roll that Stephen copies says at Dompierre in Normandy) before moving with his monks to the site of Savigny, where there were ruins.[56] However, there is documentary evidence to believe that Vitalis had been given spiritual direction of the male monastery dedicated to the Holy Trinity at Mortain around 1105 by William of Mortain, along with property, both of which were returned to Savigny by the 1118 agreement.[57]

---

52 Golding, "Robert, Count of Mortain."
53 Venarde, 1, 22. Baudri's biography was written around 1118 and Andreas's biography around 1120.
54 For instance, see the *Rule of St. Benedict*, which in discussing the four sorts of monks, notes that people should not undertake this sort of religious life as novices, but only after a period of proof (*Sancti Benedicti regula monasteriorum*, ed. Benno Linderbauer [Bonn: Peter Hanstein, 1928], 19 [*capitulum* 1]).
55 *Bernard*, for instance, 27–8. Geoffrey, writing around 1147, mentions Robert as well as Vitalis and another hermit-reformer-monastic founder Ralph of La Fûtaie.
56 For Dompierre, see below, II: 13; Orderic, 4: 331.
57 *Vital*, 144–5. See above, p. 13.

These disagreements among the sources are not enormous, but to modern eyes they are irritating. Was Vitalis a hermit or a leader of monks, or both, and when and where? For how long? What we have to conclude is that these kinds of details didn't matter to any of those who chronicled Vitalis's life.

Where in this story Vitalis's preaching fits in is also unclear. As a canon, he had very likely preached as part of his priestly duties. Orderic does not give many details, even though more than half of what he says about Vitalis is about his preaching. He mentions no miracles except the gift of discernment (knowing about people's secret sins) and characterizes Vitalis's preaching as focused on reproving vices, leading the scholar John Marshall Carter to characterize it as "fire and brimstone."[58] This is quite different from how Stephen describes Vitalis's preaching; while he certainly mentions discernment in other contexts, the focus of Vitalis's preaching in the biography is peacemaking and reconciliation. Since Vitalis left behind no sermons identified as being his, we cannot know exactly the nature of his preaching, but in this case Orderic was a contemporary and was probably drawing on things he had been told during Vitalis's lifetime.

This doesn't mean that Stephen was wrong about at least some of Vitalis's preaching; there may simply be a difference of emphasis between the two authors, based on each man's concerns (that is, his positionality). As I pointed out above, Orderic mentions a sermon on reconciliation on at least one occasion, before the battle of Tinchebray in 1106.[59] William of Mortain held the castle at Tinchebray and supported Duke Robert in the battle against King Henry.[60] One can imagine William bringing Vitalis with him, particularly if Vitalis was already directing the church at Mortain, to plead with his cousin Henry in hopes of escaping from the trap in which he was positioned. Indeed, the Savigny manuscript of Robert of Torigni's chronicle expands on this point, noting that everyone involved heard mass said by Vitalis before the battle.[61]

---

58 John Marshall Carter, "'Fire and Brimstone' in Anglo-Norman Society: The Preaching Career of St. Vital of Mortain and Its Impact on the Abbey of Savigny," *American Benedictine Review* 34, no. 2 (June 1983): 166–87.

59 King Henry I of England completed his systematic campaign to deal with his brother Robert, duke of Normandy, in 1106. He was besieging the castle of Tinchebray when Robert decided to chance an open battle, which he lost. Robert was taken prisoner and remained one for the remainder of his life (another twenty-eight years). Charles Wendell David, *Robert Curthose, Duke of Normandy* (Cambridge, MA: Harvard University Press, 1920), 171–6, gives an accessible account of the events.

60 As reported by the historian Henry of Huntingdon. For these details see David, *Robert Curthose*, 179n16.

61 RT, 1: 127n5. On the manuscript, see 1: iv–v. The manuscript contains the version of the chronicle up to 1156, and the additions have been published as the *Chronicle of Savigny*. See also *Vital*, 178, for a discussion of this story. Moolenbroek thinks that this was quite probable, and it is worth remembering that Henry of Fougères, the son of the original donor and a man who knew Vitalis in life, had become a monk at Savigny at the end of his life and died not much before this manuscript was composed.

This is a detail Orderic would have had good reason to report (whether factual or not); he had lived through these events, which occurred in his adulthood, and he was deeply concerned with the political disorder Normandy had experienced under Robert Curthose. However, if Vitalis preached other sermons on the subject of peace, Orderic does not say; instead he says that Vitalis preached to encourage moral order, particularly that of women. Stephen was also interested in moral order, as two of the stories he tells about Vitalis involve the reform of women of ill reputation (I: 9, II: 8). Stephen also comments that Pope Calixtus II (r. 1119–24) had said that no person north of the Alps had been as publicly forthright about the pope's shortcomings as Vitalis (II: 12). But Stephen was more concerned in the biography with the problem of violence, perhaps because when he wrote he had just participated in a process of formal reconciliation between Henry II and his rebellious sons. Hence, perhaps, his focus on Vitalis's preaching of peace and forgiveness.[62]

If Vitalis preached at Tinchebray (and why not?), he was already noted as a preacher by 1106. But how much before then had this happened? Robert of Arbrissel, who was probably around the same age as Vitalis, was already preaching by 1095, when Pope Urban II (r. 1088–99) came to France to preach the First Crusade and granted him a license to preach.[63] Vitalis might easily have been preaching at the same time as well, although under whose license we aren't told. Jacqueline Buhot argues that the three hermits (Robert, Vitalis, and Bernard) went on preaching tours together, which puts Vitalis's activity in the same period as Robert's.[64] It does seem likely, then, that Vitalis was licensed around the same time as Robert.

Once we get to the founding of Savigny around 1112, there is more datable information, primarily from the documentary evidence, although it is far from sketching in a life that lasted for another ten years. As I noted above, Savigny's foundation charter is extant, along with a number of confirmations of it. A copy of the charter for the monastery of nuns that Vitalis also founded is extant, although Moolenbroek has concluded that it is a medieval forgery intended to backdate the claim of the nuns to property that later came into their hands.[65] Pope Calixtus II

---

62 For more about this issue, see chapter 5.
63 Venarde, 13–14 (this is drawn from Baudri of Bourgueil's biography of Robert).
64 Buhot, "L'Abbaye Normande," 4. Stephen reports that Vitalis preached at the council of London in 1102 (II: 4).
65 Moolenbroek (*Vital*) treats the donation charters extensively. I am not enumerating them here (some are more problematic than others, matters he also discusses extensively) because they really don't shed much light on Vitalis's life, apart from testifying to the esteem in which his monastery was held in his lifetime.

issued a charter ordering the protection of Savigny in September 1119 at Angers, and, as I said above, Vitalis was reported to have attended the council at Reims called by that pope.[66] Vitalis appears in donation charters as well, as the founder of an exciting new house attracting patronage.[67]

So between 1112 and 1122, when he died, Vitalis was the abbot of Savigny. However, the narrative sources tell us little about Vitalis's monastery. Although Savigny became an order (briefly and after Vitalis's death) and then was absorbed by the Cistercians, his approach to the monastic life does not seem to have been identical to that of the Cistercians. Orderic, writing before Savigny entered the Cistercian orbit (in 1147), tells us that Vitalis "did not imitate the customs of the Cluniacs [from the monastery at **Cluny**] or others who had submitted themselves to monastic observances for some time, but adopted the recent institutions of the new monks as he chose," suggesting that he picked and chose among the new options before him in this age of experimentation. He does not mention the dress of Vitalis's monks, whereas he specifically mentions the white robes of the Cistercians. Orderic then goes on to say that on Vitalis's death, his successor, Geoffrey of Bayeux, imposed new customs that were strict to the point of harshness.[68]

And then came Vitalis's death, well attested to, not least by the extraordinary mortuary roll his monks compiled and carefully preserved. The moment of his death may have been the height of his fame. Much of what happened next comes from a document written in the mid-thirteenth century, the *Miracles of the Saints of Savigny*. It reports that when the **abbey** church was demolished in the late twelfth century, to permit the building of a new one, the bodies of five holy people, including Vitalis, were moved to a chapel. Various figures were said to be present at the time, although, as Moolenbroek points out, no twelfth-century source reports these events and no bishops were said to be present.[69] The narrative then reports that in 1242, the abbot requested permission to put the **relics** – the remains were now being treated as relics – in the new church, which duly occurred on May 1, 1243, although again no bishop was said to be present and hence no **canonization** could have occurred.[70] In the wake of this event, treated in the narrative as a **translation** (the removal of a saint's body from one place to another), Ralph III

---

66 *Vital*, 100; on the council of Reims, see below, p. 139. As I mentioned earlier, Orderic attended, as did Norbert of Xanten, another reforming contemporary and saint (*Vita Norberti archepiscopi Magdebergensis*, in *Monumenta Germaniae historica, Scriptores* 12, ed. Georg Heinrich Pertz [Hannover: Hahn, 1856], 677).

67 The English royal family became significant patrons; see Francis R. Swietek, "King Henry II and Savigny," *Cîteaux: Commentarii cistercienses* 38, nos. 1–2 (1987): 14–23.

68 Orderic, 4: 333.

69 *Vital*, 82.

70 *Vital*, 83.

wrote to the pope requesting formal canonization in 1244, but it did not happen.[71] Vitalis was canonized only in 1738 by the Cistercian General Chapter.[72]

So Vitalis lived the life of a deeply respected and locally well-known man of holy reputation. It may be that had his order persisted, he would have become more than that. As it was, his **cult** (the practice of venerating him as a saint) seems to have been restricted to the local area, although it was certainly kept alive there. That does not mean he is an unimportant figure; it simply means that he was an "ordinary" saint.[73] But most locally venerated holy men and women probably didn't have full, formal biographies. It took an investment to create and preserve one; an author had to be found, for one thing, who could compose a decent biography in Latin. The author of Vitalis's biography was considerably more than that: he was a man of unusual talents who brought with him an agenda of his own. I now turn to that author, Stephen of Fougères.

---

71 *Vital*, 84. For formal canonization, see chapter 3.

72 Lindy Grant, "Savigny and Its Saints," in *Perspectives for an Architecture of Solitude: Essays on Cistercians, Art and Architecture in Honour of Peter Fergusson*, ed. Terry N. Kinder (Turnhout: Brepols, 2004), 111.

73 On the distinction between "ordinary" and "extraordinary" saints, see Janine Larmon Peterson, *Suspect Saints and Holy Heretics: Disputed Sanctity and Communal Identity in Late Medieval Italy* (Ithaca, NY: Cornell University Press, 2019), 29–35.

CHAPTER TWO

"Strive to rise swiftly from the dust": The Author Stephen of Fougères

When Stephen of Fougères died in 1178, his friend Robert of Torigni (d. 1186) wrote a charming obituary notice. Robert says that God had mercy on Stephen and wanted to give him time to repent of the frivolities of his earlier life, in which he had written "many rhythmic songs and much joking prose for the applause of men," and so sent an apparition:

> The bishop told a monk, a man known to us, about a marvelous vision that came to him before his death. For some person appeared to him and said these verses to him, in a soft hiss:
>
> Stop daring to play;
> Strive to rise swiftly
> From the dust.[1]

The soft hiss (*levi sibilo*) is a nice touch, giving the messenger a demonic aura. Robert may be alluding here as well to an incident in another work written by Stephen, the *Life of St. Firmat*, in which the saint, who is a physician, comes home to find a devil perched on his moneybox. Firmat is prompted by this encounter to take up the holy life.[2]

1 RT, 2: 73 (my translation of the Latin).

2 *Life of St. Firmat* (below, p. 153). It is also possible that Robert was thinking of Gregory the Great's *Moral Lessons on the Book of Job*, 30: 12 (Gregory the Great, *Morales sur Job, Livres xxx–xxxii*, ed. Marc Adriaen, trans. nuns of Wisques [Paris: Cerf, 2009], 48–9), where Gregory, talking about the need to vary the kinds of lessons for different audiences, notes that a soft hiss calms a horse but

Robert goes on to list Stephen's Latin works, the only way we know that Stephen was the author of the lives of Vitalis and Firmat, since the author is not named in either manuscript. Robert also mentions a fifty-line poem on old age that Stephen had written for him, which ended with one of the above lines. That poem seems not to have survived. Robert does not mention Stephen's **vernacular** work, the *Book of Conduct* (*Livre des manières*), but Stephen names himself at the end in requesting the prayers of his readers:

> God have mercy on you for your prayers
> For Master Stephen of Fougères,
> Who has shown us the modes of conduct
> Which are customary for many people:
> Which to set aside and which to take up,
> Which to flee from and which to embrace,
> Which to praise and which to reprove,
> So that we may give our souls to God.[3]

That Stephen put his name on his vernacular work and didn't on his Latin hagiographic work reflects **generic** expectations (that is, the type of work each one was; for more about this, see chapter 3). Sulpicius Severus did not name himself in his *Life of Saint Martin*, which was massively influential as a model, so **hagiographers** often did not identify themselves. In contrast, vernacular works often ended with a reference to the author or singer. For example, the last line of *The Song of Roland* is "Here ends the ancient tale that Turoldus relates."[4]

Context and positionality

In this chapter, I am going to dig into Stephen's life for two reasons. One relates to the simple issue of what historians call the "**sourcing heuristic**," namely answering all the "W" questions about a **primary source**, here *The Life of St. Vitalis*. We

---

urges a puppy on. This was the kind of work he was undoubtedly familiar with; it was available in the library of Bec, where his career began. (See Jenny Weston, "Manuscripts and Book Production at Le Bec," in *A Companion to the Abbey of Le Bec in the Central Middle Ages (11th–13th Centuries)*, ed. Benjamin Pohl and Laura L. Gathagan [Leiden: Brill, 2017], 158n58.)

3 *LM*, 13, 105 (my translation of the French). Earlier editors thought that this meant that the poet was translating something written by Stephen into French, but Lodge thinks there is no reason to hypothesize this, since Stephen obviously spoke French and Robert of Torigni tells us that he wrote vernacular songs during his days in the chancery.

4 Simon Gaunt and Karen Pratt, trans., *The Song of Roland and Other Poems of Charlemagne* (Oxford: Oxford University Press, 2016), 133.

already know the answer to "who" in this case – Stephen of Fougères – but that really doesn't give us much information by itself. All of the other questions are equally important to understand the **context** in which an author created a given work and are fundamental questions that historians ask about every source, even if they can't always answer each of them. But the second reason to research the author of a literary work is to come closer to understanding the kinds of choices that authors, even anonymous ones, make from among the possibilities available to them; that's a kind of context also. Although Stephen tells us he got information from trustworthy informants, presumably the **monks** of Savigny, it is highly unlikely that he simply took dictation from them, just as it is highly unlikely that they passed on everything they had heard about Vitalis. While he and they clearly concurred in seeing Vitalis as a holy man (if he hadn't thought so, he would not have written the hagiography), as an accomplished writer it was his job to shape the work into an appropriate literary form.

Not only would Stephen include the material he considered proper to a hagiography and exclude other material – and I will write more extensively on this issue in the next chapter – but his own interests would also govern his selection of the contents and his ideas about presentation. In other words, the text would be an expression of his **positionality**, which would be shaped by his lived experience. I'll make the case at the end of the chapter that Stephen's positionality was crucial in the form the story takes.

This chapter, therefore, has three parts. The first part is biographic; that is, I will follow Stephen's career to the degree to which this is possible, given the resources at my disposal. If I were writing an article about Stephen, there might be more that I might do, but I will provide enough material to get a "feel" for his life trajectory. This part of the chapter, therefore, is straightforward factual research, something everyone understands to be part of history, although there is silent interpretation through my selection of facts and my creating a narrative from them. The second part of the chapter will explore the question of why Stephen undertook to write the works he did, including the *Life of St. Vitalis*. This second part involves more obvious inference and interpretation. In discussing this material, I will be highlighting some facts, the interpretations of other scholars, and some of my own.

In the third part of the chapter, I will put together the pieces and provide an argument about at least one way in which Stephen's positionality affected the shape he gave to *The Life of St. Vitalis*. Here my interpretive moves are the most obvious to a history student because they are literary. In providing this interpretation, I am treating the text not as a simple transparent account of a factual past nor as a complete invention, but as a shaped response to the context in which it was created, in which Stephen selected what he included from among things he thought were true. I've done the same in writing this chapter, adding and deleting factual information many times and rewriting the prose. The reader needs to remember that my work is as positioned as Stephen's is.

Investigation of the author: Who was Stephen of Fougères?

Although scholars have known of Stephen of Fougères for decades and have written about the rough outlines of his career, they have not generally put the pieces together to create a full portrait. It has long been known that he was a clerk in Henry II's **chancery**. Indeed, his is one of only two hands whose writer can be named; his handwriting has allowed scholars to identify sixteen surviving **charters** he wrote (and more may very well surface). Generally, however, the scholars interested in Stephen's chancery career have not been interested in his life once he left the chancery.[5] Literary scholars, on the other hand, have offered brief biographies of Stephen but have not done more than mention his chancery career. In what follows, then, I've tried to draw together the bare facts amassed by previous scholars across all of the phases of Stephen's career.

Although it is tempting to see Stephen of Fougères as a member of the ruling family of Fougères, the original patrons of the **monastery** of Savigny, Stephen never suggests that he was related to the family, and most scholars, following the work of Hippolyte Pigeon, have concluded that he simply came from the town and thus acquired the **toponym**.[6] Although Savigny and Mortain were in Normandy, in the **diocese** of Avranches, Fougères was in Brittany and in the diocese of Rennes, near to where the borders of Normandy, Brittany, and Maine came together (see Map 1). In this part of Brittany, French was the vernacular language, and local nobles were thoroughly integrated into the society outside of Brittany's borders.[7] So when Stephen became the bishop of Rennes later on, he was a local man, although he had been away for quite some time. It also means that his

---

5 See T.A.M. Bishop, Scriptores regis: *Facsimiles to Identify and Illustrate the Hands of Royal Scribes in Original Charters of Henry I, Stephen, and Henry II* (Oxford: Clarendon, 1961) and "A Chancery Scribe: Stephen of Fougeres," *Cambridge Historical Journal* 10, no. 1 (1950): 106–7. Nicholas Vincent also discusses Stephen in his article "The Court of Henry II," in *Henry II: New Interpretations*, ed. Christopher Harper-Bill and Nicholas Vincent (Woodbridge: Boydell & Brewer, 2007), 278–334, in various places as well, but he does not follow him from the chancery.

6 Hippolyte Pigeon, "Étienne de Fougères et les Cisterciens," *Cîteaux: Commentarii cistercienses* 31 (1980): 181; *Vital*, 53; *LM*, 13–14.

7 Judith Everard, *Brittany and the Angevins: Province and Empire, 1158–1203* (Cambridge: Cambridge University Press, 2000), 7–8, 10–12.

vernacular was French, not Breton, which mattered in Henry II's court, where, as Nicholas Vincent has pointed out, people paid attention to accents and origins.[8]

We know nothing about Stephen's family except that he must have had at least one sibling, because his nephew Peter appears in documents from Rennes as early as 1170, eventually as an **archdeacon**, and at length Peter became bishop of Rennes himself.[9] Our first information about Peter's career, however, is that he was a canon at the **Augustinian** house of Saint-Pierre de Rillé in Fougères, which may mean that Stephen's family remained in Fougères.[10]

Stephen's career suggests that his family must have been prosperous, because he was well educated. There were a number of places where he might have acquired his early education. There was a school in a **priory** of Marmoutier in Fougères, and of course the canons of Mortain, not far away, also ran one.[11] However, he clearly had advanced education as well. In the passage from the *Book of Conduct* that I quoted above, he calls himself "master" (*mestre*), and he appears in Latin documents he drew up or witnessed as "master" as well. While the term "master" in the twelfth century did not imply a specific degree, as it came to later, it did mean that the individual was considered highly educated by his contemporaries.[12] A surviving copy of Peter Lombard's commentary on St. Paul's *Epistle to the Romans* and *First Letter to the Corinthians* belonged to Stephen.[13] The Lombard taught at Paris; Stephen may have studied there, as did other of his contemporaries. Thomas Becket (1118–70), Stephen's contemporary and superior in the chancery, spent a year at Paris, although he was not nearly as learned as Stephen.[14] A younger contemporary and court clerk, Walter Map (c. 1140–c. 1210), was also educated at Paris and was similarly termed "master."[15] It is possible that Stephen

---

8 Vincent, "Court of Henry II," 325–6.

9 *Cartulaire de Saint-Melaine de Rennes suivi de 51 chartes originales* (Rennes: Presses Universitaires de Rennes & Société d'Histoire et d'Archéologie de Bretagne, 2015), 91, where Peter attests to a confirmation made by Stephen of previous donations to the monastery of Saint-Melaine.

10 Rillé was closely associated with Savigny, however, so here is another connection between Stephen and his family and that monastery (*GC*, 14: 790–1). Peter appears as a witness in a charter of 1170 (*Cartulaire de Saint-Melaine*, 90–1), where he is identified as Stephen's nephew; is not identified as belonging to the diocese of Rennes; and where he witnesses after William, the abbot of Fougères.

11 B.-A. Pocquet du Haut-Jussé, "Étienne de Fougères," in *Dictionnaire d'histoire et géographie écclesiastique*, vol. 15, ed. R. Aubert and É. van Cauwenbergh (Paris: Letouzey et Ané, 1963), 1224.

12 In a notice he drew up of an accord between Henry II and the monastery of Mont Saint-Michel in 1166, Stephen is also called master (RT, 2: 286). He also witnessed a document in 1165, in which he is also designated as "master" (Robert William Eyton, *Court, Household, and Itinerary of Henry II* [London: Taylor and Co., 1878], 88).

13 Pigeon, "Cistercians," 185n16. This is the book in which Stephen wrote an account of the achievements of his inaugural year, which I will discuss below.

14 Frank Barlow, "Becket, Thomas [St Thomas of Canterbury, Thomas of London]," *ODNB*, https://doi.org/10.1093/ref:odnb/27201.

15 C.N.L. Brooke, "Map, Walter," *ODNB*, https://doi.org/10.1093/ref:odnb/18015.

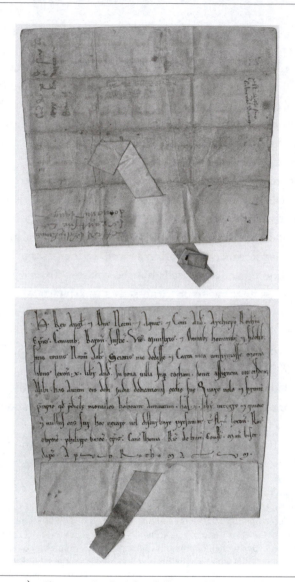

FIGURE 2 (A AND B): *Charter in Stephen's hand (front and back). (Archives Départementales de Calvados 2H/133/1.)*

This charter, tentatively dated between 1156 and 1161, was written by Stephen. As T.A.M. Bishop has noted, Stephen used an adapted "book hand" (a formal hand normally used to copy books) rather than cursive (a faster and more connected hand typically used in documents) to draft his charters, which makes them fairly clear and easy to read. This charter was drafted at Rouen ("Apud Rothomagum" is written across the bottom of the charter) and granted the nuns of Notre-Dame-du-Pré near Lisieux £10 Angevin to be collected at Bonneville-sur-Touques, until the king granted them this sum elsewhere, in honor of the dedication of their church. Three bishops (Lisieux, Evreux, and Bayeux) witnessed, alongside Thomas Becket (in his capacity as chancellor), the king's constable, and the royal seneschal.

studied some law, since a **chirograph** issued in Stephen's name in 1174 of the settlement of a property dispute between Savigny and Saint-Melaine, a monastery in Rennes, cites the legal maxim that more recent laws overrule older ones.[16] (Chirographs were formal legal documents copied two or three times on the same piece of parchment, with the word "chirographum" written between the copies. The copies would then be cut apart using a wavy or jagged cut through the word, so that they could be matched up for authentication, and each party would get a copy sealed with the other party's seal.) However, Stephen was extremely unlikely to have composed the text of the settlement himself (he had clerks for that), so it may only be that the drafter of the agreement had legal knowledge. But even if Stephen, himself an experienced clerk, dictated the text, to cite a maxim of this kind doesn't necessarily imply very *deep* formal legal knowledge.

Stephen's chancery career

Since V.H. Galbraith has identified Stephen's hand, we know that Stephen had joined the English royal chancery by 1157.[17] Thomas Becket became chancellor in 1154, so it is tempting to speculate that the two men met in Paris and that Stephen got his job though this connection, but we really don't know how Stephen ended up at the court. What we do know, however, is that Henry II (r. 1154–89) was having to rebuild the institutions of royal government, which had collapsed under his predecessor, King Stephen (r. 1135–54). After years of civil war in England, it was important for the new king to project a powerful image, and effective administrative structures were part of that.[18] Competent men were needed to do the work, which was not simply menial. While chancery clerks copied things, they also drafted documents and might use characteristic turns of phrase, as Stephen did (this is how his authorship of some documents has been determined).[19] However, it is also possible that Stephen came recommended by Henry of Fougères, who eventually became a monk at Savigny but who had been a staunch supporter of Henry II when Henry was still just the duke of Normandy.[20]

---

16 *Cartulaire de Saint-Melaine*, 138–9.

17 Anthony Lodge, "The Literary Interest of the 'Livre des manières' of Étienne de Fougères," *Romania* 93 (1972): 480.

18 Nicholas Karn, "Nigel, Bishop of Ely, and the Restoration of the Chancery after the 'Anarchy' of Stephen's Reign," *Historical Research* 80, no. 209 (2007): 299–314.

19 V.H. Galbraith, "Seven Charters of Henry II at Lincoln Cathedral," *The Antiquaries Journal* 12, no. 3 (1932): 269–78; Bishop, "A Chancery Scribe," 106.

20 Everard, *Brittany and the Angevins*, 36. Henry's son Ralph seems to have been loyal to Henry II until 1164 (ibid., 55).

Under Henry II, the royal chancery, or at least part of it, travelled with the king, although the financial office, the **exchequer**, resided at Westminster.[21] That means both that scribes travelled fairly widely and also that the king would have come to know many of these individuals on a personal level, because he was frequently in their company. The surviving charters that Stephen copied and/or witnessed place him at Lincoln, Rouen, Brill (in Buckinghamshire), Windsor, Portchester, Fécamp, Fougères (his home town!), Lyons-la-Forêt, Thouars, Tours, and Surgères while still attached to the chancery.[22] This is certainly a very partial account of the places he would have gone, because these are only the places from which some surviving charters were issued. The important point here is that he travelled widely within Henry's domains and would have met many of the movers and shakers of Henry's empire. It would have been a test of his people skills as well as his competence as a scribe, in other words, his competence as a courtier.

Probably no scholar has described Henry's court so richly or well as Nicholas Vincent, who outlines numerous points worth considering in relation to Stephen. Vincent surveyed the witnesses to over three thousand of the surviving charters of Henry II and catalogued the number of people who witnessed at least fifteen times. (He notes that given the nature of documentary survival and that only the most solemn of the charters survived, with very few of the numerous writs and directives the chancery also produced being saved, this is undoubtedly a significant undercount.) Stephen appears in twenty-five of those charters (including some witnessed in his later life as canon and bishop). Many people we know were at the court do not appear at all, so Stephen's multiple appearances there are a sign of continued favor, as well as availability, although the historian Galbraith thought Stephen acted as the **chancellor**'s deputy and so was particularly important.[23] Henry II was known to take a liking to people and not to change his mind lightly once he had, so to be part of that inner circle was significant.[24]

The court of Henry II

Equally important, to be a member of the court of Henry II was to enter an environment with many highly educated people, many of whom had literary aspirations.

---

21 Karn, "Nigel of Ely," 300–1. Karn notes, however, that the treasurer sometimes travelled with the court, leaving a president to handle day-to-day affairs (302).
22 Bishop, "A Chancery Scribe," 106–7.
23 Vincent, "The Court of Henry II," 288–91. Some 116 men appear on the list, so Stephen was in a fairly small company (Galbraith, "Seven Charters," 274).
24 Vincent, "Henry II," 295, referencing Gerald of Wales (c. 1146–c. 1223). Only one of the clerics on Vincent's list failed to become a bishop (ibid., 294).

This court produced an extraordinary quantity of writing of all kinds.[25] The Latin writers of the later period of Henry's court, such as Peter of Blois (c. 1130–c. 1203), Walter Map, Gerald of Wales (Gerald de Barry, c. 1145–before 1223), and Gervaise of Tilbury (c. 1150–c. 1220), are probably better known than those at the court at the beginning of Henry's reign; all of these men entered royal service either at the end of Stephen's chancery career or after his departure in 1166. But John of Salisbury (also Paris-educated) was a slightly older contemporary and a major literary figure of Stephen's period. John (d. 1180) worked for the archbishops of Canterbury, but it was a small world. John's *Entheticus in dogmate philosophorum* (*Interpolation into the Teachings of the Philosophers*) and his *Policraticus* (*The Statesman*) were both written around the time that Stephen entered the chancery and were both dedicated to Stephen's first boss, Thomas Becket. The *Entheticus* is a verse satire, while the *Policraticus* was a lengthy treatise about the court and governance, along with many other things.[26] Stephen knew the *Policraticus*, which he used as a source in the *Book of Conduct* in a number of places.[27] Literary composition was as competitive as anything else in this very competitive court, and it was a court hungry for entertainment. Great storytellers like Walter Map could gain a reputation, as Gerald of Wales reported.[28]

Henry's court was also a collection point for vernacular literature in French. (Nothing has survived in English from that period and not all courtiers learned it.)[29] Quite a lot of literature in French was either explicitly commissioned by the king and his wife, Eleanor of Aquitaine (1122–1204), or dedicated/offered to them,

---

25 Vincent, "Henry II," 320.

26 Perhaps the swiftest introduction to John and his work is David Luscombe, "Salisbury, John of," *ODNB*, https://doi.org/10.1093/ref:odnb/14849. The word *entheticus* is Greek, not Latin, and is generally not translated. John wrote other works, particularly the *Metalogicon*, where in a famous passage he describes Bernard of Chartres saying that moderns saw further because they were dwarves standing on the shoulders of giants, but I have limited my references to him here to the works that would have been read and discussed at the court.

27 Keith V. Sinclair, "L'inspiration liturgique du *Livre des manières* d'Etienne de Fougères," *Cahiers de civilisation médiévale* 40, no. 159 (July–September 1997): 261. Stephen's familiarity with the *Policraticus* appears in his discussion of hunting in *laisses*, 16–18, among other places. See, for example, Kerstin Hård af Segerstad, *Quelques commentaires sur la plus ancienne chanson d'états française*, *Le* Livre des manières *d'Étienne de Fougères* (Upsala, Sweden: Edv. Berling, 1906), 26, 29, 34.

28 Walter Map, *De nugis curialium: Courtiers' Trifles*, ed. and trans. M.R. James, revised by C.N.L. Brooke and R.A.B. Mynors (Oxford: Clarendon, 1983), xxii. On the hunger for entertainment, see Vincent, "Henry II," 319–20.

29 Walter Map jokingly said that Henry II knew of every language as far as the Jordan, but he spoke Latin and French (Map, *De nugis*, 37). Peter of Blois seems never to have learned to speak English in all his years in England, as he says in one of his letters. R.W. Southern, "Blois, Peter of," *ODNB*, https://doi.org/10.1093/ref:odnb/22012.

as Karen Broadhurst has laid out.[30] While none of Stephen's works from this period has survived, at least that we know of, he was a contributor to this literary
interchange through the songs and stories Robert mentions in his obituary.

Stephen seems to be referring to this period of his life in his *Book of Conduct*
when he laments the "dissipation" of his youth:

> I repent of my foolish life,
> For great fear seizes me
> When I remember I gave my whole youth
> Completely over to foolish purposes.
>
> Nothing good, so much evil!
> I find nothing that might please God!
> [missing line]
> So that my heart has neither rest nor ease.
>
> So much evil, nothing good!
> I am the tree that gives no fruit.
> God who damns and pardons,
> Knows who deserves the flame or the crown.[31]

To modern ears, this all seems a little harsh, but medieval moral authors might
be expected to engage in a little instructive self-criticism, without anyone necessarily taking it too much to heart.

Stephen's post-chancery career

Another point that Vincent makes about the circle around Henry II is that with
the notable exception of Becket, they were remarkably loyal to the king for the rest
of their careers. Geoffrey Ridel (d. 1189), who succeeded Becket as chancellor and
who became an archdeacon of Canterbury, was excommunicated twice for his actions on behalf of the king against Becket, but he eventually became the bishop of
Ely, one of the richest dioceses in England.[32] Stephen also clearly remained loyal,

---

30 See Karen M. Broadhurst, "Henry II of England and Eleanor of Aquitaine: Patrons of Literature in
French?," *Viator* 27 (1996): 53–84. She is more interested in situations in which money or other pay-
ment changed hands; I'm simply interested in what French literature was floating around in the court.

31 *LM*, 102, ll. 1257–61, 1269–73 (my translation). Jacques T.E. Thomas, *Le Livre des manières* (Paris-
Louvain: Peeters, 2013), pp. 98, 273, suggests this for the missing line: "I know it well, and it weighs
on me" (my translation).

32 A.J. Duggan, "Ridel, Geoffrey," ODNB, https://doi.org/10.1093/ref:odnb/23618. On the wealth of
Ely, see James A. Brundage, *The Medieval Origins of the Legal Profession: Canonists, Civilians, and
Courts* (Chicago: University of Chicago Press, 2008), 240n79.

which may have been a factor in his next appointment, for in 1166 he was rewarded with a promotion to the office of **cantor** in the **collegiate church** of Saint-Évroul at Mortain, where Vitalis's career had begun; Henry had become count of Mortain in 1159.[33] Given that Mortain was close to the border with Brittany, I suspect that this appointment was a way for Henry to place an agent with local knowledge and connections in a politically unsettled region. Whether this was the occasion upon which Stephen began to use the title of royal **chaplain**, or whether this title had been granted to him earlier as a sign of royal favor, sometime around this time he was granted the title and he used it for the rest of his life.[34]

While a canon of Mortain, Stephen seems to have continued to travel with the king. Two charters Stephen drafted in favor of Mont Saint-Michel in 1166, when he had taken the position as cantor, were created at Fougères, when Henry's army captured the town from its rebellious lord, Ralph.[35] Ralph was probably reacting to events earlier in the year when Henry had forced the duke of Brittany, Conan IV, to abdicate in favor of his daughter Constance, to whom Henry engaged his own son Geoffrey. (I am indebted here to Judith Everard's work on Brittany.) While some of the Breton nobility acquiesced in this regime change (some of them also held lands in England, including Conan), other nobles revolted; Henry then carried out two campaigns and squashed the rebellion.[36]

It is not clear what role Stephen played in assisting the king in his efforts in these years. However, it must have been quite satisfactory, for Henry engineered Stephen's election in 1168 as bishop of Rennes, a city over which Henry had just taken control.[37] As bishop, Stephen continued to serve the king as an "active partner" of Henry's **seneschal** at Rennes.[38] When the Breton revolts were sufficiently

---

33   Henry's cousin, who had held the county, died in that year, which meant the office went back to the duke of Normandy (Thomas K. Keefe, "William, earl of Surrey," *ODNB*, http://www.oxforddnb .com/view/article/46707). Later, Richard I (r. 1189–99) gave it to his brother John (r. 1199–1216), but Henry hung onto it until his death, no doubt because of its strategic importance.

34   Robert of Torigni, when he writes of Stephen's appointment, mentions that he was a royal chaplain but does not explain further (RT, 2: 2). Stephen is noted in some documents of c. 1166 as a chaplain.

35   Léopold Delisle, *Recueil des actes de Henri II, roi d'Angleterre et de Normandie concernant les provinces françaises et les affaires de France*, 3 vols., ed. Élie Berger (Paris: Imprimerie Nationale, 1916–27), 1: 402–4, 402n1, and 404n1. The dating clauses referring to Stephen as cantor appear only in the cartulary of Mont Saint-Michel. However, the hand of the one original has been identified as that of Stephen. In the next year (probably), Stephen was with the king in Surgères in Poitou, where he was one of the witnesses (Robert of Torigni was another) when Henry II recognized the liberties of the burghers of Pontorson. Stephen is there named as the king's chaplain and the cantor of Mortain (ibid., 1: 417).

36   This is a synopsis of the events described by Everard, *Brittany and the Angevins*, chap. 2.

37   Everard, *Brittany and the Angevins*, 67.

38   Everard, *Brittany and the Angevins*, 68. Stephen mentions in his account of his inaugural year's activities that William witnessed the transfer of property by the monks of Melleray to the diocese of Rennes in the cathedral chapter house.

quelled, Henry sent his son Geoffrey, then nine, to Rennes to receive the homage of the Breton barons, and Stephen was there with the bishop of Saint-Malo and Robert of Torigni to greet him.[39]

But even though Stephen now had a diocese to administer (and everything that can be gleaned about his activities suggests that he was a serious and capable administrator), he remained a loyal friend and servant to the king. On August 24, 1169, Stephen visited the **papal legates** charged with negotiating between Henry and Becket at Domfront, along with the king. (I will say more about the "Becket controversy" below.) While he is not mentioned by anyone as being present in the negotiations carried out at Bayeux later in the month, he was present at Bur-le-roi in early September as the negotiations continued, so it is reasonable to think he had been part of the negotiations all along.[40] After Becket's murder, Henry had to negotiate his reconciliation with the Church, which he did at Savigny in May 1172. Robert of Torigni is remarkably terse about the nature of these negotiations, so it is not clear which bishops would have been involved or if Stephen was there.[41] But he was certainly present at Le Mans in December of that year, where he witnessed a grant to the nuns of Locmaria (in Quimper in Brittany) along with the papal legates.[42] He was at Henry's court at Caen sometime between 1172 and 1175, where he witnessed a charter for the nuns of St. Mary of Lisieux.[43] He was one of the witnesses who ratified the agreement between Henry and his sons on October 10, 1174, at Falaise, and he was present in 1175 at the reconciliation between Henry II and his eldest son, also named Henry (the Young King, 1155–83), in April at Bur-le-roi.[44] I have found no indications, however, that Stephen ever set foot on the English side of the Channel after 1166, although, of course, he may have done. (This is one of the limitations of using charter evidence to track someone's movements in the Middle Ages; one can speak only about places where a charter has survived that someone witnessed or composed, not all the places they may have gone that have left no such traces.)

Stephen as bishop

I've been concentrating on Stephen's relationship with Henry II, for reasons that will become clearer below, but as I said above, he was also a serious and effective

---

39 RT, 2: 13.

40 Eyton, *Court, Household, and Itinerary*, 124, 128.

41 RT, 2: 31–2.

42 Delisle, *Recueil*, 1: 581.

43 Delisle, *Recueil*, 2: 28 argues for either 1172–3 or 1175; Eyton, *Court, Household, and Itinerary*, 177–8, opts for the Christmas court at Caen in 1173.

44 Delisle, *Recueil*, 2: 21–4; Eyton, *Court, Household, and Itinerary*, 187.

bishop of his diocese. There are relatively few surviving diplomatic sources (charters and other documents of this kind) from Brittany through which to track
him,[45] but Stephen commented on his own activities as bishop in his personal
copy of Peter Lombard's commentary on the *Epistle to the Romans*:

> The lack of writers consigns deeds worthy of memory done by earlier peo-
> ple to oblivion, from which great harm comes to church property and dig-
> nity. For that reason, I Stephen, bishop of Rennes such as I am and chaplain
> of the king of England, propose to transmit to memory those things I rea-
> sonably acquired for the use and honor of our church, not led to win a
> title of foolish glory, but hoping in this little way to assist my soul, so that
> whoever may read these things with a devout heart and a well-meaning
> voice shall not fail to say, "May the soul of Stephen of Fougères, bishop of
> Rennes, rest in peace."[46]

Stephen went on to list what he had done in the first year of his episcopacy,
which was mostly to acquire property for the church of Rennes, to rebuild one of
the episcopal houses and the church attached to it, to settle a grievance over property, and to build a chapel in the bishop's garden to Mary and St. Firmat. He also
purchased property from the **Cistercians** of Melleray and resettled the peasants
on it whom the Cistercians had turfed off when the monks acquired the property,
keeping only the manor house and woods, although the peasants were allowed
to use the woods for firewood and building supplies. Many of Stephen's contemporaries complained about the Cistercian practice of clearing land of its inhabitants when they were given it, so this appears to constitute a gentle rebuke or at
least a conscious act of restitution.[47] As the author of Stephen's biography in the
Dictionary of Ecclesiastical History and Geography points out, many of Stephen's
surviving acts involve him settling or witnessing the settlement of quarrels.[48] It is
also worth noting that Stephen was still referring to himself as a royal chaplain in
this document, as he did in the charter he had drawn up of a settlement between

---

45 Everard, *Brittany and the Angevins*, 5–7.
46 RT, 2: 2, n4.
47 For the whole text, see Hyacinthe Morice, *Mémoires pour servir de preuves à l'histoire ecclésias-
tique et civil de Bretagne*, vol. 1 (Paris: Éditions du Palais Royal, 1974), 672–3; the excerpt quoted
above is my translation. For contemporary critiques of the Cistercians (as well as praise), see Bede
K. Lackner, "Friends and Critics of Early Cîteaux," *Analecta cisterciensia* 34, nos. 1–2 (1979): 17–26.
Walter Map wrote a series of anecdotes blisteringly hostile to the Cistercians in his *Courtiers' Trifles* (Map, *De nugis*, 77–113), and Orderic's treatise on the new orders expresses both admiration
for their piety and critique of their practices (Orderic, 4: 325–7).
48 Pocquet du Haut-Jussé, "Étienne de Fougères," 1224.

the monks of Saint-Broladre and Mont Saint-Michel that he adjudicated in 1170.[49] Clearly once a royal chaplain, always a royal chaplain.

In the *Book of Conduct*, Stephen writes extensively of the obligations of the bishop, and it is hard not to see this as a reflection of his sense of his responsibilities. Kerstin Hård af Segerstad, in her study of this text, notes that this portion of Stephen's poem hews particularly closely to the sentiments of the **canonists** about bishops (and also to the *Policraticus*). The bishop should be chaste and humble and generous in alms:[50]

> Wherever he goes, he ought to preach
> Whenever he is face to face with his people.
> He should censure all of the vices for them,
> Praise good and reprove evil.[51]

In fact, this is what Stephen was doing in his vernacular book.

Why did Stephen write?

My discussion above has provided a fairly extensive overview of what sort of person Stephen was. He was a faithful clerk and courtier with a lifelong dedication to his king. He was both educated and cultivated, a man often called upon to make peace in both the secular and ecclesiastical worlds. He had spent at least ten years in an intensely literary court to which he had clearly contributed, even if we don't know exactly what he wrote there. When he became a bishop, he seems to have taken those responsibilities seriously too.

What these observations do not explain, however, is why Stephen chose (or was chosen) to write the three works of his that survive, when he did so, and for whom he wrote them. While some medieval writers seem to have written on their own initiative – Walter Map, for instance, set down his courtier's trifles as the culmination of a lifetime of oral storytelling – many wrote either because they were asked to do so or because they hoped to please someone with the gift of a written work. Writers often included this information in the prefaces of their texts, by writing a dedicatory letter, or by asking for a work to be vetted.

Modern people don't tend to think of literary works as operating as a kind of **social capital**, yet for medieval writers, literary compositions could be written to

---

49 RT, 2: 292.
50 Hård af Segerstad, *Quelques commentaires*, 25–9.
51 *LM*, 73, ll. 329–33 (my translation).

appease rage, to gain attention and favor, or to cement friendships. Thus Lambert of Ardres (d. after 1206) says he wrote his history of the counts of Guines and lords of Ardres to regain the favor of Count Baldwin II, who was a man capable of holding a lifelong grudge. (It didn't work.)[52] Similarly, Wace (d. after 1174) may have offered his *Romance of Brut* to Henry II in hopes of some sort of compensation; he seems to have received a position in Bayeux either because of that work or because of work he did afterward on his *Romance of Rou* [*Rollo*].[53] Finally, to provide a humbler example, Jocelyn of Brakelond reports that when he was casting around for a gift for the Feast of the Circumcision (January 1) for his rather difficult abbot, he created a list of the manors belonging to the abbey and their annual incomes as a gift.[54]

Unlike these other figures, however, Stephen was himself a powerful man at the time he wrote the works we've been talking about. It is therefore unlikely that he was expecting a reward or preferment for his literary work. It seems more likely that he was doing favors for friends (as he wrote the now-lost poem for Robert of Torigni), filling a perceived need, or striving to rise from the dust through edifying words.

The Life of St. Firmat

In the case of St. Firmat, it is easy to see why a biography was needed. Firmat was officially **canonized** on June 10, 1156; that is, his body was solemnly taken from its tomb by the archbishop of Rouen and the bishops of Évreux, Avranches (the diocese in which Mortain was located), and Coutances. An altar was then consecrated to him by the bishop of Avranches, and he was ceremonially reburied.[55] But an official canonization meant that a **liturgy** was needed to celebrate his feast days (both the date of his death in April and the date when his body was moved to its new site in June), and a biography was normally required to be read on these occasions. Perhaps the canons did not feel up to writing such a life themselves at the time of the canonization, for Robert of Torigni's comments suggest that Stephen was not replacing an existing biography. Since, as far as we know, Stephen's connection to Mortain began with his appointment as cantor, it seems most likely that Stephen wrote the biography after that happened.

---

52 Lambert of Ardres, *History of the Counts of Guines and Lords of Ardres*, trans. Leah Shopkow (Philadelphia: University of Pennsylvania Press, 2001), 186.

53 Jean Blacker, "Wace," *ODNB*, https://doi.org/10.1093/ref:odnb/28365.

54 Jocelyn of Brakelond, *Chronicle of the Abbey of Bury St. Edmunds*, trans. Diana Greenway and Jane Sayers (Oxford: Oxford University Press, 1989), 56–8. January 1 was not the New Year at this time, so this was not a New Year's gift (gift giving at this time was an old tradition).

55 RT, 1: 299.

Precisely when is still uncertain. While there is little in the biography that allows us to date it – Firmat died around 1095, and there are no obvious references to any particular period of time – Stephen's decision to create the chapel dedicated to Mary and to St. Firmat in his first year at Rennes implies that he had either already written the saint's biography or that he was engaged in doing it. And given Stephen's eminence and the fact that he was already an experienced writer, it makes sense that he was either asked to do this or took it on himself as a contribution to the community he had joined, or perhaps even a little of both.

The Book of Conduct

The genesis of the *Book of Conduct* is more nebulous. Stephen could certainly have chosen to write it off his own bat, perhaps as a response to some of the moral treatises circulating in his time. However, a reference to a countess of Hereford in the *Book of Conduct* suggested to Hård af Segerstad and Lodge that the book was dedicated to her, given to her, and/or, perhaps, requested by her. Who is meant is something the two scholars don't agree on. Hård af Segerstad thought she was Dametta Goyon, whose father was Adam of Hereford. Lodge identifies her as Cecily, who went through three husbands before her death around 1204. The earl of Hereford was the first, but Cecily continued to use the title of countess for the rest of her life.[56] Whichever of the two ladies she was (and I'm inclined toward Cecily), Stephen invokes her when he discusses women who have no children, who share their goods with the poor. He then says,

> The countess of Hereford
> Will know whether I am right or wrong.
> She had children, but they are all dead.
> Now all her joy is in God.[57]

It is difficult to know for certain if Stephen knew Cecily, although his comments imply that he knew her personally. Furthermore, the family of her third husband,

---

56 Hård af Segerstad, *Quelques commentaires*, 88–9; *LM*, 17–18. Her second husband was William of Poitou, but by 1162 she had married Walter of Mayenne; she died around 1204. Hård af Segerstad rejects the identification of Cecily, because Roger, earl of Hereford, was already dead when Stephen was writing. However, when Roger died, Henry II did not permit his brother and heir to assume the title of earl (the English counterpart of "count"), which left Cecily to use it. It may also be that Stephen met her before Roger's death in 1155 (depending on when he came to court). See David Crouch, "Roger, earl of Hereford," *ODNB* https://doi.org/10.1093/ref:odnb/47203.

57 *LM*, 100, ll. 1204–8 (my translation).

Walter III of Mayenne, had a long relationship with Savigny going back to the founding, and they were an important family in this border region.[58]

Stephen's intentions for the work are a little less clear. It could certainly have served as pious reading for a lay audience, given that it was written in the vernacular. As Hård af Segerstad noted, the *Book of Conduct* drew on vernacular sources like *The Romance of Alexander*, as well as the Bible and the *Policraticus*, and these vernacular references might well have been a result of Stephen wishing to meet a lay audience where it was coming from.

That said, the *Book of Conduct* is an unusual work. It has the distinction of being the first surviving moral work written in the French vernacular about different classes of society, although contemporaries were penning Latin versions of this kind of text, usually satires about vice. However, in contrast to the authors of satires, who urged moral reform through often harsh mockery, Stephen recognized the need of most people to live in the world and offered advice on how to live honestly in such treacherous circumstances, while not ignoring the sins that different classes of people were prone to.[59] In other words, it is sermon-like in its approach but is ultimately practical in its expectations. The organization is essentially liturgical, as it treats the different groups in society in the order in which a priest would have prayed for them in the common prayer for the faithful. That prayer would ordinarily have been delivered in the vernacular, which can help explain why the text survives in a manuscript otherwise dedicated to sermons.[60]

While the *Book of Conduct* makes no overt reference to historical events that might permit it to be dated, Anthony Lodge, the editor, points to the inclusion of two saints in the **litany** (a prayer asking for a series of holy figures to pray for one) that forms the end of the poem. St. Melaine, who appears in the last verse, was the third bishop of Rennes and the patron saint of the most important monastery in Rennes, so Stephen was clearly writing after he became bishop.[61] But Lodge also argues that the St. Thomas who appears in the litany has to be Thomas

---

58 *LM*, 18n13. A document issued by Calixtus II in 1119 addresses the lords of Fougères and Mayenne, along with others, saying that Savigny had been placed under his protection and urging them to protect it as well (*Vital*, 99). As Moolenbroek notes, members of the family appeared as witnesses to documents relating to Savigny (*Vital*, 107) and as donors to the monastery, connected as they had been to Vitalis through his stint as a hermit (186–7). Cecily's husband Walter appears in a letter from his father Geoffrey confirming the properties of Savigny donated by his family in an act of 1168 (Auvray, 3: 174).

59 *LM*, 33, 35.

60 For this argument, see Sinclair, "L'inspiration liturgique," 262–3. Lodge (*LM*, 9–10) describes the manuscript, most of which contains sermons of Hildebert of Le Mans. The entire manuscript, however, is copied in one hand and may have come from the monastery of Saint-Aubin in Angers.

61 *LM*, 19; 104, ll. 1325–6.

Becket, who was canonized in February 1173, which implies that the composition was after that date.[62] Thomas, who has recently re-edited and translated the work, however, thinks Lodge is being overly precise.[63]

The Life of Vitalis

I want to postpone the question of *when* Stephen wrote the *Life of St. Vitalis*, for which there is no *explicit* **internal evidence** (that is, reference to some datable event), because it is connected to what I'm going to discuss in the third section of this chapter, namely how Stephen's positionality affected what he wrote. This demonstrates the ways in which some of the questions we ask as historians are intertwined, making us go backward and forward between different approaches to arrive at our interpretations. Instead, I want to consider why the monks would have wanted a life of their founder to be written, when he was not officially canonized and their order was no longer independent.

First, it is clear that although he was uncanonized, Vitalis was viewed as a saint. Robert of Torigni calls him one in Stephen's obituary. And although Vitalis had not been canonized, Moolenbroek, in his extensive monograph, suggests that the monks were planning at least a local canonization campaign, and a biography would have been useful in that regard (although, as is clear from the case of St. Firmat, not essential).[64] He notes that when Savigny joined the Cistercian order, it was **filiated** directly to Clairvaux (that is, for Cistercian organizational purposes, Clairvaux was Savigny's mother house).[65] Bernard of Clairvaux, the most important Cistercian saint, was officially canonized on January 18, 1174, so perhaps the monks were inspired by that campaign. Furthermore, Savigny, which had been fairly eclipsed after it joined the Cistercians, was undergoing a period of revitalization under Prior Haimo. Haimo had begun building a new church in 1173, when he died. In addition, the monks may have wished to have Vitalis recognized on the Cistercian **calendar**. Finally, around the same time or a little later, biographies were written of Geoffrey (Vitalis's successor and the man responsible for the creation of the brief-lived **order of Savigny**), Haimo, and Peter of Avranches.

---

62 *LM*, 20–1.

63 Thomas, *Livre*, 10.

64 *Vital*, 72–5.

65 Cistercian houses all belonged to a filiation that connected them to one of the four original daughter-houses of Cîteaux: Clairvaux, La Ferté, Morimund, and Pontigny. Houses created by colonization from an existing house automatically were the daughter-houses of the founding establishment. Houses that joined the order were assigned to a filiation. Savigny was thus placed close to the center of the Cistercian order. See Moolenbroek, *Vital*, 72–5, for what follows.

In other words, the life of Vitalis seems to have been part of a regular program of commemoration at the monastery.[66]

That, of course, does not explain why *Stephen* was asked to write the biography. True, he was from Fougères, and the lords of Fougères were major patrons of the monastery, while Savigny held property in Fougères. Savigny is close to Mortain (21 km), where Stephen was a canon and Vitalis had been before him. The female Savigniac house of Neufbourg (Abbaye Blanche) was just outside Mortain as well, and Stephen may well have had contact with the nuns. In addition, as bishop of Rennes, Stephen had regular contact with the monks of Savigny, who owned property in his diocese; he adjudicated their property disputes and confirmed their holdings.[67] Savigny is only 76 km from Rennes by modern roads, or only two days travel (one if a person was really booking it on a horse). But there is, perhaps, a closer connection. Here it seems fitting to return to the question of Stephen's positionality.

Stephen of Fougères and the Becket controversy

There were several major crises during Stephen's reign as archbishop of Rennes that probably had an effect on his writing, but the most significant was the Becket controversy, which began just before Stephen became a canon at Mortain. Although scholars are very familiar with the particulars, it is worth briefly going over them here for readers who are less acquainted with the issues. As I have mentioned above, Becket was once Henry II's chancellor and friend, and Stephen's superior in the chancery. No cleric that Henry II trusted rose higher than Becket, who became the archbishop of Canterbury, the most important religious figure in England.

Henry clearly supposed he was gaining a loyal supporter, as he did with all the other men he favored. However, Becket began to steer an independent course as archbishop of Canterbury. Henry was deeply concerned that **clergy** who committed secular crimes like murder were being let off easily in church courts, where they had a right to have their cases heard, and the king issued legislation at Clarendon in 1164 to have them tried in secular courts. However, Becket insisted on the Church's jurisdiction over these individuals, even though most of the English bishops sided with the king. After a threatening confrontation, Becket fled to France, where he remained for the next six years. The Cistercian order

---

66 See *The Lives of the Monastic Reformers*.
67 See, for example, *Cartulaire de Saint-Melaine*, 132–3.

FIGURE 3: *The murder of Thomas Becket, reliquary casket, between 1173 and 1180. (New York, Metropolitan Museum of Art, Acquisition number 17.190.520; public domain, Creative Commons.)*
This reliquary was made to contain a relic of Thomas Becket. This long panel shows the murder, while the other long panel shows Becket's body tended by monks of Canterbury. The monks began making relics immediately after the murder by dipping pieces of cloth into Becket's blood, making Becket into an almost instant saint. The psalter (a copy of the book of Psalms) from which the image on the cover of this book comes, which is roughly contemporary with this casket, also has a scene of monks with Becket's body, suggesting that these two depictions were a common pairing. Since Thomas was canonized in 1173, the casket and the picture are among the earliest witnesses to the growth of Thomas's cult, but many others followed, as his cult became widespread, and his shrine at Canterbury became a major pilgrimage site. Images of his martyrdom can be found in murals, mosaic, ivories, metalwork, glass, and sculpture as well as manuscript paintings created in France, England, Germany, Italy, and Spain within a couple of decades of his death. The powerful resonance of his story helps explain the need for Stephen's efforts to redeem his king.

initially sheltered Becket at Pontigny, out of Henry's reach, but in 1166 Henry threatened to seize the order's property in England, and the order backed down.[68] In the meantime, Becket issued excommunications against the bishops who had crowned Henry's son Henry as king, further angering the king.[69]

At the time Stephen became bishop (to remind you, this happened in 1168), intensive negotiations were going on about the circumstances under which those who had been excommunicated in the controversy (which included Stephen's former superior, Geoffrey Ridel) might be absolved and Becket might return. Stephen participated in these negotiations, as I mentioned above, meeting with the papal legates and witnessing agreements. Becket returned to England in 1170 and was murdered in his cathedral at the altar shortly after Christmas. It was widely believed that Henry had either deliberately or inadvertently ordered the murder, because the knights who killed the archbishop reportedly cried out "Royal! Royal!" as they pushed their way in.

Henry's supporters responded in various ways to the murder. Robert of Torigni, who was updating and continuing the great chronicle of Sigebert of Gembloux (c. 1030–1112), quite simply does not mention the murder at all in his entries for 1170 and 1171, although in writing about events in 1172, he refers to Becket as "Thomas, of pious memory."[70] Nonetheless, it was clear even to those who loved him that Henry was going to have to atone in some way, and intense negotiations followed the murder. While these negotiations were held in various places, much of the discussion took place at Savigny, which had long enjoyed patronage from Henry's family.[71] Stephen was certainly present for at least some of these negotiations, as I've noted above.[72] If Stephen spent time at Savigny during the negotiations, it would have offered an opportunity for Haimo (who was still alive at the time) to approach him to write a biography of Vitalis.

And here we come to the reason I am arguing both that Stephen had to have been writing the biography after July 12, 1174, and also that the events of that summer shaped the story that gives this book its title. It is worth quoting the whole

---

68 Swietek, "King Henry II and Savigny," 15–16.

69 He is generally known as Henry the Young King, because he died before his father did and therefore never ruled independently, although in some medieval reckonings he is given a number.

70 RT, 2: 32. In one of the manuscripts, a marginal note was added in the notice for 1171 that Thomas was canonized in the following year (RT, 2: 26 and n7). Robert seems to have begun his year at Christmas (so Christmas 1170 would be given at the beginning of the entry for 1171); the author of the note, however, would be correct if that person was following Paris usage, in which the year began at Easter. Since Thomas was canonized on February 21, 1173, this would, by Paris usage, still be 1172.

71 Swietek, "King Henry II and Savigny," 17–19.

72 See above, p. 42.

story here at length (for the second time, because it is the passage that opens the introduction). Stephen gave it two chapters.

6. But we should not pass a matter over in silence that he told one of his disciples, because of that man's authority. One time, he found the countess weeping and troubled by great sobbing and sorrow. He quickly asked the reason for her sorrow and learned from her own mouth that the count did not respect her and had presumed to beat her. The venerable man was moved by her pain and said that he was angry that the count had presumed to do such things to her and that the bond between himself and the count would have to be broken, unless the count agreed to refrain from visiting such injuries upon the lady.

7. So then it happened that Vitalis left Mortain and did not let the count know about his departure. But when it was announced to the count, the count followed him without delay and once the count had given him a pledge that he would make satisfaction [for his misdeed], the count got him to return. But the reason he left remained hidden and only those two knew it. When they returned and secretly entered the chapel, the count, who begged for compassion, began to implore the venerable man not to hesitate to whip him as much as he wished. The prince took off his clothes and stood nude before the reverend man who stood over him and struck him with bitter blows. But as the prince humbly begged Vitalis to have mercy on him, the venerable man chastised him as much as he wanted to with the descending switches.

Here is what Robert of Torigni, Stephen's friend, wrote about Henry's penance for Becket's murder.

The humility with which he [Henry] visited the tomb of the blessed martyr Thomas is noteworthy. When he saw the church of Canterbury, he got down from his horse, and dressed in linen clothes and with bare feet, he walked to it through the marshes and sharp stones with the greatest devotion. He was so devout in his prayers at the tomb of the glorious martyr that he moved the onlookers to tears. He went there on Friday and he spent the whole night there fasting. But when morning came, he went to the monk's chapterhouse and submitted himself to their blows, imitating the Redeemer, who gave his back to the lash. Of course, the Redeemer did so for our sins, the king, because of his own.[73]

---

73 RT, 2: 51 (my translation).

Although it is unlikely that Stephen was present as Henry did his penance (as I said above, we have no evidence that he ever crossed the Channel again after 1166), this story circulated widely in Henry's realm and Stephen would have heard about it. Perhaps there was gossip when, in October of the same year, Stephen was at Falaise, witnessing the reconciliation of Henry with his rebellious sons. Stephen could also easily have read his friend Robert's account.

But it isn't only similarity between these acts of penance that binds these two stories. Penance in both cases was being administered to a count of Mortain, something contemporaries would have been well aware of, but which for us, from our own positionality, is overshadowed by Henry's royal title and so many other more important titles (such as duke of Normandy) that seem to us much more politically significant. And Robert was Henry's great-great-uncle, the brother of his great-grandfather. It was all connected.

Using the past to make sense of the present

This raises an important question, one we need to think about in relation to hagiography, where the moral significance of the narrative is often more important than whether an event actually took place. Did Stephen make this story up? Did Vitalis ever really beat the count? As historians we simply have no way of knowing. We have one account – Stephen's – that reports this event. It is vague about details: which wife was being beaten – Robert of Mortain had two – or when during Vitalis's service this happened. Moolenbroek thought there was a core of truth in the story and that Stephen may have heard about it while he was the cantor at Mortain, although it is the only story in the biography set at Mortain;[74] if Stephen had collected stories of Vitalis's life there, why are there not more of them? But the story as we have it clearly (at least to me!) reflects Stephen's world, not Vitalis's, so we are left in doubt, which is often the case for historians. I think it most likely that Stephen constructed the story, perhaps from pieces of information gathered from those he consulted, or at least seriously embellished a story that perhaps began as something else, but there is no way to know for certain.

In the final chapter of the book, I'll turn to one of the issues raised by this story, namely how medieval people viewed domestic violence and when they began (if they began) to be concerned about it. But here I want to argue that this story gave

---

74 *Vital*, 67, where he says that there is nothing unreasonable in this story (after a long discussion of the possibly oral origins of the story) and points out that it conforms to penitential practices of the time.

Stephen a way of talking about events that probably had disturbed him deeply and resolving them satisfactorily. The story does not exonerate the count for his actions: he was guilty. Similarly, Henry had sinned gravely (even if it took him some time to acknowledge it). But the story presents the count as genuinely penitent and receiving his punishment in the proper spirit of mind. This is the frame of mind in which Robert suggests the king received his punishment. Contemporary readers must have seen the same connections I see between two counts of Mortain accepting their punishment with humility (a sentiment that appears in both Stephen's narrative and Robert's).

Stephen's concern about Henry's sin also appears obliquely in the *Book of Conduct*. In that book, the section on how kings ought to behave ends with these verses:

> Above all things, he should love the Church
> And those who serve God,
> Clerks and monks of many types
> And black nuns and grey nuns.
>
> And if the clergy does him dishonor
> Or greater or lesser harm,
> He should still do them honor,
> Not for themselves but for the Lord.
>
> The king who does these things,
> And dedicates himself to doing so,
> Will have pardon for his sins
> And will be crowned king with God.[75]

Here Stephen again seems to be encapsulating the events of his time. Becket had done the king dishonor (and in earlier verses in this section of the poem Stephen mentions those raised up by the king who prove ungrateful), but the king handled it wrongly. He should have continued to honor this man who was doing him harm, for God's sake. However, if he applied himself to better conduct, this would ensure his salvation.

Likewise, it is hard not to see Stephen thinking about these issues in his section on the archbishop. After saying that it wasn't for him to criticize an archbishop, who had authority over a bishop such as himself, and exploring the virtues of the

---

75 *LM*, 68, ll. 173–84 (my translation).

good archbishop, including a love of peace and humility (things critics of Becket felt he lacked), Stephen remarks that the archbishop should believe that there is no glory greater than in the cross, and that

> For this reason, he ought to both think and say
> That he is ready for martyrdom,
> Without dispute or contradiction
> To tolerate for God the one who wishes to kill him.[76]

Thus Stephen obliquely refers to Becket's death.

The story of the count's penance is the most overt way in which Stephen's positionality is reflected in the life of Vitalis. However, his positionality probably played a role in his selection of the contents overall. To recap: Vitalis was first a canon of the collegiate church at Mortain and then, when Robert of Mortain died in 1095, he seems to have become a hermit and also the informal director, it would seem, of monks, which he did for seventeen years, until he was given land to found a monastery around 1112. Stephen's narrative mentions Vitalis's early life up to his stint as the count's chaplain. Stephen then jumps immediately to the founding of Savigny, with no mention of Vitalis's many years as a hermit. Writers more contemporary to Vitalis were deeply interested in this period of his life, which was undoubtedly when he established his reputation for holiness.

However, the sources available to Stephen did not treat this part of Vitalis's life. It is possible Stephen had read Orderic's or Robert's treatises on the new orders, although Robert is most interested in Vitalis having been a companion of Bernard of Tiron and Robert of Arbrissel, a chaplain of the count of Mortain, and the founder of Savigny.[77] Furthermore, the mortuary roll doesn't provide much factual information about Vitalis at all. Geoffrey Grossus in his biography of Bernard of Tiron has a lot to say about Vitalis as the venerable leader of a community of hermits, but we have no evidence that Stephen would have read this biography.[78] Moolenbroek suggests that Stephen may have picked up some stories at Mortain and he clearly was told stories by the monks of Savigny, but their stories would most likely have come from his period as their abbot.[79] There is only one miracle story from Vitalis's childhood, and the discussion of his education is rather non-specific. We

---

76 *LM*, 77, ll. 457–60 (my translation); see also p. 117 for Lodge's comment on this passage.
77 RT, 2: 188–9.
78 *Bernard*, 12 and 12n6. The biography may never have left the region around Tiron. The original does not survive; the two early-modern copies were made from a thirteenth-century copy.
79 *Vital*, 59f.

can speculate, as I discussed in the first chapter, but not know for sure. But to the monks of Savigny and perhaps also for Stephen himself, matters such as family, early life, and even long stints in the woods were simply not the most important parts of Vitalis's life. And Stephen was writing this life for the monks.

The impact of audience

The intended audience probably also plays a role in Stephen's other works. Although the *Book of Conduct* seems to have been written for Cecily, countess of Hereford, because of the extensive reference to her in the text (the only individual explicitly referred to there), Stephen is unlikely to have intended his poem only for her.

Cecily had no need, for instance, to hear about how kings should behave (or how women might have sex with each other, but shouldn't). As Sinclair has argued, Stephen was preaching in the vernacular as a priest and a bishop.[80] I mentioned above that the text was preserved in a manuscript with sermons, among other works, and it is not unreasonable to think that a priest might take some inspiration from it and build a sermon around it, perhaps even read portions to a lay audience.

The audience Stephen wrote for may also have influenced the form of the *Life of St. Firmat*. The life of Firmat is so different in character from the life of St. Vitalis that scholars have been reluctant to attribute it to Stephen. Part of the difficulty is that one of the episodes, when Firmat was drafted as the bishop of Constantinople on his return from a pilgrimage to Jerusalem, seems completely inconsistent with what Stephen was likely to have known about the state of affairs between the eastern and western churches and is completely ahistorical to boot. The editors of the ***Acta sanctorum*** version of the biography included this part of the text, but they removed it from the main text and suggested that it might be some sort of interpolation.[81] Jean Leclercq, in his edition of a previously unedited sermon/treatise of St. Firmat, refuses (more or less) to name Stephen as the author at all; he simply refers to "the biographer."[82]

---

80 See Sinclair, "L'Inspiration liturgique," 263, for his discussion of how a priest would deliver the common prayer of the faithful.

81 *De s. Guilielmo*, in *Acta sanctorum, April III* (Antwerp: Michael Cnobaris, 1675), 334–41. For a more complete edition, see Pigeon, "Saint Guillaume Firmat, évêque et confesseur (Part 1)," *Mémoirs de la Société Académique du Cotentin* 13 (1897): 57–80, and "Vie de saint Firmat, patron de Mortain (suite)," *Mémoirs de la Société Académique du Cotentin* 14 (1898): 32–59.

82 Jean Leclercq, "L'Exhortation de Guillaume Firmat," in *Analecta monastica*, 2nd series (Rome: Herder, 1953), 28–44. As Leclercq points out, Stephen (or "the biographer") depicts Firmat as a hermit, yet the sermon sings the praises of the monastic life. However, at the very end of the biography, Stephen refers to Firmat saying goodbye to the "brothers" before dying, so there is some oblique acknowledgment of Firmat's community life.

However, Stephen may have felt that his job in composing this life for his community was simply to include morally useful stories that people were telling about the saint and not to edit them for probability.[83] There is a charming playfulness to some of the stories, nearly all of which involve **lay people** rather than monks. In one, the saint turns some stolen eggs he has been offered into frogs until the embarrassed would-be donor agrees to return them to the owner. He loves and is loved by animals; he can tickle a fish out of a pond but then returns it unharmed to the water. In another story, a thief who has stolen a tunic is forced to wander lost in the woods until he returns it.[84] Leclercq points out that although Firmat's exhortation (as he calls it) is clearly directed to **Benedictine** monks, as it sings the glory of the cloistered life and references the rule of St. Benedict on several occasions, the biography makes only the slightest of references to a monastic career. Leclercq explains this by suggesting that since the biography was destined for a community of canons, the author was being tactful in not mentioning this element of Firmat's career.[85] It is worth remembering, however, that the collegiate church was also a parish; the inhabitants of the castle were expected to attend services there. One can hypothesize that these stories, then, suited an audience that was not simply composed of canons but would also include lay people and students at the school.

Conclusion

In chapter 5, I will have more to say about some of the themes in the *Life of St. Vitalis* and how they reflected Stephen's concerns and those of his contemporaries, but I hope my remarks have clarified one of the puzzles presented by medieval sources and not just hagiographies. Although they often purport to speak about the past, and, depending on what was available to their authors, they may do so with accuracy, they always speak also about the authors' presents. In some cases,

---

83 While Vitalis left no written trace apart from the charters in which he appears, a treatise on the life of the cloister attributed to Firmat has survived; it is not clear whether Stephen knew it (D.G. Morin, "Un traité inédit de S. Guillaume Firmat sur l'amour du cloître et les saintes lecture," *Revue bénédictine* 31 [1914–19]: 246). Although Stephen refers to the saint always as Firmat, he was venerated as William at Fougères, where his body ended up. Raison suggested that two different individuals might have been blended together to create this single saint. See Abbé Raison and R. Niderst, "Le mouvement érémitique dans l'ouest de la France à la fin du XIe siècle et au début du XIIe siècle," *Annales de Bretagne* 55, no. 1 (1948): 8. Another suggestion is that Bernard of Tiron was said to have used the name "William" when he was in hiding, avoiding election as abbot, and that these two saints might have run together. This seems less likely, as Firmat is generally believed to have died in 1095, while Bernard lived until 1117. Finally, Firmat may have been his name in religion.
84 See below, pp. 163, 169, for these stories.
85 Leclercq, "L'Exhortation," 28–9.

when the narratives are written by contemporaries or near contemporaries, the divergence between author and subject is minimal, although such biographies are necessarily partial and positioned. The biographies of Becket are an example of this, many of them written by contemporaries (each with the author's own "take" on his holy subject). But when subject and author were separated by a significant period of time, it is the author's concerns that dominate the narrative, even where the factual content is accurate.

Still, authors were not writing in a vacuum. If they wanted audiences to respond to their work, they had to meet at least some of the audiences' expectations and desires. The existence of holy people was a given in the Middle Ages, and saints were heroes as much as Lancelot or Roland. So when Stephen set out to write his biography of Vitalis, he was launching his craft into a sea already afloat with other examples. In the next chapter, therefore, I turn to hagiographic writing as a genre, and how we might approach these biographies in an analytic way.

CHAPTER THREE

✠

"Men who built the Holy Church": *Hagiography and Genre*

Since we can read the lives and deeds of many men who built the Holy Church by their words and works and examples, it is highly unworthy that the life of such a great man should be passed over in fruitless silence and that it should not be transmitted in writing for the knowledge of those who come afterward. (Prologue)[1]

When Stephen of Fougères sat down to write his biography of St. Vitalis, he had already encountered many biographies of saints (as he says in the quotation above), and these undoubtedly and necessarily shaped the way he thought about his task and his ideas about what a saint was. At the same time, ideas and rules about what constituted sanctity and holy behavior changed over the course of the western Christian Middle Ages. Dramatic new forms of sanctity were being introduced in Stephen's time; the movement of holy women known as the **Beguines** was just gathering steam at the end of Stephen's life. Even more dramatic revisions of holiness were to come with the **Dominicans** and **Franciscans** of the thirteenth century. This did not, however, mean that older forms of sanctity simply disappeared.

What follows first, then, for the purpose of making some context available, is a summary of some of the important changes; it relies heavily upon the scholarship of André Vauchez and Robert Bartlett to flesh out the story of sanctity in the Middle Ages, but it draws on a few other scholars as well. Then I'll turn to some

---

1 Although the Latin text reads "men," *virorum*, male people were not the only saints, even though men outnumbered women by a large margin in the ranks of the venerated. In the Romance languages, groups of men and women are generally discussed using the male gender: in the same way, Gregory of Tours (538–94 CE) includes a woman, Monegundis, in his collection *Life of the Fathers*.

of the issues surrounding the **genre** of **hagiography** and how Vitalis's biography fit into changing notions of both sanctity and hagiography. Finally, I will provide some analysis of the biography itself.

Becoming a saint

From local holiness to canonization

One significant change, underway in Stephen's lifetime, although it was fully instituted only after his death, was the process of **canonization**. During the age of the martyrs, when Christianity was illegal, simply dying for the faith made one a member of a select holy company. When Christianity was legalized, a person became a saint when that person's life was regarded by the local community as so holy that **cults** (simply the name given to the veneration of particular saints) arose in celebration.[2] While bishops might give some formal recognition to the holiness of such people, the designation of a saint depended on community consensus.

Stephen was writing in a middle period in the long history of sanctity. It was still the case that communities played a crucial role in recognizing a person as a saint, but once the community had done that work, local bishops could confirm the community's judgment through a formal act of recognition, giving the saint a more official standing. This is what happened for St. Firmat. It did not happen for Vitalis, although the monks of Savigny may have hoped to make this happen at some point in the future.[3] Starting in the early thirteenth century, popes claimed to be the only ones who could make someone an official saint, although until 1234 it was still possible for local bishops to do so. Even after that, however, some holy people continued to be locally venerated as saints, and this continued to be an essential step toward someone being formally recognized. The papacy did not attempt to stamp these cults out, provided that these individuals were orthodox in belief and virtuous in life.[4]

---

2 André Vauchez, *Sainthood in the Later Middle Ages*, trans. Jean Birrell (Cambridge: Cambridge University Press, 1998), chap. 1; Robert Bartlett, *Why Can the Dead Do Such Great Things? Saints and Worshippers from the Martyrs to the Reformation* (Princeton, NJ: Princeton University Press, 2013), chap. 2 for developments in the period after the age of martyrdom; chap. 5 for a discussion of cults as a phenomenon.

3 See above, p. 45.

4 On the necessity of an existing cult to set canonization in motion and continued veneration of uncanonized individuals, see Bartlett, *Why Can the Dead Do Such Great Things?*, 59–61; Peterson, *Suspect Saints*, chap. 1 ("Tolerated Saints").

So was Vitalis even a saint?

Some of the tentativeness about what constituted sanctity and when it might be reasonable to conclude that someone had achieved it is evident in Vitalis's **mortuary roll**. The circular letter that prefaced the roll is, in Moolenbroek's words, "quasi-hagiographic," while the entries from several of the monasteries that added to the roll imply that Vitalis was to be regarded as a saint.[5] But the purpose of a roll was to solicit prayers for the dead person from the **monasteries** visited by the emissaries (as well as to create **communities of prayer** between religious institutions) and presumably the saints, who had led holy lives and were dearly loved by God – hence their miracles – would not seem to require such prayers.[6] One might regard this roll perhaps as the **monks'** way of crowd-sourcing their belief in Vitalis's sanctity, while not being so arrogant as to make an explicit claim.

However, by the time that Stephen was asked to write the biography, it was clear that the monks of Savigny believed that Vitalis *was* a saint. There were miracles. Still, the events that made Vitalis notable in his own day, his power as a preacher, were decades in the past. It is difficult to feel the charisma of someone long dead, unless that person's shrine is a font of miracles, like the shrines of the Virgin Mary at Paris or Rocamadour. Furthermore, the order that grew from Vitalis's foundation at Savigny had been absorbed by the **Cistercian** order, displacing him as a founder. As a consequence, outside of the limited circles of western Normandy, Vitalis was probably not much remembered. Stephen's task, therefore, was to produce hagiographic materials that would be true to the knowledge of the saint passed along in the communities with which he had been associated (Mortain and Savigny) and that would also be convincing to others who might read or hear the biography, when Vitalis's accomplishments were no longer still vivid in the Anglo-Norman world.

Medieval "genres," modern genres

To see how Stephen accomplished this dual task, we need first to understand what the conventions of hagiography were upon which Stephen was drawing. The notion of genre can help us understand this. Genre is a modern literary term, not a medieval one, so I want to be careful in using it. Some medieval scholars have

---

5 *Vital*, 14, 23–4.

6 Although, as Moolenbroek points out (*Vital*, 23), generally holiness of life did not preclude the possibility that a holy person had some minor sins that required forgiveness, and even if such a person did not, the prayer would help the soul of the one doing the praying.

been extremely uncomfortable with using the idea of genre at all, arguing that since the term is modern, we shouldn't use it or that medieval texts were so fluid that it makes no sense to speak of genres. But scholars who do accept that medieval readers sorted their reading into different types of material and who are comfortable with using the term genre (I am obviously one of them) would agree that we can use the term as long as we recognize that medieval genres didn't function in the way that modern genres do, as classificatory schemes used institutionally both to describe and to delimit literature, as in modern libraries.

Most research library classification systems depend on genre (among other things) to sort their wares, and these are generally uniform across many institutions. In fact, many libraries purchase their cataloguing data rather than classifying books themselves, since so many books are published and libraries may house a million volumes or more.[7] Library systems tend to be governed by both content and form: fiction and non-fiction; history and science; prose and poetry; geography and period; and other finer-grained categories besides. Public libraries tend to separate books by genre (general fiction, mysteries, science fiction, romance, or graphic novels) and also by audience (children, young adults, adults), as well as non-fiction topic.

The categorizations used by booksellers are more like those of public libraries than research libraries. While novels, for instance, in a research library may be sorted by the geographic and temporal origins of the authors and then alphabetically, in a public library or a bookshop, geography (unless the book is written in a language other than English) and time (unless the book is deemed a "classic" and is shelved with older literature) may not matter. Meanwhile, the other categories come into play, sorting books by genre and audience. These classification systems allow people to find the type of book they are looking for, when they aren't sure what they are looking for but know the sort of thing they like. There is always, as there was in the Middle Ages, a measure of **generic** vagueness: Should a science fiction novel in which love blooms be put in romance? Should a romance with a mystery at its center be put in mysteries? What to make of the "young adult" novels very popular with "old" adults? The sorting principle may come down to similitude – this book is like *that* book, which is shelved in the young adult collection – or authorship – this author generally writes mysteries, so despite being a romance, the book belongs among mysteries. Occasionally a book will come

---

7 Purchasing this material may lead to amusing and replicated mistakes. My own institution's library persists in classifying Michael Crichton's novel *Eaters of the Dead* as an historical text, despite the introduction, offered by a Dr. Fraus-Dolus (Fraud-Deception in Latin), and a plot clearly modelled on *Beowulf* (Michael Crichton, *Eaters of the Dead* [New York: Knopf, 1976], 5–6).

along that is declared to be "genre-busting," which means that those who would classify it are perplexed about where to put it, at least until it spawns imitators. And despite these conventions, all booksellers are free in theory to organize the books in any way they want (even if none do); libraries (public or research) are generally constrained by shared classification systems such as Dewey decimal, Library of Congress, Anglo-American Cataloguing, or Resource Description and Access.

Medieval library catalogues often did organize texts into categories when they were listed, but they did not always do so. However, I wonder if the function of medieval library lists wasn't more for inventory purposes than for actually finding books. In a small library of a few hundred books, a knowledgeable librarian might simply direct a reader toward a desired text or find the book and give it to the reader.[8] And books of a type may not have been shelved together. This was clearly the case in the Cotton library (a post-medieval example), where books were listed by the bookcase, shelf, and location on that shelf where the book was originally found. In that library, histories (for instance) were scattered across the cases and shelves, as the 1777 catalog makes clear.[9] And not all books possessed by medieval institutions appeared in library lists either. Books kept in the church for regular use would not necessarily be listed, and I have to think that there would have been a monastic *samizdat* (underground copying and circulation) of secular, vernacular, or illicit reading material. So medieval libraries aren't where we can best see medieval conventions.

What did medieval people themselves say about different types of literature? One way of seeing which texts belonged together in their minds is when copyists copied texts together. In the previous chapter, I mentioned that Stephen's *Book of Conduct* was copied in a manuscript containing sermons, all written in one hand, so the copyist obviously thought that his text was a sort of sermon. That all the texts were in the same hand is important here, since loose pamphlets were vulnerable and might be bound into a book with other pamphlets of the same size,

---

8 Thus in the list of books that Philip of Bayeux gave to Bec in Normandy around the middle of the twelfth century, the books were topically grouped, with biblical materials, commentaries, and theological writings of the Fathers of the Church first, although a history of the Normans appears among these books. But a roughly contemporary list from Bec, which contains many of the same volumes, was organized differently. See Laura Cleaver, "The Monastic Library at Le Bec," in *A Companion to the Abbey of Le Bec in the Central Middle Ages (11th–13th Centuries)*, ed. Benjamin Pohl and Laura L. Gathagan (Leiden: Brill, 2018), 176.

9 *A Catalog of the Manuscripts in the Cottonian Library* (London: S. Hooper, 1777). For histories see pp. 1ff., which provide an index to the contents of the individual texts as well as a listing. (The British Library, which inherited the collection, still identifies the Cottonian manuscripts in this way, although the bookcases, identified by the busts of the classical figures atop them, were long ago rendered into ash.)

but with different contents and origins. Therefore, scholars consider whether the same hand is found throughout a manuscript or whether the texts are of the same date or show other signs of being continuously copied or deliberately grouped.

However, medieval people themselves reported that they mentally grouped together works with similar contents. The opening of the fourteenth-century *Wars of Alexander* remarks that, after dinner, people generally want to hear a story, and the author then lists what different people like: tales of the martyrs ("legends of the saints who lost their lives for our Lord's sake") takes first place in the list.[10] Similarly, the *South English Legendary* of the thirteenth century explicitly attempts to lure readers who might otherwise turn to epics or other stories about wars, by suggesting that this form of writing offered spiritual warfare just as full of gore.[11] Successful parody also requires that readers be familiar with conventions (otherwise they won't get the jokes).[12] There are parody saints' lives, such as the life of St. "Nemo" [No One], which plays with the joke, also found in the *Odyssey*, of treating "no one" as a name.[13] This suggests that readers knew what a saint's life ought to be like.

Generic change and continuity

So what would readers expect, and how did this change over time? The overwhelming majority of miracles performed posthumously by saints (that is, after the saint has died) in all periods were (and are) "therapeutic miracles," miracles of healing.[14] This is hardly surprising, given the absence of the medical knowledge and tools necessary to treat many illnesses before the nineteenth century. So this is a great form of continuity. However, canonization seems to have shifted the emphasis in biographies of the saints from miracles performed by the living saint to posthumous miracles, even though two of the great saints of the twelfth and thirteenth centuries, St. Bernard of Clairvaux and St. Francis (d. 1226), performed

---

10 Walter Skeat, ed., *The Wars of Alexander* (London: Trübner, 1886), 1 (my translation); for a discussion of this text in relation to genre, see also K.S. Whetter, *Understanding Genre and Medieval Romance* (Aldershot: Ashgate, 2008), 3–4. Whetter's book gives a useful overview of scholarly debate over genre.

11 Beth Crachiolo, "Seeing the Gendering of Violence: Female and Male Martyrs in the South English Legendary," in *A Great Effusion of Blood? Interpreting Medieval Violence*, ed. Mark Meyerson and Daniel Thiery (Toronto: University of Toronto Press, 2004), 148.

12 Whetter, *Understanding Genre*, 1, 14.

13 Bayliss, *Parody in the Middle Ages*, chap. 3, "Mock Saints' Lives." The life of St. Nemo was popular in a variety of versions for several centuries.

14 Christian Krötzl, "Miracula post mortem: On Function, Content, and Typological Changes," in *Miracles in Medieval Canonization*, ed. Sari Katajala-Peltomaa and Christian Krötzl (Turnhout: Brepols, 2018), 158, gives a figure of 70–95 per cent (this would be for posthumous miracles).

very few posthumous miracles, as Robert Bartlett points out.[15] Toward the end of the Middle Ages, there also seem to have been more "remote" miracles, that is, miracles that were not performed at the saint's shrine or through contact with a relic but by direct prayer to the saint, often followed by trips to the saint's shrine in thanksgiving, as in the case of the resurrection of William Cragh, examined by Robert Bartlett and Jussi Hanska.[16] However, such miracles also occurred in the earlier period, and Gregory the Great (d. 605) in his *Dialogues* explains that this happens because remote miracles strengthen weak faith and remind people that the saints are everywhere.[17] Finally, there is evidence that audiences in the fourteenth and fifteenth centuries particularly liked gruesome retellings of the torture and death of the martyrs, usually saints from early Christian times.[18] What is hard for many modern readers to grasp is that many people *enjoyed* hearing about the saints as much as many modern people enjoy seeing movies about superheroes. Books like *The Golden Legend* (a collection of saints' lives written by James of Voragine in the second half of the thirteenth century) exist in many manuscripts and translations into most of the medieval vernaculars and were read or heard in all sorts of circumstances by all sorts of people.[19]

Changes in notions of sanctity over time

Still, while there are some significant continuities in sanctity – the importance of healing, the necessary endorsement of the community – there were changes over time, determined by the context in which the saint lived. Most of the earliest

---

15 Krötzl, "Miracula post mortem," 158, on the prevalence of posthumous miracles; Bartlett, *Why Can the Dead Do Such Great Things?*, 342–5. Bartlett does preface this observation, however, by noting that many people thought posthumous miracles were special (343–4).

16 Krötzl, "Miracula post mortem," 159ff.; Jussi Hanska, "The Hanging of William Cragh: The Anatomy of a Miracle," *Journal of Medieval History* 27 (2001): 121–38; Robert Bartlett, *The Hanged Man: A Story of Miracle, Memory, and Colonialism in the Middle Ages* (Princeton, NJ: Princeton University Press, 2006). While it was not authenticated by the canonization proceeding that eventually did canonize Thomas of Cantilupe (d. 1282), the miracle began (after the hanging), by the lady having a penny bent in a vow to St. Thomas to save the hanged man. Upon his revival, she, her (probably dying) husband, and the man went in pilgrimage to Hereford.

17 Gregory the Great, *Dialogues*, trans. Odo John Zimmerman (New York: The Fathers of the Church, 1959), 109.

18 Crachiolo, "Seeing the Gendering of Violence," 148–9. Her larger argument is that female suffering was particularly graphically depicted in the *South English Legendary*.

19 Over a thousand manuscripts of the text have survived, sixty-nine of them in Italian, French, Dutch, high and low German, English, and Czech. For an introduction to this medieval best seller, see Jacques le Goff, *In Search of Sacred Time: Jacobus de Voragine and* The Golden Legend, trans. Lydia G. Cochrane (Princeton, NJ: Princeton University Press, 2014), particularly the preface and first chapter.

saints after the age of martyrs were **clergy**: monks, nuns, and hermits, with some popes and bishops thrown in (some of whom had been monks or hermits, like Martin of Tours [d. 397 CE]) and some theologians (some of whom were monks or bishops). If they were **lay people** originally, like Queen Radegund (sixth century) or St. Rictrude of Marchiennes or Queen Balthild (seventh century), they ended their lives in monasteries, places they were depicted in their biographies as always having longed for. Only in the tenth century did any religious people who had not left the world, such as Gerald of Aurillac (d. c. 909) or Queen Matilda of Saxony (d. 968), come to be viewed as saints. Virtually all saints after the martyrs and before the eleventh century came from aristocratic families (St. Anthony and St. Martin are notable exceptions to this generalization). In a society that was quite hierarchical, in which to join a monastery or to become a bishop one had to come from a family with significant resources, it was only natural that most saints would come from the ranks of the elite.

There was, however, some softening of the lines as significant social changes transformed medieval society beginning in the late tenth and early eleventh centuries, a process sometimes called the commercial revolution. Medieval agriculture became more productive, the commercial economy expanded, and new professions emerged. While high ecclesiastical offices were still monopolized mostly by aristocrats, some offices came to be held by talented men of somewhat more modest social backgrounds. This is the background of Abbot Samson of Bury (d. 1211), who through his appointment as abbot became the lord of the barony of St. Edmunds and controller of one of the richest towns (and monasteries) in England.[20] Stephen of Fougères fits in here also; he became a bishop through service, supported by education, not through the social rank he was born into. Education, then as now, could be a powerful engine of advancement, and the growth of the economy permitted the expansion of schools: Stephen, as well as both of his holy protagonists, was highly educated.

This new society had different needs and therefore required some different sorts of saints (while more traditional holy people continued to be venerated). In the eleventh century, older monastic traditions were revived and given new shapes. New orders of hermits appeared, as well as orders that aimed at returning to a more austere monastic life. We can see both those trends in the life of Vitalis, but also in the Cistercian founders, in St. Romuald (d. 1027), the founder of the

---

20 Jocelyn of Brakelond gives a vivid portrait of Samson in the *Chronicle of the Abbey of Bury St. Edmunds*. Although one of his relatives was a knight, his decision to join Bury seems to have been a strategic move as he looked for a place to park his considerable education. See Jocelyn, *Chronicle of the Abbey of Bury St. Edmunds*, 12, 22.

order of **Camaldoli**, and St. Bruno (d. c. 1101), the founder of the **Carthusian order**. In addition, as Lester Little argued some time ago (in a book still well worth reading), discomfort with the growth of a profit economy triggered a reactive embrace of religious poverty.[21] St. Francis is probably the most famous proponent of it, but it is worth noting that Robert of Arbrissel, Vitalis's contemporary, was accused by Marbode of Rennes of bringing the Church into disrepute because he wandered the French roads ragged and dirty and preached to women (imitating Christ, as Robert would have seen it).[22]

Robert's efforts (and Vitalis's) were part of a powerful religious reform movement intended to reform both lay and religious behavior. This required lay people to be taught what was expected of them, which occurred through an increased emphasis on preaching. In the second half of the eleventh century, wandering preachers licensed by a bishop or by the pope brought the message to lay audiences. While their methods were not always welcomed, their oratorical skills helped a new notion of sanctity to develop. In their wanderings they reached people whose parish priest was not capable of preaching well, or at all, or people who might be negligent church-goers, and particularly they reached women. In other words, preaching enhanced the relationship between the **laity** and the Church. The orders of **regular canons**, founded in the first half of the twelfth century, also involved ministry to the laity through parish work. Norbert of Xanten (d. 1134), the founder of the **Premonstratensians**, perhaps the most famous order, came to be venerated as a saint.[23]

So saints are products of their time periods; that is, they are positioned (as are their biographers and as are we all). However, in raising the question of the **historical context**, I want to caution against seeing the environment as irresistibly determinative. Individuals might well display singular, novel, and individual behaviors. St. Francis is the first noted stigmatized saint (that is, he was believed to bear the marks of Christ's wounds on his body), but he was followed by other stigmatized saints.[24] Still, people continued to be inspired by the more conventional religious behavior they saw. Christina of Markyate was moved to the religious life

---

21 Lester Little, *Religious Poverty and the Profit Economy in Medieval Europe* (Ithaca, NY: Cornell University Press, 1978).

22 For Marbode's letter and Venarde's commentary on it, see Venarde, 88–100.

23 An accessible general introduction to these new orders (including the Cistercians) is C.H. Lawrence, *Medieval Monasticism*, 3rd ed. (Harlow: Longman, 2001), 146–98 (chaps. 8 and 9).

24 See Carolyn Muessig, "Signs of Salvation: The Evolution of Stigmatic Spirituality before Francis of Assisi," *Church History* 82, no. 1 (March 2013): 40–68, for the pre-Franciscan stigmata; Cordelia Warr, "Visualizing Stigmata: Stigmatic Saints and Crises of Representation in Late Medieval and Early Modern Italy," *Studies in Church History* 47 (2011): 228–47, on later stigmatized saints.

by observing the **Benedictine** monks of St. Albans; Marie of Oignies (d. 1213), often considered the first "Beguine" saint (and an "extraordinary saint"), as a girl would follow behind the Cistercians.[25] People who long for a holy life (and those who write about them) might still prize traditional forms of holiness.

The horizon of expectations and the life of Vitalis

Any saint's life, then, might be entirely traditional; might be traditional with some innovative features; or might be extremely unusual in many ways. How can we know which is which? The short answer is that we can't from a single source. Each biography presents the same challenge as any single primary source of a given kind. It simply is what it is. We can only get an idea of how typical or unusual a source is by comparing it to other things of its kind. So it matters what biographies and collections of miracles Stephen had read, because they shaped his notion of the "**horizon of expectations**" for these works.

The "horizon of expectations" is a term coined by the literary scholar Hans Robert Jauss to address literary questions, such as how to differentiate truly literary texts from formulaic offerings of a "read 'em and forget 'em" sort and how to explain generic changes across time. A horizon of expectations is formed by all the texts that might be read as being of a particular type. It is a horizon, because the texts vary across a range. We might think of it as a bell-curve of expectations, with most texts sharing a goodly number of particular attitudes and types of contents, with a few outliers at the tail end that share only a few. This structure leaves room for new or unusual material – Jauss argues that truly literary production demands it – while allowing readers to be easily drawn into the material.[26] Over time, the characteristics of the works within a genre might slowly shift through innovations.

At the beginning of this chapter I cited Stephen referring to the "lives and deeds of many men" (he says "men," which would include female men), and these provided the horizon of expectations not just for what he wrote but also – and this is a crucial point – for what he was told, because his informants would also have their ideas of sanctity shaped by what they had heard and read. He was writing the life of a monastic saint, not a martyr, and one with a relatively conventional religious career for his time, so these would be the models that both he and his informants

---

25 Talbot, *The Life of Christina of Markyate*, 5–6; Jacques de Vitry and Thomas of Cantimpré, *Two Lives of Marie of Oignies*, trans. Margot H. King and Hugh Feiss (Toronto: Peregrina Publishing, 1993), 53.

26 Hans Robert Jauss, *Towards an Aesthetic of Reception*, trans. Timothy Bahti (Minneapolis: University of Minnesota Press, 1982), esp. 22f.

would draw on. Vitalis, unlike Firmat, did not suddenly become pious after a very secular life (which was one model for sanctity in this period).[27] Instead, he was a pious boy whose religious commitment deepened into the fervor of a holy man. There was a long tradition of just such saints, beginning in the fourth century with St. Antony of Egypt (d. 356 CE) and St. Martin of Tours. The cults of both saints spread across western Europe, and their lives were widely read and imitated. As I mentioned above, Stephen may have been imitating the life of St. Martin when he did not name himself as the author of Vitalis's life. There are also many echoes of Gregory the Great's biography of St. Benedict (d. 547) in Stephen's biography of Vitalis, as Pigeon has argued.[28] Vitalis, like Benedict, shunned a worldly career, lived as a **hermit**, and ended up founding a religious community.

Benedict was a particularly apt model for the founder of a monastery dedicated to a revitalization of the monastic life in this period; the Cistercian movement that Savigny eventually joined presented itself as strictly adhering to the original form of Benedict's rule.[29] Furthermore, Benedict founded an order, and founding a new monastic order was a sure road to sanctity in the early twelfth century. The Cistercian founders, Robert of Molesme (d. 1111) and Stephen Harding (d. 1134), were both venerated as saints. (Bernard of Clairvaux was not technically a founder, but he was certainly the brightest Cistercian star and a powerful inspiration for the growth of the order.) Norbert of Xanten (the Premonstratensians), Bernard of Tiron (Tiron), and Robert of Arbrissel (Fontevrault) all founded orders. And as I mentioned before, contemporaries grouped Robert, Bernard, and Vitalis together in their accounts as preachers.

Although preaching was an important part of all three men's careers (and of Norbert of Xanten's as well), I do not know of any person who was canonized in this period simply for being a great preacher; apparently St. Francis was a compellingly charismatic preacher, but he was also the founder of an order. Peter the Hermit (d. 1115), who preached the First Crusade and then went on it, may have blown his chance for canonization when he attempted to escape from the siege of Antioch and was caught; while he achieved later respectability, it is difficult to imagine that such a major flaw would have been forgotten.[30]

---

27 Firmat had been a physician before becoming a hermit, and Stephen expresses in that story the suspicion that greeted those who made money in service professions. On this point, see Little, *Religious Poverty*, 33 (on fees in the universities, including those for students studying medicine), 39 (on the "sale" of knowledge), and 175 (on scholastic thinking about "service" professions).

28 Pigeon, "Étienne de Fougères," 185.

29 On this feature of Cistercian life, see Burton and Kerr, *Cistercians in the Middle Ages*, 14–15.

30 Peter Tudebode, who participated in the First Crusade, gives the unedifying story of Peter's attempted escape. See Peter Tudebode, *Historia de Hierosolymitano itinere*, trans. John Hugh Hill and Laurita L. Hill (Philadelphia: The American Philosophical Society, 1974), 48. Peter remained with the crusade after this episode and then returned to Europe, where he died.

Finally, the revival of the practice of being a hermit was also a feature of the eleventh and twelfth centuries. The founders of orders of hermits – Romuald of Ravenna (d. 1027; Camaldoli), Bruno of Cologne (d. 1084; La Chartreuse), and John Gualbert (d. 1073; Vallombrosa) – were all venerated as saints. But not only founders were seen as holy; St. Firmat is depicted as fitting into the hermit mold, but not as founding anything.

Form and audience in the saint's life

What traits appear in the life depend on a number of different issues: the saint himself or herself as a person who lived a particular life in which holy actions were defined in particular ways; the community around the saint, which remembered the things that constituted its notion of the saint's holiness and forgot others that were less exciting or pertinent to the community, and which perhaps even invented a few things; the views of the biographer (shaped by the time at which the story was being told); and finally the ways in which the biographer expected the text to be used. So, as historians, we have to ask questions about all of these things.

Use and form have to be related because the form of a text is shaped by how it is intended to be used. The question of usage has come up already in chapter 2, when I discussed why Stephen might have written this life. If Vitalis was being locally venerated at Savigny, which seems likely, there would have been prayers said for and to him and perhaps a **liturgy** written for his feast day, in which readings from his *vita* would have been a traditional part. Saints' lives were generally written to be read in chunks, perhaps at various times during the day, and thus often had relatively uniform chapters. The life might also be read in the monastic **chapter**, the daily meeting of the monks to transact the monastery's business.[31] Or it might be part of the reading St. Benedict prescribed for mealtimes, to prevent monks from engaging in idle gossip.[32] Stephen's life of Vitalis is organized into neat and compact chapters to fit all of these functions.

The life of Firmat as we have it, however, was not organized in this way. Instead, it features four long sections, perhaps the result of a different intended use. At Mortain, where the **canons** served a lay congregation and had a school, the canons would have needed material that might speak to that lay audience, perhaps by being drawn on for sermons. Not only are some of the stories humble and

---

31 Bartlett, *Why Can the Dead Do Such Great Things?*, 510–13, explores some of the reasons people wrote saints' lives, including straightforward devotion.

32 See Benedict, *Sancti Benedicti regula monasteriorum*, 49–50 (cap. 38), where the rule says that meals should not lack reading and provides for a weekly reader.

homely, but women appear in a number of the stories too, including the saint's mother, who encourages his conversion (perhaps imitating St. Augustine). Firmat goes on pilgrimage, something a few local people might have done. The miracles are also striking: Firmat is led by a crow he has raised (echoes of Elijah and the ravens); and he is miraculously identified so he can be seized and forced to become the patriarch of Constantinople (there is a hint here of the *Life of St. Alexis*, which was widely known when Stephen was writing).[33] In short, the life of Firmat may have been written with this audience in mind (whether Stephen wrote it or someone else), while the life of Vitalis seems more clerical in its audience.

Making sense of the *Life of St. Vitalis*

To his contemporaries, Vitalis was all of these things: a famous preacher, a hermit, and the founder of an order. But the different people who wrote about him stressed different things about him, based on their own **positionalities** and the audiences they imagined for their works. For Geoffrey Grossus, the biographer of St. Bernard of Tiron, Vitalis's life as a hermit and as a man who trained other hermits was the most important thing about him, because his stature enhanced Bernard's. Ralph of la Futaye appears in Bernard's biography for the same reason.[34] So how can we determine what was important to Stephen and his contemporaries about Vitalis?

It is often a surprise to students that historians not only read things but also count them. One way we can find out what was important to Stephen is to sort the stories he tells into categories and count them. This is a method that Peter Burkholder has used with his students, and it provides purchase on often slippery material or mountains of detail.[35] I went through Stephen's text sorting the

---

33 In the story, Alexis is born in Rome, but when he takes up the religious life on his wedding night, he flees to Edessa. After living as a beggar there for decades, his holiness is divinely announced and he flees again to avoid public acclaim. One of the earliest surviving versions of the text appears in the *St. Albans Psalter*, made at the English monastery of St. Albans but given to Christina of Markyate by her friend and spiritual advisee, the abbot of St. Albans. The psalter has been digitized, transcribed, and translated, and may be accessed at https://www.abdn.ac.uk/stalbanspsalter/. However, the legend was already widely known in the eleventh century. See Paolo Golinelli, "Sicut alter Alexis: The Saint Alexis Model in Medieval Hagiography," in *Church and Belief in the Middle Ages: Popes, Saints, and Crusaders*, ed. Kirsi Salonen and Sari Katajala-Peltomaa (Amsterdam: Amsterdam University Press, 2016), 141–2.

34 There does not seem to be a surviving biography of Ralph of la Futaye, except in the necrology of the monastery he founded. However, he appears twice in the biography of Bernard of Tiron (*Bernard*, 27–8, 27n5, 87).

35 Peter Burkholder, "Connecting the Curricular Dots: Designing the World History Survey with Gen Ed in Mind," at the 133rd Annual Meeting of the American Historical Association, Chicago, January 5, 2019. Burkholder uses a Google spreadsheet, which allows the students to work on a common document.

stories into categories and noting themes when they appeared, using an Excel spreadsheet. Some findings were hardly surprising. Most of the stories involved miracles, hardly startling or unconventional in a saint's life! Even so, in the next chapter of this book, you'll see that some of what I am characterizing as "non-miraculous" might be taken as miraculous by a medieval reader, for example, the ability to learn quickly. Would that be a miraculous gift from God or simply a natural talent? Stephen depicts it as a divine gift, if not quite a miraculous one. Nearly all of the chapters about Vitalis's death involve miracles of various kinds, including a failed attempt to carry off his body.[36] However, the posthumous miracle stories form only a small portion of the biography as a whole (nine of the forty-one chapters) and the beneficiaries are generally clergy, suggesting that at the time Stephen was writing, the cult had not moved much beyond the monastery.

Of the miracles that occur when Vitalis is alive, three miracles are about his escapes from attempts on his life (one where the attempt is only intended but never acted on), while in four stories Vitalis miraculously brings about peace. In fourteen stories, God is said to have aided the saint in some way (not always in a way *we* might characterize as miraculous), thereby showing Vitalis to be a "friend of God," while seven of the miracle stories involve healing, including most of the posthumous stories. Vitalis is also credited with one of the most significant and rarest of miracles, the resurrection of a dead man. Thirteen of the chapters reference Vitalis's preaching, a figure that includes both miracle stories and those without miracles.

So we might put the findings in a table in this way:

Is said to be aided by God (not always miraculously)	14
Vitalis's preaching	13
Chapters without obvious miracles	11
Miraculous healings (including posthumous miracles)	7
Miraculously makes peace among enemies	4
Personal austerity	4
Escapes attempts on his life	3
Puts an end to female sexual transgression	2
TOTAL	58

---

36 The classic exploration of this hagiographic theme is Patrick Geary, *Furta sacra: Thefts of Relics in the Middle Ages*, rev. ed. (Princeton, NJ: Princeton University Press, 1990).

The categories and their characterizations here are mine, and another reader might sort the miracles differently. You will also note that the numbers add up to more than forty-one, because some chapters draw on more than one theme. But this process does provide a sort of frequency table that is helpful. That Vitalis is aided by God is very frequently mentioned – sometimes, but not always, to explain a miracle. Stephen is particularly careful to stress that the miracles are God's work, done *through* Vitalis, not wonder working on Vitalis's part (that is a man with theological training speaking!). Preaching and peace-making are also obviously major concerns of the narrative, as they come up over and over again.[37] That Vitalis spent a major part of his life as a hermit is not, however; Stephen does mention that Vitalis was a hermit, but none of the miracles hinge on his being one.

A life reduced to a few elements

If I were to characterize these findings, I would say that Vitalis's role as a preacher is foremost in Stephen's mind, along with his general virtues and his friendship with God. There is very little about Vitalis acting as the abbot of Savigny, which is striking, particularly if we compare it to the biographies of Robert of Arbrissel, which culminate in his founding of Fontevrault.[38] Although Vitalis's years as a hermit are stressed in the biography of Bernard of Tiron – he is referred to as "divine Vital" – there is also almost nothing in Stephen's account about Vitalis's years as a hermit, even though this is the period in which he established the religious credentials that made him such a notable figure in his own day. Jessica Leach has pointed to a very similar phenomenon in the case of Marie of Oignies.[39]

Preaching, however, occupies a great number of episodes, as I've shown. While preaching increased dramatically in importance in the late eleventh century, it became a central concern in the twelfth century and was one of Stephen's concerns

---

37 Peacemaking appears in the second life of Robert of Arbrissel and also in the life of St. Norbert. I will discuss this issue in the final chapter. For a deeply insightful discussion of the violence of the knights, see Richard W. Kaeuper, *Chivalry and Violence in Medieval Europe* (Oxford: Oxford University Press, 1999), esp. chap. 4.

38 Venarde, 25, where he points out that the second life of Robert is largely about his direction of Fontevrault. About half of the first life by Baudri is about the establishment of his community.

39 *Bernard*, 28. On the second issue, Jessica Leach, in her PhD dissertation, "A Network of Holy Women: Early Thirteenth-Century Women in the Low Countries" (Indiana University, 2017), 78, points to this phenomenon in relation to Marie of Oignies. It is unlikely that Marie would have been venerated without the seventeen years she spent selflessly nursing lepers. It was the reputation for holiness that she created through these actions that encouraged the canons of Oignies to welcome her to their community, where they hoped her holiness would be a draw. However, neither of her biographers gives more than passing attention to this part of her life.

as well. I mentioned above that in the *Book of Conduct* Stephen describes preach-ing as an obligation of the bishop (and he was clearly thinking about his own obligations in that regard). But before he says that, he says that bishops ought to ordain good and wise priests, legitimately born of whatever status, and then goes on to say

> He should not ordain anyone a priest
> If he wants to give him a church
> Unless he knows how to preach
> And teach his congregation well.[40]

Preaching is also significant in the biographies of Vitalis's contemporaries (Nor-bert, Robert, and Bernard), so we can think of inspiring preaching as a measure of holiness that is relatively new in this period, but widely shared. Interestingly, however, Stephen does not mention Vitalis preaching at Tinchebray. This may be because it represents a failure on the part of the saint (after all, the battle took place and Vitalis's patron, the son of the donor of the land Savigny stood on, was captured), and such stories of failure might only feed cynicism about Vitalis's ho-liness. When Walter Map wants to criticize the Cistercians, for example, he tells stories about how St. Bernard failed to resurrect a dead boy or to expel a demon.[41]

Also striking are the attempts on Vitalis's life. Stephen tells of two separate incidents in which Vitalis's enemies try to kill him, and one in which murder is contemplated but not acted upon (II: 2–4). Monasteries were certainly not places of sweetness and light, and the saints might be attacked. St. Benedict's monks at his first monastery were reported to have attempted to poison him because they hated the discipline he imposed, and a local priest who was jealous of the saint also tried to poison him.[42] Jocelyn of Brakelond describes something that sounds suspiciously like a murder attempt on Abbot Samson, again probably stemming from tensions within the monastery.[43] Yet none of the active attempts Stephen mentions are plots by Vitalis's monks against him. Moolenbroek dismisses these stories as improbable, although they speak to real social issues of the twelfth

---

40 *LM*, 73, ll. 321–4 (my translation).
41 Map, *De nugis*, 79–81.
42 Gregory the Great, *Dialogues*, 62, 70–1.
43 Jocelyn, *Chronicle of the Abbey of Bury St. Edmunds*, 29. Samson was awakened by a voice and found a lit candle sitting by straw; the door was locked with a key and the windows were tightly shuttered. Jocelyn does not say that this was a murder attempt, although later on Samson accused the monks of plotting to stab him (105).

century, as I will show in the final chapter.[44] For now, we may just want to observe that these stories stand out.

Conclusion

It should be clear from this account that Stephen's biography of Vitalis is focused only on the things he felt were important for his audience to know about the saint (as well as a few concerns of his own, as I pointed out in the last chapter). We are told about Vitalis's mother and father, but not much else about his family. One brother is mentioned in passing, but the sister who may have entered the religious life is not mentioned; the house founded by her brother is also not mentioned, although the nun cured by drinking a potion made with hairs from Vitalis's garment would almost certainly have been one of the sisters of that house (II: 10). Vitalis's life as a hermit is not much discussed, nor does Stephen even say much about his work as abbot of Savigny. In addition, almost nothing in Vitalis's life – at least, not as Stephen presents it – was particularly novel or unexpected, although it was all very earnest. There were some quotidian healing miracles. There was one less common miracle, the revival of a man otherwise destined for hell; Bartlett, reporting statistics compiled by Pierre-André Sigal and Ronald Finucane, notes that fewer than 3 per cent of healing miracles involve resurrections.[45] It is not surprising, then, that when Vitalis's body and those of the other "saints" of Savigny were reburied, the **reliquary** created for his body showed, among its scenes, this incident.[46]

This makes the story referred to in the title of this book stand out even more distinctly. As Burkholder's students discovered, the significance of a given incident in a text is not necessarily related to the frequency with which incidents of that type appear. I've argued in the previous chapter that the story of the count being beaten is powerfully significant to what Stephen was up to, but it is not particularly significant to Vitalis's sanctity. Significance, in other words, is always contextual, in relation to a particular issue and not to others. If Stephen had left this story out, Vitalis's sanctity would very likely not have been in question, but we would have less of an idea of the impact of the murder of Becket on Stephen and his contemporaries.

As far as the biography is concerned, what Stephen wrote was not the story of a spectacular and innovative luminary. Vitalis did not have to innovate (much)

---

44 *Vital*, 63. Moolenbroek thinks these stories are intended to show heroic courage and readiness to die for God (and they do that, of course).

45 Bartlett, *Why Can the Dead Do Such Great Things?*, 353.

46 *Vital*, 83–4.

to please the community that venerated the saint. To them, Vitalis was their holy man. So what if he was much like other holy people? Holy people were all alike. For that reason, Gregory of Tours, writing in the sixth century in his *Life of the Fathers*, explained his choice to use the singular of "life" rather than the plural:

> It is better to speak of the "Life of the Fathers" rather than the "Lives of the Fathers," the more so since there is a diversity of merits and virtues among them, but the one life of the body sustains them all in this world.[47]

Of Vitalis's merits, Stephen and the monks of Savigny had no doubts.

From the modern perspective, this biography, as the life of a saint, is ordinary in comparison to other contemporary lives, as I've said.[48] If we had a particular devotion to the saint or to Savigny or indeed to the Cistercian order, for whom Stephen's biography of Vitalis and of the other saints of Savigny have been translated, we would no doubt see this life differently.[49] For us as historians, however, materials like these can allow us to get a better sense of people's experience and concerns in a given time and place. That is one of the premises of microhistory, of which this is a kind.[50] And I will be doing just that in the next two chapters.

---

47 Gregory of Tours, *Life of the Fathers*, trans. Edward James (Liverpool: Liverpool University Press, 1986), 28.

48 As Peterson, *Suspect Saints*, 29f., argues, local pious people might be more "relatable" than the flamboyantly ascetic individuals that the Church as an institution came to champion. Vitalis's miracles correspond well to those worked by the late-medieval Italian urban saints she discusses.

49 See *The Lives of the Monastic Reformers*.

50 István Szijártó, "Four Arguments for Microhistory," *Rethinking History: The Journal of Theory and Practice* 6, no. 2 (2002): 209–15.

CHAPTER FOUR

✠

"These are not our inventions": Miracles and Doubt

I am about to say marvelous things and it may be that these things will be judged to be uncertain by some people because of their greatness, but I swear to God, whom I desire to serve with all my mind's focus, that these are not our inventions that we include here, but we know these things from the narrative of men of the faith living in holy religion. (II: 7)

Stephen of Fougères inserts this comment just after he has explained that Vitalis, when he was officiating at the altar, consumed a spider that had fallen into the chalice, but he took no harm from eating the spider. This is hardly surprising to modern readers, who are probably aware that they consume insects all the time, although medieval readers seem to have been particularly wary of spiders.[1] But the marvel was yet to come: later on, the same spider exited the saint's body through his foot. Here modern readers would draw the line. How could he know it was *the same* spider? How could a spider exit someone's foot? Stephen rushes in to point out that God was responsible for greater marvels, such as permitting a

---

1 Graham C.L. Davey, "The 'Disgusting' Spider: The Role of Disease and Illness in the Perpetuation of Fear of Spiders," *Society and Animals* 1, no. 2 (1990): 17–25. Spiders were commonly believed to poison liquids they fell into and to be poisonous themselves. Notker the Stammerer in the ninth century told a story about Charlemagne watching a spider bite a cleric on the head while the cleric was saying mass, and the cleric's head swelled up and he died (Notker Balbulus, *The Deeds of Charlemagne*, in *Two Lives of Charlemagne*, trans. David Ganz [Harmondsworth: Penguin, 2008], 82–3). Readers may also think of tarantism, the dance Italians in Apulia engaged in after being bitten by a spider. Although there are references as early as the eleventh century, they become common in the fifteenth century. See Jean Fogo Russell, "Tarantism," *Medical History* 23 (1979): 404–25.

woman to give birth to a child and remain a virgin, in other words, that God could permit a living entity to exit from an intact body. He ends with these words:

> Let the faithful man hear this, so that he may be made the more ardent and devout. Let the doubter hear this, so that he may be confirmed more robustly in faith. Let all hear this, so that the virtue and faith of this man may be known and the magnificence of the Lord may be glorified. (II: 7)

Stephen clearly expected at least some of his audience to be skeptical of accounts of miracles. In fact, this is the second time that Stephen has raised the issue of incredulity. He writes earlier,

> We describe true things, even if they are not things we have seen. We ask whether he would have been able to do these things, except through divine power. Why should the One who is known to have done much greater things, indeed all things, not be believed also to have done these things through His servant? In saying these things, let us protect ourselves with a battlement of caution, lest we stray from the truth. And let us commit the whole matter to God, to whom nothing is impossible. (I: 11)

My purpose in pointing to these statements of Stephen is not to accuse him of falsity or of foolish credulity, nor am I questioning his belief in the truth of what he was writing – there is no way apart from what he wrote to determine what he thought or believed within the constraints that historical evidence place on us. Instead, I want only to point both to his awareness that *others* might not believe and to his anxiety on that account.

Two problems of belief

The medieval believer's problem

This anxiety was not new among Christians. One could say it began with Christianity, which has at its heart a supernatural event, the Incarnation of God in the person of Jesus. The **Christian apologists** were determined to prove that their beliefs were consistent with rationality, were a form of philosophy, not the delusions of a bunch of illiterates. Central matters of Christian faith were difficult for even some Christians to get their minds around, hence Tertullian's argument in *On the Flesh of God* (c. 203–206) against those who insisted that God had not become incarnate as Jesus but only appeared to have a physical form. The difficulty of convincing people of the existence of the miraculous reached new urgency in the eleventh century, as attempts to teach the Christian population what they ought properly to believe through more systematic instruction gathered steam. For example, the miracles of St. Foy, collected and written down in the early eleventh century by Bernard of Angers (d. 1059), a man educated in the great cathedral school of Chartres, contain miraculous punishments wreaked on those who did not believe in the power of the saint or those who scoffed at the saint's **reliquary** statue.[2]

Bernard was a classmate at Chartres of Berengar of Tours (d. 1088), whose writings raised questions about the most central and commonplace miracle newly being taught at the time: the conversion of the bread and wine of communion into Christ's body and blood through **transubstantiation**. There were many aspects to this debate over what happened when a priest blessed the wine and bread, but at least one relates to the evidence of the eyes and mouth. The bread and wine looked like bread and wine and tasted like bread and wine. If Christ was present after the consecration, in what sense was He present? How was one to know about the invisible and miraculous change?[3] Miracles might provide some support for this assertion, as in miracles in which a host bled like flesh or looked like flesh or the priest looked into the chalice and saw blood or hosts in which a miniature Christ appeared, but these were not daily occurrences.[4] It was a matter of belief. It is worth mentioning on the other side that some Christians not only believed but also thought of consecrated hosts as having magical properties. They were equally likely to be miraculously disabused of their attempts to act on these understandings.[5]

---

2 For example, the saint punished a man who wished her reliquary statue would fall so he might collect any valuables that were knocked off, and crippled a girl who refused to stand for her reliquary statue (Bernard of Angers, *The Book of Sainte Foy*, trans. Pamela Sheingorn [Philadelphia: University of Pennsylvania, 1995], 79–81). One of Firmat's posthumous miracles is of this kind.

3 For any discussion of the Eucharist, Miri Rubin, *Corpus Christi: The Eucharist in Late Medieval Culture* (Cambridge: Cambridge University Press, 1991) is essential. For an introduction to the intellectual elements of this issue, see Gillian R. Evans, "Berengar, Roscelin and Peter Damian," in *The Medieval Theologians*, ed. Gillian R. Evans (Oxford: Blackwell, 2000), 87–90.

4 See Rubin, *Corpus Christi*, 108ff., in the section "Teaching the Eucharist with Miracles." Robert of Torigni, Stephen's friend and contemporary, peppers his chronicle with these kinds of miracles.

5 On this point, see Sofia Boesch Gajano, "The Use and Abuse of Miracles in Early Medieval Culture," in *Debating the Middle Ages: Issues and Readings*, ed. Lester K. Little and Barbara H. Rosenwein (Oxford: Blackwell, 1998), 337–8, where she discusses attempts on either side of the year 1100, as transubstantiation was being established as doctrine, to secrete consecrated hosts and use them for magical purposes. Later anti-Semitic legends also attributed to Jews the desire to attack Christ through host desecration. See Robert C. Stacey, "From Ritual Crucifixion to Host Desecration: Jews and the Body of Christ," *Jewish History* 12, no. 1 (Spring 1998): 11–28.

Similar anxieties to those expressed by Stephen pepper the biographies of other saints as well. Jacques de Vitry (d. 1240) says almost the same thing Stephen does to those who disbelieve in the miracles of Marie of Oignies:

> There are many sensual people who do not have the Spirit of God, although they are considered to be prudent among themselves. They deride and despise those things which they do not understand. The apostle spoke against them when he said "Extinguish not the spirit; despise not prophecies" (1 Thess. 5:19, 20). They extinguish the spirit the more it is in them, and they despise prophecies because they scorn spiritual people, thinking them to be either insane or idiots, and they consider prophecies and the revelations of the saints to be fantasies or illusions of sleep. "The hand of the Lord is not shortened" (Isa. 59:1) and there has been no time since the beginning when the Holy Spirit did not work wondrously in his saints (cf. 2 Thess. 1:10), either openly or secretly.[6]

There were undoubtedly people who simply did not believe in the miraculous, or even in God, but Christianity as a faith could not do without it because of the theological centrality of the Incarnation (God taking on human flesh and walking the earth as Jesus). For that reason, St. Anselm (d. 1109) devoted considerable energy to attempting to prove in a series of treatises both God's existence and the necessity of the Incarnation.[7]

For medieval people, then, as for us, the miracle was contested; they were aware that miracles might be made up or events that appeared miraculous might have natural explanations. Nancy Partner cites some medieval examples of these kinds of skepticism: William of Newburgh (1136–98) refused to accept as a saint a man who died squabbling over loot from the houses of local Jews, although a cult had begun around the man, which William saw as arising from both ignorance and fraud.[8] He also provided a natural explanation for the sudden deaths of a group of men redigging a well, suggesting they were asphyxiated by some poison they uncovered.[9] Still, he accepted the existence of the miraculous and of demons.

---

6 De Vitry and Thomas of Cantimpré, *Two Lives*, 49.

7 The *Proslogium* and *Monologium* (the existence of God) and *Cur Deus homo* (Why God Became Man), all included in Anselm, *Basic Writings*, 2nd ed., trans. S.N. Deane (La Salle, IL: Open Court, 1962).

8 Nancy F. Partner, *Serious Entertainments: The Writing of History in Twelfth-Century England* (Chicago: University of Chicago Press, 1977), 73–4, 191–2; on this whole incident, see also E.M. Rose, *The Murder of William of Norwich: The Origins of the Blood Libel in Medieval Europe* (Oxford: Oxford University Press, 2015). Partner (217) also quotes Richard of Devizes's comment that people who understand nature recognize that changes in the sun or moon have no moral significance.

9 Partner, *Serious Entertainments*, 140.

Even when ordinary explanations seemed difficult, however, medieval people did not necessarily conclude that the events had been miraculous. One of the most widely discussed examples among modern scholars of an unusual event, one I have mentioned before and which was, in the end, not accepted as a miracle, is the story in the dossier of Thomas of Cantilupe, the thirteenth-century bishop of Hereford, in which William Cragh, a Welshman, was executed for rebellion but revived some hours after being cut down. The wife and family of the man who gave the order claimed it as a miracle of St. Thomas. The testimony of the survivor, when the papal questioners caught up with him some years later, was more equivocal, seeming to attribute the miracle to Mary. But the commission in the end did not accept these events as definitively miraculous; Thomas of Cantilupe was canonized on the basis of other miracles thought to be more convincingly demonstrated.[10]

Such decisions were seemingly often made on the basis of what the witnesses considered to be likely or natural and what seemed beyond what nature might be able to produce. Steven Justice, in a trenchant discussion of our problem as modern scholars with medieval belief, points to a miracle of Christina of Markyate, in which she reported having been present in spirit at a service conducted by her friend and supporter Geoffrey of St. Albans. Her interrogator was at first inclined to see her testimony as an imaginative recreation, until she reported that Geoffrey had worn a cope of the wrong color for the liturgical occasion. As Justice points out, this was not something her interlocutor imagined she could have guessed, so he accepted that she must have seen it in spirit.[11]

Justice makes another point that is worth thinking about in this connection. Modern people, including scholars, seem to see belief as an all-or-nothing proposition – one either believes or doesn't. Yet for medieval people, belief was often an act of will.[12] There is an edifying story in Joinville's memoir of St. Louis that illustrates exactly this point. Louis (IX; r. 1226–70) has been lecturing Joinville (1224–1317) on belief, and the king tells his friend that one should believe the doctrines of the faith so automatically that one does not require further discussion. Louis then tells Joinville the story of a learned cleric who was troubled by a doubt concerning transubstantiation and confessed this to the bishop of Paris.

---

10 On this case, see Bartlett, *The Hanged Man*, and Hanska, "The Hanging of William Cragh." Bartlett does not report the outcome of the inquiry, but Hanska does (138). Steven Justice, "Did the Middle Ages Believe in Their Miracles?," *Representations* 103, no. 1 (Summer 2008): 6–7, notes that this was a natural part of such inquiries, because what is miraculous must be measured against what is natural.

11 Justice, "Did the Middle Ages Believe in Their Miracles?," 16.

12 Justice, "Did the Middle Ages Believe in Their Miracles?," 12f.

The bishop then inquired whether the cleric enjoyed these doubts. When the man said that he hated them and asserted he would rather die than deny the truth of transubstantiation, the bishop reassured him that God would reward him for persisting in belief despite these doubts, which clearly originated in the devil.[13]

So Stephen of Fougères may have expected medieval readers to believe what he said or to doubt it, whether loudly or quietly, or perhaps to strive to believe it. He does not assume that they will simply take his word on the matter, but whether they do or do not is not relevant to his purpose, which is providing a demonstration of the holiness of a man whose sanctity was already beyond doubt, for the benefit of those who would venerate him. As Aviad Kleinberg has pointed out, this was always the work of the medieval **hagiographer**: to give an account of the life of a person that he (or occasionally she) believed to be a friend of God, even if no one else did.[14]

The modern problem of belief

There may be some modern readers who will read the life of St. Vitalis and accept all of the miraculous events as factual. It is not my argument that they should not do so. However, I think it extremely likely that most of the miracles will be explained in realistic terms by modern readers (one of Vitalis's companions noticed a spider crawling away from the saint's foot and assumed it was the same spider Vitalis had swallowed), dismissed as coincidence, or rejected as fabrications.

Furthermore, many events, presented as miracles in this and other hagiographic writings, would not necessarily strike modern readers as miraculous. For instance, the sixth-century historian and hagiographer Gregory of Tours tells how he became very ill with fever and was unable to eat or drink. He called upon St. Martin of Tours for help and became sufficiently better that he was able to begin to travel to the saint's tomb to pray. While on the road he again became so ill that his friends wanted to take him back home to die there. He begged them, however, to carry on, and if he died to bury him near the saint, so they continued on their way. Not only was Gregory ill, but another of his clerks was so ill that he became comatose. However, three days later, both men were better.[15]

---

13 Jean de Joinville, *The Life of St. Louis*, in *Chronicles of the Crusades*, trans. M.R.B. Shaw (Harmondsworth: Penguin, 1963), 173–4.

14 Aviad Kleinburg, *Prophets in Their Own Country: Living Saints and the Making of Sainthood in the Later Middle Ages*, rev. ed. (Chicago: University of Chicago Press, 1997), esp. chap. 3, "Wild-eyed Witnesses and Partial Observers."

15 *De miraculis santi Martini episcopi*, in PL, 71: 935–7 (Book 1: 32–3).

To a modern reader this sounds suspiciously like a case of adult chickenpox, for Gregory describes the little blisters on his colleague. That only one of his **clergy** also seems to have caught it would make sense, because those who had had the disease as children would have been immune. Furthermore, while adults can become seriously ill with chickenpox, they usually do recover.[16] To Gregory, however, his recovery was due to the intervention of St. Martin.

Gregory's miracle seems "natural" to us, but even very odd miracles can have a naturalistic explanation. Stephen tells one of these, and it should caution us not to be too swift to reject medieval accounts of miracles as inventions. Stephen says that when Vitalis was a little boy, he went to the Channel (about 6 km from his home) to swim with some other children. While he was in the water he was attacked by a fish, which clung to him as he left the water. As the editor of the Latin life suggests, the fish in question was likely to have been an octopus.[17] Although octopuses are not commonly found in the Channel's cold waters, blooms are known. There was a great bloom in 1950 and an earlier bloom in 1899–1900 in the region of the Channel Isles. In the 1950 bloom, an English fisherman caught an octopus with a 30-inch arm span, and some octopuses caught at Dartmouth had spans of 4 feet. Because the Channel is not the natural habitat of octopuses, the cephalopods were hungry, and boys at Cherbourg were fishing them out using small bits of bait to which they would cling.[18] We may imagine a small boy picking his way through a tidal pool, spotting an octopus, and having the octopus grab on for dear life. Given the relative infrequency of blooms and the oddity of octopuses for those not used to them, stories about one would have been told and retold. So what seems a totally improbable story becomes a possible one. In fact, the apparent improbability of the story led me to ask questions about its possibility, which in turn led me to the literature on octopus blooms.

Many of the other stories in Stephen's narrative present the same ambiguity, having naturalistic explanations (for us, at least) as well as miraculous ones. In

---

16 *The Merck Manual of Diagnosis and Therapy*, 17th ed. (Whitehouse Station, NJ: Merck Research Laboratories, 1999), 2331, notes that "[t]he risk of severe or fatal disease increases in adults," and adults may contract pneumonia with chickenpox. Retrospective diagnosis, however, is a treacherous business. See Piers D. Mitchell, "Retrospective Diagnosis and the Use of Historical Texts for Investigating Disease in the Past," *International Journal of Paleopathology* 1, no. 2 (2011): 81–8. Mitchell argues that in the past, disease was socially diagnosed as opposed to biologically diagnosed, notes that descriptions of disease in the past depended on beliefs about disease that we may not share with past people, and explains that we may not always be able to diagnose what diseases people suffered, based only on documents.

17 Sauvage, 361n1.

18 See W.J. Rees and J.R. Lumby, "The Abundance of Octopus in the English Channel," *Journal of the Marine Biology Association in the United Kingdom* 33 (1954): 515–36.

one of the miracles, Vitalis successfully prevents a revenge killing. One knight had "handed over" a man to be killed (perhaps acting through some legal authority), and the dead man's brothers were set on avenging their sibling's death. Vitalis became involved when the potential victim was present while Vitalis was preaching, presumably about the beauties of peace, and he asked the saint for help. The brothers were summoned and Vitalis asked one of the brothers to make peace with their potential victim:

> This man, however, replied that he felt such hatred toward that man that the magnitude of his hatred could not easily be expressed in words and that it was painful for him to see the man still alive. When the holy man responded to this and asked if it were possible for him to uproot the flame of hatred from his heart, the man is said to have answered in the following way: "If I had one foot in paradise but the other in hell, I would gladly withdraw my foot from paradise, if I could get the revenge I desire in hell!" (I: 10)

The saint first dismissed the angry man and then called him back; the saint placed the potential victim on the ground, spreading his arms into a cross, and Vitalis invited the would-be avenger to strike. Instead, the would-be avenger was struck by a fit of trembling, and he too fell to the ground, after which reconciliation took place.

Some modern people might dismiss this story as a complete fabrication. After all, it had happened at least half a century before. Some might whisper that it never happened (and some medieval people might have whispered that as well). After all, a very similar story was told about St. John Gualbert, the founder of a monastery at Vallombrosa, who forgave the murderer of a kinsman, a man who had similarly thrown himself to the ground, arms spread into a cross. And this is how the first part of the epic *Raoul de Cambrai* ends, with Berthier, who has killed Raoul in revenge for Raoul burning the convent in which Berthier's mother was a nun, seeking reconciliation in this manner with Raoul's kin.[19]

Or if it happened (and who is to say that the historical Vitalis didn't get the idea from reading or hearing about John Gualbert?), perhaps the saint only used ordinary human powers of persuasion to avert this crisis. Others might see this as a ritual interaction, in which the would-be avenger was provided with a way to walk back words expressed in anger and grief and to avoid the potential legal

---

19 Atto, *S. Joanis Gualberti vita*, in PL, 146: 672; *Raoul de Cambrai*, trans. Jessie Crosland (London: Chatto and Windus, 1926), 164–8 (*laisses* 238–41).

consequences of murdering his opponent. It might also be explained as the genuine fear, which expressed itself in a faint, of the avenger in the face of the power of the holy man. Finally, it might be explained as coincidence, a man bent on revenge whose body failed him at a critical moment. For Stephen, however, the theme is divine justice, and he admits of no doubt that in order to promote peace and justice, God seized the knight and rendered him powerless.[20]

Some modern people, of course, still believe that God's hand can be seen in seemingly natural events, such as recovery from serious illness; they may even see God's hand in their suffering the illness in the first place, as a form of chastisement or lesson. The difference, however, is that they may not convince their peers that the event had divine origins. This is not surprising, because we are the heirs of two great intellectual developments: the transformation of historical methods (and therefore what we know about the past) and the scientific revolution.

I will not spend a great deal of time on the scientific revolution, except to say that our views of medieval scientific thought are often blurred by the assumption that medieval people would believe anything and were essentially irrational, even though they sometimes subscribed for quite rational reasons to practices that we see as irrational.[21] Furthermore, we shouldn't overestimate the speed at which science obliterated the miraculous, for the claims of the miraculous were powerfully reinforced by the Counter-Reformation.[22] The medical historian Jacalyn Duffin, herself in her capacity as a physician having been an assessor of a miracle attributed to Marie-Marguerite d'Youville (1701–71), points out that as the understanding of physicians changed over time, so too did the notion of what might be a miraculous cure, without, however, ever eliminating the inexplicable (to some) or miraculous (to others) cure.[23] However, the general trend in the sum of miracles *is* downward, as can be seen in places like the Marian shrine at Lourdes. Only eleven of the seventy official miracles were recognized in the past half-century, while twenty were recognized in 1908. The penultimate official miracle occurred

---

20 On the threat posed by the knights and the response of clerical writers to it, see Kaeuper, *Chivalry and Violence*, esp. chap. 4.

21 See, for example, Richard Kieckhefer, "The Specific Rationality of Medieval Magic," *American Historical Review* 99, no. 3 (1994): 813–36; see also Partner, *Serious Entertainments*, 120f., on William of Newburgh's struggles to understand prodigies and her response as an historian to accounts of miracles.

22 See, for example, Albrecht Burkardt, *Les clients des saints: Maladie et quête du miracle à travers les procès de canonisation de la première moitié du XVIIe siècle en France* (Rome: École française de Rome, 2004).

23 Jacalyn Duffin, "The Doctor Was Surprised; or How to Diagnose a Miracle," *Bulletin of the History of Medicine* 81, no. 4 (Winter 2007): 699–729; see 701–2 and notes for a bibliography on the intersection of medicine and the miraculous. Duffin was given the xray of a patient and asked the prognosis, without being told of the outcome.

in 1989, but it was declared miraculous only in 2013, twenty-four years later. The most recent miracle (from 2008) was recognized in 2018.[24]

The development of historical methodologies, however, has also played a role, even for the devout. Historical criticism was not unknown in the Middle Ages, but it was not necessarily applied to historical narratives but instead was used in law and theology. Bernold of Constance, writing between 1070 and 1091, developed criteria for adjudicating between conflicting laws in the later eleventh century which included historical considerations, such as when and where a law was issued and for what purpose. These methods were further articulated by Peter Abelard in the prologue of his treatise *Yes and No* (1115–17), where he outlined the criteria for deciding between conflicting biblical passages and writings of the Fathers of the Church. Abelard's purposes were theological, but his criteria also included the historical. Finally, Gratian, in his *Concordance of Discordant Canons* (c. 1140), a compilation of church law that aimed at organizing and rationalizing it, applied the same criteria. These kinds of arguments became part of the medieval lawyers' stock in trade.[25]

It is hard to say when writers of historical narratives began to apply such criteria. Many twelfth-century historians probably simply chose the narrative they considered true among competing narratives. William of Malmesbury (c. 1090–c. 1142) often gave different versions of a story and explicitly left it to the reader to make the determination. Stephen of Fougères probably did not tell all the stories he might have told – there is no way to know what he left out – although it seems fairly clear that he was more reliant on what monks at Savigny told him than he was on the biographical details in the **mortuary roll** of Vitalis, which he refers to only at the end of his narrative. He was not alone among twelfth-century historians in preferring narratives conveyed to him by trusted informants over written accounts and in not worrying too much about factual accuracy.

Most modern scholars would put the date at which historians began to apply "historical" criteria to evidence from the past considerably later than the twelfth century. Lorenzo Valla is often credited with inventing historical criticism with a treatise he wrote against the so-called Donation of Constantine (*Declamatio*, 1440), a document that purported to grant the pope jurisdiction over the western

---

24 The website lists 70 cures (of the 7,000 attributed to Mary at the shrine) that have been declared officially miraculous (https://www.lourdes-france.org/en/miraculous-healings/). When I first consulted the site, there were 69 official miracles; the site was then down for a few years and the seventieth miracle had been added (and the page renamed). This should remind you that evidence may change over time!

25 On the methodology, see George Makdisi, "The Scholastic Method in Medieval Education: An Inquiry into Its Origins in Law and Theology," *Speculum* 49, no. 4 (1974): 640–71.

Roman Empire. Valla searched earlier sources that should have mentioned the Donation but didn't, and he compared the language of the document to that current in the early fourth century. As Anthony Grafton points out,

> Parts of his argument came, as Riccardo Fubrini has shown, from Nicholas of Cusa, who had already pointed out the absence of the *Donation* from sources where one would expect it to appear. But no later text showed more dramatically than Valla's how the sharp blade of criticism could cut its way through the contradictions and errors of tradition.[26]

This doesn't mean that historians were applying these techniques in their work around this time. By the sixteenth century, however, legal practice had blossomed into history that required its authors to check facts extensively, if not always to document them with citations.[27]

So far I've been talking largely about historical narratives, but hagiographic texts would seem to be a special case. It is true that historians sometimes saw their task as documenting the actions of God in the world, imbuing events with religious meaning. This was the foundation of ecclesiastical histories, which didn't only discuss religious events but also chronicled the political and social events of their day; John Ward has shown how these concerns shaped Orderic's history.[28] However, they did not necessarily approach or present all historical events as the active work of God.

Hagiographers, on the other hand, wanted to show the holiness of their biographical subjects, and while holiness of life was the real criterion for being a saint, the ability to work or request God to perform miracles was proof of the holiness of one's life.[29] Gregory the Great ends the first book of his *Dialogues* (a book overflowing with miracle stories) with this point, arguing that virtue in life is the real test of holiness but also that miracles attest to that virtue. Miracles would then seem to be a necessary part of such a biography.[30]

---

26 Anthony Grafton, *The Footnote: A Curious History* (Cambridge, MA: Harvard University Press, 1998), 73–5. Since Valla served the king of Naples, who was fighting the pope at the time, his treatise was not disinterested. However, history is by its nature not disinterested. Historians always write about the past with something particular they want to say.

27 Grafton, *The Footnote*, 132 ff., suggests that the transfer occurred through legal scholars like François Baudouin and Jean Bodin to historians like Jacques-Auguste de Thou (who did not use footnotes) and Étienne Pasquier (who did).

28 John O. Ward, "Ordericus Vitalis as Historian in the Europe of the Early Twelfth-Century Renaissance," *Parergon* 31, no. 1 (2014): 1–26.

29 Bartlett, *Why Can the Dead Do Such Great Things?*, 336ff.

30 Gregory the Great, *Dialogues*, 51–3.

Furthermore, many hagiographers saw the holiness of the saints to be all of a piece and so were happy to attribute miracles and actions they read about in other hagiographies to the one they happened to be writing. The spider miracle, for instance, appears in several saints' lives of this period: in the life of Conrad, bishop of Constance (where the spider exits from his mouth); in one of the lives of Robert, abbot of La Chaise-Dieu (told about a holy man named Bernard, perhaps Bernard of Tiron, where the spider exits through his arm); and in the life of Norbert of Xanten (where it makes its exit through his nose).[31] The world of medieval saints seems to be full of spiders, ready to be consumed with the communion wine at a moment's notice! Medieval people certainly noticed all the discrepancies and similarities, but the Reformation and Counter-Reformation brought debates about sanctity into high relief. Catholics were uncomfortably aware that the veneration of the saints might be characterized by Protestants as idolatry and miracles as trickery, and that this was throwing their beliefs into disrepute. And they had to deal with their own niggling doubts as well.

This brings us to the Jesuit scholar Heribert Rosweyde (1569–1629). After becoming a novice in the Jesuit order in 1588, he studied and then taught in Douai, where he was noted for consulting the libraries of local monasteries. He then studied in Louvain and was ordained in 1599. He became the prefect of studies in Antwerp in 1603. Rosweyde envisioned (as did many of his contemporaries) a collection of saints' lives that would be purged of foolish or incredible stories. Eventually he was given leave by his superiors to undertake the project. Rosweyde died relatively young, but his work was continued by Jean Bolland (1596–1665) and the society he founded, now known as the Bollandist Society, which produced the *Acta sanctorum* (*The Deeds of the Saints*), a massive collection of saints' lives organized according to the saint's day in the calendar that was intended to put the study of hagiography on a scientific footing.[32]

---

31 Bernard of La Chaise-Dieu, *The Tripartite Life of Robert, Abbot of Chaise-Dieu*, in *The Lives of the Monastic Reformers, 1: Robert of La Chaise-Dieu and Stephen of Obazine*, trans. Hugh Feiss, Maureen M. O'Brien, and Ronald Pepin (Collegeville, MN: Cistercian Publications, 2010), 98; *Vita Chounradi episcopi Constantiensis*, PL, 170, 870; *Vita Norberti*, 672. Bernard of Tiron had an oblique connection to La Chaise-Dieu; see *Bernard*, 15–17.

32 On these details, see Robert Godding, "L'oeuvre hagiographique d'Héribert Rosweyde," in *De Rosweyde aux Acta Sanctorum: La recherche hagiographique des Bollandistes à travers quatre siècles*, ed. Robert Godding, Bernard Joassart, Xavier Lequeux, and François de Vriendt (Brussels: Society of Bollandists, 2009), 35–62, esp. 35–8. For an English account by a member of the society, see Hippolyte Delehaye, *The Work of the Bollandists Through Three Centuries, 1615–1915* (Princeton, NJ: Princeton University Press, 1922), or David Knowles, *Great Historical Enterprises: Problems in Monastic History* (London and New York: Nelson, 1963).

The Bollandists did not include Stephen de Fougères's life of Vitalis in the *Acta sanctorum*, although they noted the saint's existence.[33] It is more likely that this was because the editors did not have access to any manuscripts of the text than because they would have had difficulty with any of the contents.[34] They did have access to the *Life of St. Firmat*, and they excised the part of the text that concerns Firmat's election as bishop of Constantinople. The editors pointed out that this was highly improbable, given that the western and eastern Christian churches entered a schism in the middle of the eleventh century, making the election of an obscure westerner to the patriarchal see totally incredible, not to mention the difference of languages. They were less bothered, however, by the saint's miracle, where he turned stolen eggs into frogs and then back into eggs so that the thief could return them.[35] In other words, the editors were applying historical criteria to decide what was historically possible, but they were not applying either scientific or historical reasoning to determining the authenticity of miracles themselves.

The volume of the *Acta sanctorum* containing the *Life of St. Firmat* was published in 1675. With the coming of the eighteenth-century "Age of Reason," hagiography was swept aside as a source of history because of its problematic nature, not to be retrieved until scholars developed new methods of turning texts intended to enhance and elicit belief into evidence for historical understanding, methods we are still working on and of which this book is a part.[36]

The "cultural work" performed by miracles

So where does this situation leave us? As historians, we cannot say whether any of these miracles actually took place. We were not present. There is no physical evidence one way or another. We have only a single written account to go by. The best we can say is that the author of the account thought it important to record the event and that some contemporary people believed in its facticity, some people believed that it was possible or the kind of thing that might have happened

33 *AASS*, I (January 390, on January 7). It is not entirely clear why Vitalis was assigned to this day. He died on September 16 and, as the entry notes, his elevation was celebrated on May 1 in Avranches.

34 The biography was published in the first volume of the journal begun by the Bollandist Society in the nineteenth century, the *Analecta Bollandiana*.

35 *De s. Guilielmo*, col. 337 for the story of the eggs, 338–9 for the narrative about Firmat's election as bishop of Constantinople. The editors even question whether Stephen, so obviously well educated, would have written such a passage which was (to them) so obviously wrong. As you may recollect, this is an issue that I have discussed above, p. 57.

36 For an illustration of this problem, see Nancy Partner's comments about Mary Augusta Ward's novel *Robert Elsmere* (1888) in *Serious Entertainments*, 183–5, and its implications for our understanding of the marvelous.

(without necessarily drawing a specific conclusion about this incident), some people believed in the miraculous but perhaps not that this specific event was a miracle, and some were skeptical of the miraculous entirely. The distribution of belief does not seem to have been markedly different in the past from the situation in the modern day.[37] I should add that when I said something of this sort once at a conference, I met with vigorous disagreement from another historian, who argued that science has told us miracles don't happen. This is actually an argument about whether all the learned sciences are intertwined, and he and I are obviously on different sides of the argument. I see arguments from the nature of science as lying outside of history, not as being part and parcel of it, although they may be compatible, while he took the opposite view. This larger question is something you'll have to figure out for yourself, but now you know where I stand on it.

Given that I would argue that we don't have evidence either way, perhaps we are not very far along yet. But accepting that people in the past wrote about miracles does not mean that we need to accept what they said without subjecting it to the same kind of interrogation as any other written evidence. Although we cannot determine whether a miracle actually occurred – as a theological or scientific judgment this would stand outside of the discipline of history – or even if the events described in our narratives happened (also true for anything appearing in a single narrative if there is no outside evidence), we *can* accept the text as a fact. It exists. And we can ask instead what cultural work the author intended the miracle to do, what meaning it was intended to convey to the readers, or what it contributed to the hagiography as a whole. In the case I started with at the beginning of this chapter, the miracle shows that Vitalis was supernaturally protected from harm, both in swallowing the spider and in having the spider exit his body without going through a natural opening. So part of the work this miracle does is to show that Vitalis's authority was similar to that of other saints.

Of these saints, one of the most significant for the Savigniacs would have been St. Benedict, as I argued in the last chapter, whose rule they followed both before and after they were absorbed by the **Cistercians**, and as the parallels between

---

37 See, for example, Rodney Stark, "Religious Competition and Roman Piety," *Interdisciplinary Journal of Research on Religion* 2 (2006): 4–5, where he argues that even in societies with compulsory religious membership, unbelief exists. Stark bases his comments both on anthropological studies of preliterate societies and the historical record of blasphemy and theft from religious institutions. Bartlett, *Why Can the Dead Do Such Great Things?*, 596–601, discusses skeptical reception of saints, which he distinguishes from critique of the **cults** of the saints or religious practices around them.

Vitalis's life and Benedict's show as well. In his life of St. Benedict, Gregory the Great related a miracle in which the monks of Vicovara, tired of the austere and orderly life that Benedict required them to lead, tried to get rid of him by poisoning his wine. When Benedict blessed his cup before drinking, his cup shattered.[38] I am hesitant to assert that any story would have been known by all the **monks** in any given **monastery**, but I'd put money on this one being known to every monk. In Vitalis's case, the chalice did not shatter, but the mishap of the spider in the cup was a natural event that happened after the blessing, not a malicious attempt at murder, so the spider was merely rendered harmless. Nonetheless, monks might well have thought of the example of St. Benedict.

But another part of the work this miracle does is to underline the transformative power of the everyday miracle of transubstantiation. The analogy Stephen chose to defend the miracle was not random. Once the communion wine had been blessed, it was the blood of Christ, and Stephen underlines that this is what Vitalis believed at the moment he took it:

> For he truly believed that he was receiving the body and blood of the Lord.
> He had faith, not in error, that such a mystery could overcome even any venom. Indeed, all things, by the testimony of truth, are possible to the believer (Mk. 9:22).[39]

Stephen does not make any kind of issue of the spider's fate, but the spider was also protected, exiting presumably alive from the saint's foot.

Similarly, the work of promoting peace that the second miracle I discussed above carried out was critical to the concerns of the twelfth century and was something Stephen was himself worried about. In the *Book of Conduct*, he contrasts what the knights are supposed to do with what they actually do:

> The knight should take up his sword
> To punish and to stop
> Those who make others complain about them.
> He should stamp out force and rapine.

---

38 Gregory the Great, *Dialogues*, 62.

39 On the Eucharist as a central miracle, see Benedicta Ward, *Miracles and the Medieval Mind: Theory, Record, and Event* (Philadelphia: University of Pennsylvania Press, 1982), 13–18. She includes a number of accounts of transubstantiation miracles, such as a pair from the *Dialogue on Miracles* of Caesarius of Heisterbach. See also Rubin, *Corpus Christi*.

But many of them are accustomed to do nothing
So that I hear people complain about them every day,
[They say] that nothing is left for them
To have or to acquire.[40]

Although medieval clerics accepted the necessity of knights and saw their role as ordained by God, as Stephen himself says ("The clergy should pray for everyone, the knights should protect and honor everyone without hesitation, and the peasants should work"), and they believed that knights who did their duty could expect salvation ("He can very well be saved within his order if no one finds something in him to criticize"),[41] they were all too aware of activities that might send knights to hell. Stephen names lying, cheating, committing treason, and appropriating tithes, among other faults of the breed.[42]

In the passage I cited above, Stephen highlights the need for knights to be agents of justice, for the sword of the knights to aid the sword of the Church. In the case of the miracle Stephen has written about, a knight who seemingly was doing his job (exactly what Stephen described in his vernacular text) himself became the target of other knights. The miracle, then, restores order and emphasizes justice. Stephen, in speaking of the would-be avenger, addresses precisely these points:

Oh, hard heart! Oh, heart blinded by malice! Oh, diabolical anger! Oh, perverse anger! Oh, anger that cannot be satiated except by the death of another! It is written, *for the anger of man does not work the righteousness of God* (James 1:20). How indeed could someone work the justice of God, who has a heart infected with such evil that he rages after the death of another? (I: 10)

In stopping the act of vengeance, the miracle restores the knights to their proper place.

---

40 *LM*, 80, ll. 537–44 (my translation); see also p. 119 for notes to this passage. Lodge also comments that Stephen's ideas about the obligations of knights depend on the comments of John of Salisbury in his *Polycraticus*; see John Dickinson, *The Statesman's Book of John of Salisbury* (New York: Russell & Russell, 1963), 226–8, VI: 16.

41 *LM*, 84, ll. 673–6; 82, ll. 621–2 (my translations).

42 These were not new concerns in the twelfth century. See Geoffrey Koziol, "Monks, Feuds, and the Making of Peace in Eleventh-Century Flanders," *Historical Reflections/Réflexions historiques* 14, no. 3 (Fall 1987): 534f., for peacemaking miracles of St. Ursmar, and 534n11 for some other hagiographic accounts of endemic violence in the period. Koziol points out that the monks of St. Ursmar were good at creating situations in which the parties were more or less coerced into peacemaking (536), and we might argue that in the first of the stories, Vitalis does the same, by having the potential victim lie in a pose that showed his faith in God, at the same time daring the would-be killer to blaspheme by killing him.

Stephen followed this miracle with a second miracle of peace, in which the saint urged a man who had lost a hand in a fight with his enemies to make peace with them. The man took up arms against the saint but was seized by a sudden fit of vomiting and was forced to grant the saint what he wished (I: 11). It is after telling the story of this second miracle that Stephen writes his defense of the truth of things he had not seen. No doubt, many in his audience had also never seen men injured in brawls or angry at an execution make peace and doubted that as much as any event requiring more than human agency.

These observations about the work that miracles do in the text, however, do not allow the historian simply to dismiss the story of miracles, not even if the events seem natural rather than supernatural, not even if contemporaries scoffed at them, even though they also do not require the historian to believe in them. The bottom line is that belief or disbelief in miracles is a theological matter. But the miracles open a door into a world run along somewhat different lines than ours and with somewhat different assumptions. When the historian brings to a miracle the assumption that it didn't happen, this simply closes off the intellectual possibilities of inquiry. We cannot help being who we are, because we are positioned entities. That is, we come from a particular set of circumstances, have had particular experiences, and view the world through those lenses.[43] The job of the historian, however, is to attempt to the degree possible to be aware of his or her own assumptions and to set them to one side while considering people in the past, to accept what is often referred to as "the strangeness of the past," not to become a person in that time but to arrive at a greater understanding of what it might mean to be a person in that time, something historians and social scientists call **perspective taking**.[44]

This is what I have been doing in this chapter. In a previous chapter, I discussed Stephen's career, which shaped his positionality. He was a man of many loyalties: to his king, whose **chaplain** he was proud to have been; to the part of the world in which he grew up and to which he returned at the end of his life,

---

43 On **positionality** in history, see Bruce VanSledright, "On the Importance of Historical Positionality to Thinking about and Teaching History," *International Journal of Social Education* 12, no. 2 (Fall/Winter 1997–8): 1–18, and David Takacs, "Positionality, Epistemology, and Social Justice in the Classroom," *Social Justice* 29, no. 4 (2002): 168–81.

44 O.L. Davis, Elizabeth Anne Yeager, and Stuart J. Foster, eds., *Historical Empathy and Perspective Taking in the Social Studies* (Lanham, MD: Rowman & Littlefield, 2001), offer a number of essays on perspective taking, sometimes referred to as empathy. I prefer to use the term perspective taking, however, because historians need to take the perspectives even of repugnant actors, but no one would suggest that they should (or could) empathize with history's monsters.

much exalted; to his duties as a bishop, which he seems to have carried out conscientiously; to the souls in his care, for whom he wrote in both French and Latin; and to his God. I am none of these things and I do not (personally) believe in miracles. But if I set my disbelief to one side, I can speak with Stephen across the ages and find out what he can tell us about his world. That is the subject of the final chapter.

CHAPTER FIVE

✠

"They tried to kill him": Hagiography and the Problem of Violence

> When that place [Savigny] was first cultivated, some men who had earlier used the wood lying near that place for their own purposes, were set on fire with the torches of malice. Angry that he was nearby and thinking that they would no longer have the wood, they tried to kill him. One day, when he took to the road, men in cahoots with them lay in ambush and greeted him with arrows. But through God's virtue, he remained unharmed and whole among the many showers of them. So when the arrows had been launched in vain, those men, who were stupefied by this event, came out of their hiding places to him and confessed their guilt; they acquired swift forgiveness from him. (II: 2)

This miracle story, in which certain unnamed men try to kill Vitalis, was one of the miracles over which Moolenbroek cast some doubt. It wasn't Vitalis's survival in the midst of a rain of arrows that was at issue for him but rather the notion that anyone had tried to kill the saint, not just this once, but in fact several times. While I suggested in the previous chapter that we have no corroboration of most of the stories in this saint's life, this story and others in the narrative do point us toward some historical truths, namely the concerns of contemporaries in general and Stephen in particular with violence in late-twelfth-century society.

The story that gives this book its title, for instance, is about violence. We know it perhaps only because it was a good way for Stephen to frame his complicated sentiments about the count of Mortain, whose **chaplain** Stephen himself had been. However, this story also raises questions about the use of physical violence against women and what some churchmen thought about it in the later twelfth century. In this chapter, I'll be following the trail of both kinds of violence, first the domestic violence of the title story and then the larger question of violence posed by the passage at the beginning of this chapter.

Violence and the position of women

Much of the scholarly discussion of violence against women has concerned sexual violence, sometimes as it appeared in literature, a topic discussed by Kathryn Gravdal, and sometimes as it was treated in law, as in Anthony Musson's work. This obviously reflects modern preoccupations (and the specializations of these scholars), to which we are as subject as Stephen of Fougères. In the case of sexual assault, medieval views are probably not so far off ours; some deplored it, some thought men would be men or that the victims were at fault, and they nearly always found it hard to prove.[1]

This case, however, concerns domestic violence, another kettle of fish entirely. Medieval society generally accepted that certain classes of people had the right to use physical punishment on other classes of people. Schoolmasters were permitted to beat students, abbots to order their **monks** to be beaten, parents to beat their children. As Christiane Mattke points out in her article on the iconography of discipline, the use of the rod on children was validated by the Bible.[2] The rule of St. Benedict also advised physical punishment for both children and adults, although primarily as a step before expulsion for adults and only for children who were incapable of understanding how serious a penalty excommunication was.[3] St. Anselm's writings show that this saint saw a place for physical punishments, although he seems to have thought that one would form better monks through love than fear.[4]

While none of these classes of people are wives, like children, students, and monks, wives were seen as being dependent and subordinate. If we look at literature, most of which, admittedly, was written after Stephen's time, violent

---

1 On rape, see Kathryn Gravdal, *Ravishing Maidens: Writing Rape in Medieval French Literature and Law* (Philadelphia: University of Pennsylvania Press, 1991); also Anthony Musson, "Crossing Boundaries: Attitudes to Rape in Late Medieval England," in *Boundaries of the Law: Geography, Gender and Jurisdiction in Medieval and Early Modern Europe* (Aldershot: Ashgate, 2005), 84–101, where he argues that rape was seen as criminal, but proving rape was difficult in the absence of physical injury to the woman (or child). Eric Jager, *The Last Duel: A True Story of Trial by Combat in Medieval France* (New York: Broadway Books, 2005), relates the story of the last judicial combat in France (1386), which arose from a rape.

2 Christiane Mattke, "Verges et disciplines dans l'iconographie de l'enseignement," *Médiévales* 27 (Autumn 1994): 107, citing three passages from Proverbs.

3 Benedict, *Sancti Benedicti reguli monasteriorum*, caps. 28 (adults) and 30 (children).

4 Gregory B. Sadler, "Non modo verbis sed et verberibus: Saint Anselm on Punishment, Coercion, and Violence," *Cistercian Studies Quarterly* 45, no. 1 (2010): 35–61.

punishment seems to be accepted. When Kriemhild in the *Nibelungenlied* (c. 1200) boasts to Brunhild that Siegfried was the first to have sex with Brunhild, not Brunhild's husband Gunther, Siegfried promises Gunther to punish his wife and Kriemhild reports to Hagen that Siegfried had, in fact, beaten her.[5] In this case, Kriemhild appears to accept the justice of her punishment.

A more ambiguous situation occurs in Chrétien de Troyes's *Erec and Enide* (c. 1170). Erec regularly threatens to beat Enide, and she accepts his right to do so, although, crucially, he never actually lays a violent finger on her. The only two figures in the narrative who do strike women (or permit them to be struck) are villainous.[6] Chrétien's narrative, however, belongs to an idealizing literature about the power of love, which was by implication making an argument about the ideal relationship between men and women. In the *fabliaux*, which begin to appear in the thirteenth century and are less idealistic, there is considerable domestic violence (indeed violence of all kinds), generally presented for comic effect (or at least comic to medieval hearers; some of the violence is repellent and gross by modern standards).[7] In real life, we have to assume, some husbands undoubtedly threatened and sometimes beat their wives. Our question has to be how this was viewed and whether Stephen's obviously disapproving view fits in or is exceptional.

I want to start this discussion by addressing the more general question of marriage in the twelfth century, because ideas about marriage were changing and had been since the late eleventh century. In the early Middle Ages, marriage was an arrangement between families rather than between the marrying parties themselves. We have to imagine (because we have no information at all) that at the level of peasants, where relatively little property was involved and everyone pretty much knew everyone else, mutual inclination (or at least the absence of disinclination) might have played a role. As Michael Sheehan has pointed out, modern ideas about marriage developed among the elites, where initially at least, alliances and property considerations were important. While church authorities strove mightily (and not always successfully) to ensure that marriage lasted until the death of one of the parties, that is, to discourage divorce, marriage was not a

---

5 *The Nibelungenlied*, trans. A.T. Hatto (Harmondsworth: Penguin, 1969), 116, 120.

6 Chrétien de Troyes, *Erec and Enide*, trans. Carleton W. Carroll, in *Arthurian Romances* (Harmondsworth: Penguin, 1991), 72–3 (for example). The two men who strike women are the dwarf who accompanies the arrogant knight Yder (39) and the count who wishes to marry Enide, thinking Erec is dead (96).

7 Yves Roguet, "La violence comique des fabliaux," in *La violence dans le monde médiéval, Senefiance* 36 (1994): 457, has counted the acts of violence in sets of *fabliaux* and found that physical violence occurred in 37 per cent of the ones he examined, while someone was threatened with physical violence in over half.

sacrament and church input was limited (again in theory) to prohibiting close kin marriage, that is, incest.[8]

Beginning in the late eleventh century and through the twelfth century, however, the theology of marriage was worked out and marriage became a sacrament of the Church. A marriage came to exist when a couple exchanged words of present consent (which is echoed in the modern exchange of "I dos") or alternatively when they exchanged words of future consent ("I will marry you") and then had sex. These ideas were articulated by Peter Lombard, with whose writings Stephen was familiar, although this definition of marriage did not become official doctrine until 1215. The notion that spouses ought to love each other, not in the romantic sense as we might mean it but in an affectionate and companionable sense, was far older than the establishment of marriage as a sacrament (it was a feature of the Roman legal tradition), but the significance of consent must have put increased emphasis on the obligation to love one's spouse.[9]

In fact, in *Erec and Enide*, which I mentioned above, the hero and heroine fall in love and marry, and the principal tension driving the story is that love makes Erec so happy that he fails to get out of bed and do his knightly duty. One way to read the remainder of the story, then, with its threats of violence by the hero against the heroine, is that Erec loves his wife too truly to actually strike her. In contrast, the man who *does* strike her does not love her but only wants her; he strikes her in the face because Enide refuses to marry him when both think that Erec is dead, and when rebuked, he replies that Enide is his to do with as he pleases. Erec awakens at her cry and promptly slices the top of the man's head in two.

Erec and Enide is clearly presenting the marriage of the two as an ideal in a society where that ideal would have been largely unattainable. Despite the crucial significance of consent in marriage, most members of the elite continued to marry for dynastic reasons, and such unions might not include tender relations. For that reason, it is interesting that the marriage contract of Berengaria of Castile

---

8 On medieval marriage, see Michael Sheehan, *Marriage, Family, and Law in Medieval Europe: Collected Studies* (Toronto: University of Toronto Press, 1996), particularly the essays on choice in marriage partners (chap. 7) and marriage among the unfree and poor (chap. 11). I would recommend that Georges Duby's book on medieval marriage (*The Knight, the Lady, and the Priest: The Making of Modern Marriage in Medieval France*, trans. Barbara Bray [Chicago: University of Chicago Press, 1993]) be used cautiously, as the argument sometimes outruns the evidence.

9 Thomas M. Finn, "Sex and Marriage in the Sentences of Peter Lombard," *Theological Studies* 72 (2011): 45. Marriage in Roman law was based on the consent of the parties, which was expected to give rise to "marital affection."

to Alfonso IX of León, drafted in 1199, specified that if Alfonso abused his wife, he would forfeit the entire marriage gift of thirty castles.[10] Berengaria (1180–1246) was Henry II's granddaughter, although this marriage was contracted decades after Stephen's death. But it does suggest that the conversation that Stephen was a participant in was continuing past his death. So what was the conversation, and where does Stephen fit in? It would seem that domestic violence, while discouraged, might be anticipated.

Roman law did not permit a man to strike his wife with any implements (rods or whips) unless she had given him grounds that would justify divorce. Without such grounds, he had to pay her the equivalent of a third of her dowry.[11] The law does not specify, however, that he might not slap her, punch her, kick her, or pull her hair. (Since Nero was reputed to have kicked his wife Poppea to death, obviously the barring of implements did not preclude lethal violence.)[12] The law codes compiled for Germanic rulers from the late fifth through the eighth centuries do not mention domestic violence at all, only violence against women from those outside the family. These laws lay far in the past by Stephen's time, but while Roman law was being revived and studied from the eleventh century onward, it is difficult to know how or if its legal standards were being applied in practice. **Canon law** (church law) weighed in on the issue in the twelfth century, with Gratian (c. 1140), citing a sixth-century canon of Toledo, which said that clerical husbands might discipline their wives by confinement and penitential fasting (short of starving them to death).[13] An influential commentary on Gratian (which Brundage dates to 1160) specified that clerical husbands might beat their wives, extrapolating from the power of an abbot to order a monk beaten, but only for cause.[14]

However, there is some evidence that by the middle of the twelfth century, prominent clerics did not think women should have to put up with beatings. Pope Alexander III (Stephen's contemporary, r. 1159–81), in one of his **decretal letters** (letters providing a legal opinion), permitted a woman who had been abused and had fled from her husband not to return to him unless she received sufficient assurance that the beating would not happen again. The date of this decretal is

---

10 James Brundage, "Domestic Violence in Classical Canon Law," in *Violence in Medieval Society*, ed. Richard W. Kaeuper (Rochester, NY: Boydell, 2000), 187.

11 Henry Ansgar Kelly, "'Rule of Thumb' and the Folklaw of the Husband's Stick," *Journal of Legal Education* 44, no. 3 (1994): 356.

12 Suetonius, *The Twelve Caesars*, trans. Robert Graves, rev. Michael Grant (Harmondsworth: Penguin, 1979), 233 (Nero, 35).

13 Brundage, "Domestic Violence," 185.

14 Brundage, "Domestic Violence," 187. This is the *summa parisiensis* commentary.

disputed, but it may have been written while Stephen was alive.[15] This trend becomes clearer after Stephen's time. Johannes Teutonicus (d. 1245), who provided the "**ordinary gloss**" to Gratian (the commentary that students of canon law would have read alongside Gratian's text) permitted husbands to chastise, but not beat, their wives, specifically because their wives were not servants. A lay man might imprison his wife, put her on a (non-starvation) penitential diet, or refuse to eat with her if she misbehaved.[16] Imprisonment was the fate of Henry II's wife, Eleanor of Aquitaine, from early 1174 until Henry's death in 1189, for her involvement in the revolts of her sons against their father.[17]

What authorities thought, what husbands did, and what courts ruled about it, however, are three different things. Unfortunately, legal records concerning domestic abuse appear only much later; in these cases women were sometimes granted separations from abusive husbands, as one might conclude from Alexander III's decretal, but unless the abuse was frequent and severe, most women seem to have put up with it. In some of these later cases, the wife was not the one to bring the action, but the neighbors stepped in when the violence pierced the boundary between the private world of the marriage and the public world of the community. And social status sometimes mattered, as the case of Berengaria's marriage suggests: if the canonists thought an ordinary wife ought not to be beaten like a servant, how much more ought a noble woman to be spared this treatment? In a very late case (1299), the judges separated a man from his noble wife and required him to pay her a substantial pension each year because of her social status.[18]

So where does that leave us in relation to Stephen's narrative? In Vitalis's day, marriage was not yet a sacrament, although it was on its way to becoming one, and the question of violence within marriage had not been raised by ecclesiastical authorities. So these ideas about violence within marriage have to be Stephen's.

---

15 Brundage, "Domestic Violence," 188; on the decretal *Ex transmissa*, see Charles Donohue, "The Dating of Alexander the Third's Marriage Decretals: Dauvillier Revisited after Fifty Years," *Zeitschrift der Savigny-Stiftung für Rechtsgeschichte: Kanonistische Abteilung* 68 (1982): 78, 112–13 (the bulk of the decretal, according to Donohue, is about the dissolution of an incestuous marriage).

16 Brundage, "Domestic Violence," 186–7, quoting Johannes Teutonicus and Laurentius Hispanus.

17 Eleanor of Aquitaine may be the most debated and written-about medieval woman ever; a reader who is interested in the basic outlines of her life, however, could well start with Jane Martindale's biographical article ("Eleanor [Eleanor of Aquitaine], suo jure duchess of Aquitaine (c. 1122–1204), queen of France, consort of Louis VII, and queen of England, consort of Henry II," *ODNB*, https://doi.org/10.1093/ref:odnb/8618>).

18 Hannah Skoda, "Violent Discipline or Disciplining Violence? Experience and Reception of Domestic Violence in Late Thirteenth- and Early Fourteenth-Century Paris and Picardy," *Cultural and Social History* 6, no. 1 (2009): 18.

Stephen does not tell us why the count beat his wife, but the story tells us that the count had sinned in beating her and that he needed to provide some sort of assurance – a pledge – that it would not happen again. This makes Stephen the advocate and adopter of relatively new ideas about marriage. There is a slight hint about this subject in the *Book of Conduct*, where in discussing women, Stephen says that

> A good woman is an ornament
> To her lord, and she does not lie
> When she loves him and serves him well
> And advises him truly.

> If a wife loves her husband truly,
> She should not be punished by God or man;
> She should safely invoke his name
> And confide all her troubles to him.[19]

Stephen then goes on to sing of the joys of a loving marriage (the word "joy" appears four times in the eight following lines). This is the ideal that Chrétien, who was Stephen's contemporary, perhaps even someone Stephen had met, puts before the reader. St. Paul may have enjoined men to love their wives and wives to fear their husbands (as Brundage points out), but Stephen, like many contemporaries, thought love should go both ways.[20]

The larger issue of violence

The right to use violence

In chapter 4, I mentioned that some of Vitalis's miracles involve his efforts to mitigate violence. This is not something that writers before Stephen emphasized in writing about Vitalis; instead, they stressed Vitalis's concern for moral reform. There are passages in the biography that show that Stephen was also concerned with moral reform (particularly that of women, a topic you can explore on your own), and it was certainly the focus of his *Book of Conduct* (where in several stanzas Stephen distinguished himself by being one of the only medieval writers to

---

19 *LM*, 99, ll. 1161–8 (my translation).
20 Brundage, "Domestic Violence," 184 and n11; Eph. 5:33.

refer explicitly – and disapprovingly – to women having sex with each other).[21] But Stephen returns over and over again to the issue of knightly violence.

In reading about the past, we have a tendency simply to accept what stories say. That is particularly true when the stories seem, in our terms, "primitive." We shrug and accept that people in the past just weren't as enlightened as us. It's connected to "the Whig interpretation of history," a phrase coined by Herbert Butterfield in 1931.[22] What he meant by it was the assumption of progress, that history is moving "forward" and that human society is getting better and better. Historians are bedeviled by this notion of progress. While on the one hand human life expectancies have expanded dramatically on the global level, on the other hand it is hard to argue, in the wake of the Armenian genocide, the European Holocaust, the Rwandan genocide, the genocide of the Rohingya, not to mention all the other massacres, that humanity is less violent as a species now than it used to be.

But even if we don't accept the notion that human nature is somehow being improved, we may still lump all the nasty evidence of human failures together under one heading and forget about it. Sam Wineburg writes about a class in which resistance to the American civil rights movement is reduced to "prejudice." This is part of his discussion of **historical context**, which is my key point.[23] Violence (or racism or sexism or prejudice) may persist in all or most human societies, but it bears a different face and serves a different purpose in each. What this means is that rather than accepting the narratives about violence that come to us from the past, as historians we have to interrogate them, to ask what causes the violence, and to determine the context in which it occurs. So here comes the context.

In recent years, scholars of the European Middle Ages, for instance Warren Brown, have become increasingly interested in the issue of violence (all sorts of violence: wars, crimes, feuds, executions, martyrdoms), its depiction, and its contexts. What emerges from much of this research is that violence had a different place in medieval society than it does in ours.[24] As I've noted above, attitudes toward physical punishments were different, but what is most striking to modern people may be that individuals frequently felt that they had the right – and

---

21 *LM*, 97–8, ll. 1105–24; for a discussion of this passage, see Robert Clark, "Jousting Without a Lance: The Condemnation of Female Homoeroticism in the *Livre des manières*," in *Same Sex Love and Desire among Women in the Middle Ages*, ed. Francesca Canadé Sautman and Pamela Sheingorn (New York: Palgrave, 2001), 143–77.

22 Herbert Butterfield, *The Whig Interpretation of History* (London: G. Bell, 1931).

23 Sam Wineburg, *Historical Thinking and Other Unnatural Acts: Charting the Future of Teaching the Past* (Philadelphia: Temple University Press, 2001), 17.

24 See, for example, Warren C. Brown, *Violence in Medieval Europe* (Harlow & New York: Longman, 2011), but any medieval database will turn up hundreds of articles written in the last decade.

this right was legally acknowledged – to take aggressive action against others. The right to feud was one form that this took in the early Middle Ages. While legal scholars such as Patrick Wormald and Tom Lambert have argued about whether early-medieval kings desired to eliminate feuding as a solution to interfamilial aggression or were simply interested in codifying the terms under which feuding might take place, the feud was recognized to have a place.[25] Furthermore, Richard Kaeuper has pointed out that the notion of chivalry, often taken to be an attempt to limit violence, in fact required violence, because only through the use of "edged weapons" could the prowess necessary for chivalric reputation be demonstrated.[26] Medieval warfare permitted, with impunity, all sorts of violence against all sorts of people; until very late in the Middle Ages, there was no practical limitation on what fighting men might do to civilians or to one another in war, even though there were early attempts to create such limitations in the **Peace of God** and **Truce of God** movements.[27] Violence might be limited for practical reasons, however, such as the desire among elite fighters to collect rich ransoms from their peers rather than simply to kill them, but this obviously didn't apply to peasants. Taking booty was seen as legitimate well past the Middle Ages.

In the modern world, states generally attempt to monopolize the right to apply violence to solving problems. It may be that someone has murdered your child, but in many parts of the world, including Canada and the United States, this would not give you the right to use violence yourself. (There are, of course, parts of the world where "honor" killings and feud are still accepted social practices.) Even in western countries, however, there are spaces carved out where individuals can deploy violence, generally in the defense of the self or others. In the United States, "stand your ground" laws may go quite far to carve out a space for violent self-help on the part of individuals, although often dependent on who is on the receiving end, and the American culture of gun ownership means that individuals have considerable ability to use extreme violence against others, whether in self-defense or in unprovoked aggression.

---

25 See Patrick Wormald, *The Making of English Law: King Alfred to the Twelfth Century*, vol. 1 (Oxford: Blackwell, 1999), 39, who argues that King Rothari's laws were intended to curtail and contain feud; in response see Tom Lambert, *Law and Order in Anglo-Saxon England* (Oxford: Clarendon, 2017), who argues that at least Anglo-Saxon kings were not concerned with violence per se so much as violence to which an individual did not have a legitimate right and that the sphere in which kings operated (at least until the eleventh century) was extremely limited. See also the comments of Brown, *Violence*, 14–18, on feud and the problem the concept poses for historians.

26 Kaeuper, *Chivalry and Violence*.

27 Kaeuper is also a good guide to these developments. See *Chivalry and Violence*, esp. chap. 4. In that book, he notes the growth of royal power as curtailing, finally, the unrestricted right to acts of violence in war and the duel (300–1). For the Peace and Truce of God, see also Brown, *Violence*, 116ff.

That states had an interest in defining and/or restricting the use of violence is an argument made long ago by the sociologist Norbert Elias, although he framed his argument in the context of court culture. Court culture required that people who might have responded violently to insults to honor (often the trigger for feuding) were constrained to non-violent forms of competition. This worked to the degree that people wanted to participate in court culture, but as kings and great lords became more powerful, many people did want to participate. The process was not totalizing, but the power of developing states was such that in the long run it produced a "civilizing effect."[28] One can see why Elias, a Jewish refugee from Hitler's Germany whose parents died at Auschwitz, would have been preoccupied with the problem of violence. (The questions we ask arise from our **positionalities**.)

The role of governments and the culture of honor

For much of the early part of the Middle Ages, there were no states to restrain violence, at least not states in the sense of centralized bodies of governance with the power to tax, to mobilize armies, or to unilaterally impose laws. There were governing structures, but these could not fully control the behavior of the people they "governed." While this was true for nearly all of the Middle Ages, it was less true at the end of the Middle Ages than it was in the early Middle Ages. Thomas Bisson has recently argued in a dense book, however, that through the twelfth century, power was exercised through lordship and that therefore individual violence could be repressed only through lordly violence.[29] But to say that no states in our sense existed is not to deny that there were changes in medieval governance; the twelfth century was a turning point in governance, as it was in many social and political ideals.

Kings in this period were striving to increase their authority and their power. To do so, they had to tame the aspirations of their nobility, even if kings were themselves only super-nobles. David Crouch has termed the medieval nobility a "community of **honor**" and that's a useful notion.[30] The term honor was used both to refer to a holding (a piece of property) and to high reputation, and both of these needed to be defended. Richard Kaeuper has referred to a "privileged

---

28 Norbert Elias, *The Civilizing Process: Sociogenetic and Psychogenetic Investigations*, rev. ed., trans. Edmund Jephcott, with revisions by the author (Oxford: Blackwell, 2000).

29 Thomas N. Bisson, *The Crisis of the Twelfth Century: Power, Lordship, and the Origins of European Government* (Princeton, NJ: Princeton University Press, 2009).

30 David Crouch, *The Birth of Nobility: Constructing Aristocracy in England and France 900–1300* (Harlow: Pearson-Longman, 2005), 280ff.

practice of violence," and that's also a useful concept here.[31] Those who considered themselves as having a right to act violently in defense of their honors (in both senses of the word) were hard to contain and restrain, despite royal assertions of a right to do so.[32]

Warren Brown gives a number of examples of affronts to honor and the violence that ensued. For example, he relays a story told by Thietmar of Merseberg (d. 1018) about what happened when a marriage agreement was set aside by the father of the bride; it led to the abduction of the young woman from a convent. When she expressed her preference to remain with her original intended (the abductor), arrangements were made that led to a peaceful settlement (ignoring the violence of abduction, of course), and in that case no one was killed.[33] However, Brown also discusses a more deadly case: the attempt of Charles the Good of Flanders (d. 1127) to insist that members of one of the powerful families of Flanders were serfs. It led to Charles's assassination and a civil war in Flanders.[34]

We can see that culture of honor in the case of the miracle I discussed in the previous chapter, in which a man seeks Vitalis's help in deflecting his enemies (I: 10). While the circumstances of the events are not entirely clear, the intended victim appears to have been acting on behalf of public authority. The man who wished to attack him was operating within the context of honor and feud. In intervening, Vitalis was reconciling two different notions of appropriate conduct and bringing the power of God into play to restrain individual violence.

It is not possible to know whether this incident occurred or not, but in telling this story, Stephen was positioning himself among those who were attempting to restrain knightly violence, and he was in good company. Many twelfth-century clerics were highly critical of knightly violence in what they saw as bad causes and longed to put that violence to honorable and good use. While in many modern quarters the Crusades are viewed with some horror, involving as they did killing in the name of God, to many clerics crusading was precisely a good use of this kind. St. Bernard famously wrote a sermon about the Knights Templar, contrasting their pious use of violence with the violence of the jewel-bedecked, fratricidal lay knights, who were a "malice" instead of a "militia."[35] To put a stop to internal

---

31 Richard Kaeuper, *Medieval Chivalry* (Cambridge: Cambridge University Press, 2016), part 3, but see esp. pp. 155–60; also *Chivalry and Violence*, chap. 7.

32 Kaeuper, *Chivalry and Violence*, 98ff. (for France), 107ff. (for England).

33 Brown, *Violence*, 143–4.

34 Brown, *Violence*, 171ff. The most extensive medieval account is that of Galbert of Bruges, *The Murder, Betrayal, and Slaughter of the Glorious Charles, Count of Flanders*, trans. Jeff Rider (New Haven, CT: Yale University Press, 2013).

35 Bernard of Clairvaux, *In Praise of the New Knighthood*, trans. M. Conrad Greenia (Trappist, KY: Cistercian Publications, 2000); Kaeuper, *Chivalry and Violence*, chap. 4 ("Clergie, Chevalerie, and Reform").

violence, **clergy** like Stephen preached peace, and Vitalis intervened. Nor is Vitalis the only contemporary saint to quell these kinds of hostilities. The biographer of Norbert of Xanten, writing only slightly earlier than Stephen, also tells how Norbert strove to bring peace to warring parties.[36]

Pride and masculinity

The second story on the same theme, the one about the man who has lost a hand, is a less dramatic story in some ways, but here too noble pride is humbled (Stephen says the man is very rich) (I: 11). The purpose of the story was not, however, to reinforce public authority, because there is no mention of law in the story, but rather to encourage touchy nobles not to seek personal revenge. Part of the context in both miracles is the different **emotional regime** of the Middle Ages. While psychologists have generally argued that all human beings have the same emotions in their repertoires, the circumstances that trigger those emotions differ from culture to culture, as does the expression of those emotions. These differences are sometimes referred to as emotional "regimes." Medieval men in historical accounts and literature, for instance, weep openly in rage, sorrow, and pity, something that would be discouraged in, for instance, modern North American men, but North American men feel these emotions as well. William Ready offers a good introduction to these issues in his book on the history of emotions.[37] What is important for us here is that in the Middle Ages, the public expression of anger and aggression was accepted. As Stephen White has argued, public anger was related to one's sense of honor, so threatening those who threatened one's honor was one way to cope; he provides many examples of the phenomenon.[38]

Even though the second story is much briefer than the first, there are some additional things I would note about it. As I mentioned in the previous chapter, Stephen again feels the need to state that he is telling the truth after he tells the story. It almost seems that such a reconciliation was a more difficult matter than reconciliation after a death, perhaps because by being injured in this way, a fighting man might feel himself to be less of a man. In other words, it is not only a question of honor but also a more fundamental one of masculinity and social function. A person so injured might have to pass on his responsibilities or titles to others.

---

36 *Vita Norberti*, 676.

37 William M. Reddy, *The Navigation of Feeling: A Framework for the History of Emotions* (Cambridge: Cambridge University Press, 2001).

38 Stephen D. White, "The Politics of Anger," in *Anger's Past: The Social Uses of an Emotion in the Middle Ages*, ed. Barbara H. Rosenwein (Ithaca, NY: Cornell University Press, 1998), 127–52.

Lambert of Ardres, in explaining how the castellany of Bourbourg passed down to a single heiress, tells how her father, the youngest of seven sons, became the heir. Older siblings failed to produce offspring or died young, and some entered the Church, but one was blinded in a tournament and so declined the title.[39] Although I won't pursue this avenue of inquiry further here, disability scholars like Irina Metzler and the contributors to the volume that Jonathan Eyler has edited have begun to explore the burden of disease and impairment that medieval people suffered under, a topic that frequently arises in **hagiographic** sources.[40]

Medieval ideas about property

Equally interesting are the two miracle stories in which direct attempts are made on Vitalis's own life. As I mentioned above, Moolenbroek thinks that these stories are improbable. They certainly aren't mentioned in any source from the saint's time, but that makes them particularly interesting to consider.[41] What are they doing in this narrative? In contrast to the stories I've discussed above, these cases seem less about honor than about property. In the story that begins this chapter, when the monastery was founded, some local men lost access to the wood at Savigny. Angry about this situation, they ambushed the saint, but all their arrows missed. They realized their error and confessed, and the saint forgave them (II: 2). The men in question were probably peasants, who were not thought to have honors (in either sense). Aristocrats did have honors, but they wouldn't have had to do their own dirty work. They would also have had woods of their own, while the loss of access to local woodland would have hit peasants hard. Forest was an important resource in the Middle Ages; I mentioned above that when Stephen in his capacity as bishop of Rennes restored land to the peasants who had been ejected by the Cistercians, he gave them the right to use the woods. It was the only source of fuel and building supplies available to many people. But Ralph of Fougères clearly owned the land he gave away, so this situation requires some further context.

---

39 Lambert of Ardres, *History of the Counts of Guines*, 154.

40 Joshua R. Eyler, ed., *Disability in the Middle Ages: Reconsiderations and Reverberations* (Abingdon: Routledge, 2010); Irina Metzler, *Disability in Medieval Europe: Thinking about Physical Impairment in the High Middle Ages, c.1100–c.1400* (Abingdon: Routledge, 2006) and *A Social History of Disability in the Middle Ages: Cultural Considerations of Physical Impairment* (Abingdon: Routledge, 2013).

41 The life of St. Norbert also mentions an attempt on the life of the saint, but under much different circumstances. Norbert may have founded the **Premonstratensian** order, but he became the archbishop of Magdeburg, and the context was a confrontation with the citizens upon his return from a church council. *Vita Norberti*, 698–9.

We could say that Ralph "owned" the land he gave. However, ownership was often complicated by layers of claims; it makes more sense to think of ownership as comprising sets of rights. In our experience, most of those rights belong to the same individual (although things like mineral rights are sometimes not owned by people who own land). But in the twelfth century, these rights might belong to different people. Someone might hold the land as a fief or be the lord who granted the fief and have the right to the **demesne** land (the land a lord held directly that was worked to his or her profit). Someone might own the right to collect **tithes** or other sorts of taxes. Someone else might have claims on acts of labor, such as building roads or labor on one's land. Someone else might have the right to work the land or reside on it. This is what produced the many **charters** around Savigny's foundation, the original grant, and then all the confirmations by overlords: everyone had to agree to move rights over which they had some sort of claim to a new holder (or perhaps to give them up entirely).

To this we need to add the concept of an **easement** (the right to use someone else's property for a specific purpose). Modern easements may consist of a right to cross someone else's property, for instance, provided one do no harm to it. But easements are also found in medieval law. This might be the right to gather brush or to take fish. From the eleventh century on, customary rights of this kind were under threat from lords who were rationalizing their management of land and charging for things that had been free or demanding payments that they had never enjoyed before, practices that were often referred to in medieval accounts as "bad customs."[42] So it may be that these men had been used to gathering wood and feared to lose that right or worried that they would have to pay for the wood.

However, there are other aspects of ownership that come into play in Stephen's narrative, even if we just think about Ralph of Fougères's right to give the land. Although we think of ownership as meaning that an individual could do with a piece of property as he or she wished, the situation in the Middle Ages was more complicated, an issue Stephen White has explored. Although in theory such a right might exist, in practice there were often individuals who made claims on donated property. There were various ways to address the concern that relatives would find a way to take back a donation, thus endangering the soul of the donor, so relatives might be listed in the donation charter as being co-donors or as giving their consent.[43] When relatives refused their consent, this might cause future problems

---

42 See Bisson, *Crisis of the Twelfth Century*, 50, 55, and passim.

43 Stephen D. White, *Custom, Kinship, and Gifts to Saints: The laudatio parentum in Western France, 1050–1150* (Chapel Hill: University of North Carolina Press, 1988). White argues that there was a notion of individual ownership and the right to dispose of one's property, but that there was also a recognition of a claim by kin, particularly children, who would otherwise inherit, so this was a mechanism of adjudicating between competing norms.

for the **monastery** receiving the gift. Indeed, Stephen writes about how Henry of Fougères initially refused to consent to his father's gift of the land upon which Savigny was built and had to be chastised by God through illness (I: 8). Henry became a monk at Savigny when he was dying, so although the story of his initial resistance might be factual, it is also possible that his resistance was *pro forma* and that he received some acknowledgement from Savigny (a promise to celebrate his anniversary, the right to visit the monastery and enjoy its hospitality at will or to be buried there, or the promise that he would be taken in at the end of his life) in exchange for that consent.

Conflicts over property

The second story of attempted murder also seems to be about property. A knight orders Vitalis killed because he is receiving donations from the local faithful (II: 3). Stephen offers no specifics here about what the knight's claim on the offerings is, but my guess is that this is a story about tithes. Although in theory tithes belonged to churches, in practice, in the twelfth century many lay lords collected and kept tithes. Clerics thundered from their pulpits about how **lay people** possessing tithes was wrong and in many cases the message got heard. Lay people either gave or sold their tithes to monasteries, killing two birds with one stone; they cleared themselves of sin and they usually got the prayers of the monks in return.[44] William of Andres has many stories about tithes given, taken back, and unjustly held. My favorite of these involves a tithe sold by a father (Gerald of le Pire), taken back by the son (Hugh Stinkebake), and surrendered only when Hugh's wife died and was refused burial in consecrated ground, as a result of which her troubled spirit haunted people and animals.[45]

Stephen doesn't call the offerings mentioned in the texts "tithes" in the Latin, so I wouldn't necessarily have drawn this conclusion, except that at the beginning of the life (the part I quoted in the first chapter) he specifically mentions that Vitalis's parents cheerfully paid their tithes to the Church.[46] Tithes were clearly on his mind, hence my surmise. This is also a reminder not only that we can't consider a text by itself without reference to its context but also that any analysis has to draw on the whole of a given text and to recognize that people in the past may have used various terms to talk about the same thing (as do we).

---

44 John van Engen, "The 'Crisis of Cenobitism' Reconsidered: Benedictine Monasticism in the Years 1050–1150," *Speculum* 61, no. 2 (1986): 279.

45 William of Andres, *Chronicle*, 117, 251.

46 See above, p. 7, and below, p. 120.

While it may seem extreme to a modern reader to kill a cleric over property, there are enough other cases of it that there is verisimilitude in this story (even if it didn't happen). William of Andres, writing in the first third of the thirteenth century, tells a story from sometime around Stephen's day about an attempt on the life of his own abbot arising from a property dispute. The abbot had been enlarging the monastic precinct (the part within the wall) and angered a neighboring lord, whose son attempted to kill the abbot. Another monk stepped in between the abbot and the blow, receiving a mortal wound in the process. The abbot prudently left for a while.[47] So while this story may or may not have happened (again, we have no way to know), it was the kind of thing that contemporaries would know *could* have happened.

Finally, there is again an echo of the Becket affair in Stephen's telling of this incident, because he notes that the affronted knight does not try to kill Vitalis himself but sends his henchmen to do it (although they are miraculously prevented). And Stephen ends his story with a reference to martyrdom:

> By these words he showed that he would willingly undergo martyrdom for the love of God, if it happened that someone dared to inflict it, and he was prepared to die for Christ, so that he might be crowned with the palm of martyrdom. We can therefore gather that although he did not suffer a bodily passion, he kept his mind ready to undergo it. (II: 3)

Finding the context

What I have been doing in the preceding pages is twofold. First, I've been looking for the glimpses of how Stephen and his contemporaries thought about violence. A husband beats his wife. Men brawl and feud with each other, get mad, and make up. People fear losing property and take action accordingly. But these stories just tell us what they tell us until we start asking questions about them to uncover the context in which the stories are being told. The context places Stephen in the heart of changing ideas about marriage and violence within it; royal power and its attempt to contain private warfare; and changing religious ideas. Once again, we see Stephen's positionality shaping his material, directing it toward his concerns as a bishop and as the king's loyal servant, and not so much addressing the life of the cloister or the monks within it. This is the work of a man interested in moral

---

47 William of Andres, *Chronicle*, 100.

reform, but more influenced by legal ideas than the austerities of reformers like Bernard of Clairvaux.

But it was not Stephen's *purpose* to tell us all these things. Rather, in telling stories about St. Vitalis he simply brought his world into the telling for us to consider, if we choose to do so.

AFTERWORD

✠

"So that my words may not bore the reader"

However, so that my words may not bore the reader by their prolixity, let this first book end, so that the reader may grow strong and hasten the more devoutly to reading other things. (I: 15)

Stephen ends the first book of his life of Vitalis (which he suggests he initially hoped would be the only book) by saying that he will end the book there, so that the length of the work will not bore the reader. Even with the second book, however, the biography is not excessively long by medieval standards. It is much shorter than the book I have written about it. Such comments about tedium were often a commonplace, repeated by medieval authors. His readers would have understood the commonplace and the claims of busyness. They might have believed (or doubted or not believed) what Stephen said, but they would not have been surprised by what they found in this thoroughly conventional saint's life.

Stephen's audience was familiar with the conventions of writing about the saints and the historical context I have spent so much space reconstructing. They did not need a way to make sense of the narrative, but modern readers do. Our approach to the text and the uses we unintended readers put it to are very different from those of the original audience. Moreover, the ways that historians have learned to analyze primary sources are not intuitive or straightforward. They are, as Sam Wineburg has said, unnatural acts.[1] While this book cannot, without

---

1 See the title article in Wineburg, *Historical Thinking*. His point is that historical thinking is something one has to learn to do (it is different from simply thinking about the past).

boring the reader, present all the ways in which this biography can be explored or understood, or all the questions that might be asked of this kind of source, it has, I hope, presented a few. The ways I have chosen to do so are not the only ones, but they are useful ways, conditioned by my own experience as a scholar of the Middle Ages and also as someone interested in theory of history and in teaching and learning in history.

I hope it has become evident through this process that hagiographies, although they purport to present eternal verities, are as positioned as every other medieval document. They were written for particular audiences to use in particular ways by individuals with particular concerns and particular literary backgrounds. In the case of someone like Stephen of Fougères, one of the most educated men of his day with significant political connections and major religious responsibilities, these factors had a powerful effect on what was produced. As I've mentioned in the above chapters, these meant that he all but ignored the period when Vitalis was a hermit (nearly two decades of the saint's life, according to other sources) to focus on his role as a preacher, something near and dear to Stephen's heart but also something that was a concern in Vitalis's time. Stephen was reaching out to Vitalis across time just as we reach out to Stephen. Stephen updated Vitalis's story for his audience, and I've done some of that as well, translating medieval approaches to modern takes.

The purpose was also to walk you, the reader, through an analytic approach to working with these sources, utilizing a set of questions, highlighting the way in which I draw on the work of other historians, and also taking a particular theoretical stance. (As Diana Jeater has pointed out, the theories that historians apply to their material are defined largely by the questions they ask and the suppositions they make.)[2] The theoretical stance is this: that medieval people were neither stupid nor more credulous than we are, even if they sometimes believed things that seem odd to us (just as what we believe would have seemed odd to them); that the literature they created and consumed can be used by us for purposes other than the original ones, if we interrogate that literature systematically and set it in its context; that to do so well, we need to be aware of how we ourselves are positioned and how the sources we draw on are positioned; that in doing so we enter into a dialogue with the work of other scholars; and that all these things are part and

---

2 Diana Jeater, "'Theory' as the Practice of Asking Questions: Moving Second Year History Undergraduates from Knowledge Acquisition to Knowledge Construction in a UK University," in *Teaching History, Learning History, Promoting History: Papers from the Bielefeld Conference on Teaching History in Higher Education*, ed. Friedrike Neumann and Leah Shopkow (Frankfurt: Wochenschau, 2018), 77–93.

parcel of the disciplinary thought of history. Producing history is, in other words, a highly intellectual activity.

Not all of the questions I've asked of Vitalis's biography can be answered about other hagiographic writings, although it is certainly worth asking the questions, if only to see what we can find. We may not know the author or a precise date or much about the cult of the saint. Knowing an approximate date of Stephen's work has allowed me to put that information to work in my interpretation. But parts of the intellectual moves I have made can be applied even when all you have in front of you is the life of a saint.

Equally important, though, is that many of these moves can be applied to primary sources of almost any kind. The same questions would generate different answers, but all of these questions would open up avenues for historical exploration. Just as I asked why the biography of Vitalis was written, for instance, I might focus on the mortuary roll of the saint. My discussion might then be about the ways in which rolls of this time created networks of communication between monasteries and communities of prayers. Or I might ask about the purpose of Marbode of Rennes's letter to Vitalis, in which case I might explore instead the culture of letter writing and also the question of why some letters survive, while the vast majority of medieval letters, documents written for instrumental purposes like getting a poor girl a position in a monastery, did not.

In the first appendix to this book, I have provided you with a complete translation of the text I have been writing about, while in the second I have included a translation of the other biography attributed to Stephen. In the case of the first, you can check on my interpretations of the passages I have discussed and perhaps arrive at your own. You should be aware as you do so, however, that any translation involves choices made by the translator which affect the meaning. Words in one language can seldom be translated with a word that exactly mirrors the original meaning, so translators choose words based on their perception of the context (I hope you are convinced at this point that context is inescapable in history!). However, despite these warnings, I would urge you to use the translation to ask questions about the twelfth-century world and the nature of sanctity that I have not discussed in this book. Here are some questions, which certainly do not exhaust the possibilities.

In what context can we put what Stephen says about Vitalis's education? What does this text tell us about the relative place of Latin and the vernacular in the twelfth century? This narrative was used for liturgical purposes. It would be read on Vitalis's saint's day and might be read at other times, when the monks were at table, for instance. What does it tell us about religious literature of this kind, perhaps even about sermons? Some of the miracles concern legal matters. How can we understand the legal regimes of the late twelfth century? How does this text fit in with literary and theological trends of the twelfth century and ideas about sanctity? What role did preaching play in Stephen's day or in Vitalis's? Now that I've asked some questions, ask your own! My questions arise from my positionality. What can you ask from yours?

APPENDIX I

✠

The Life of St. Vitalis

About the translation

As I discussed above, in chapter 2, Stephen was a highly educated man who spent at least a decade in one of the most literary courts of his day, one to which he contributed himself, even though none of those works have survived. It should hardly be surprising, then, that his Latin is often flowery and rhetorical, although because he intended this work to be read by those who were not as educated as he was, his style is not nearly as difficult as that of some contemporaries, such as Walter Map. In this translation I've tried to capture some of his rhetorical flights without making the text too oblique for modern readers. I've often inserted a proper noun where the Latin has only a pronoun or an implied pronoun, to clarify the meaning. I've often broken up long sentences into shorter ones. I've sometimes added ideas that are implied by the Latin but not explicitly stated [in square brackets]. I've translated passive sentences into active ones. To clarify the reading, I have followed the old convention of capitalizing references to God, avoiding too many undifferentiated "hims" in the text (and I have also followed the convention of using the masculine to refer to God). Where the meaning is ambiguous, I have chosen a single clear reading, but there is as much interpretation in translating as there is in any other historical activity, so readers should know that another translator might make different choices. In fact, this text has been translated elsewhere, as part of a collection of lives of the saints of Savigny. Both my translation and theirs use the same printed Latin text, the one provided by E.P. Sauvage.[1] This different purpose (and different translator) has produced a somewhat different text.

---

1 Sauvage; *The Lives of the Monastic Reformers*, 2.

A special note is necessary about the translation of biblical references. The Bible is itself a translated document. Jewish scripture was originally written in Hebrew and Aramaic, Christian scripture in Greek. Western Christians encountered the text in various Latin translations, some based on the Septuagint translation of Jewish scripture (a Greek translation), although St. Jerome in his great translation that formed the heart of the Vulgate consulted the Hebrew as well. But his translation did not entirely replace earlier translations into Latin. Furthermore, every copy of the Bible had to be copied by hand and was thus subject to some variation, while medieval writers were often quoting the Bible from memory and were not always quoting word for word as we would understand it. Modern biblical translations have mostly gone back to the original language versions. The result is that what the Latin says is not always quite the same as what a modern Bible would have (and not all modern Bibles would have the same thing either; Biblegate, a website many people use to look up biblical references as well as to study the Bible, has sixty-odd different translations of the Bible into English). I have therefore translated the words as they appear in the biography, without reference to modern translations. However, I have given the modern numbering (and it is modern: the division of the Bible into chapter and verse came after Stephen's day). "Cf." where it appears means that Stephen is alluding to a passage without really quoting it.

The paragraphs appear in the printed version, but they are not original, so I have felt free to change them. The divisions of the text into chapters (*capitula*) is original, however. I've kept notes to a minimum; most refer to translation issues. Topics and individuals addressed in the text above may be looked up in the index. And if something cannot be found in the index, you could look it up! In these days of miracles and wonder and the internet, information is *not* scarce! (Of course, information has to be processed to turn it into knowledge.)

The text

Here begins the prologue to the Life of St. Vitalis

Since, as the authority of the angel testifies, *it is good to keep the king's secret, but honorable to reveal and confess the works of God* (Tob. 12:7), we have decided to convey to your ears in a more open manner those things we discovered written in the vernacular or that we know from the narratives of faithful men about that venerable man and first abbot of Savigny. Since we can read the lives and deeds of many men who built the Holy Church by their words and works and examples, it is highly unworthy that the life of such a great man should be passed over in fruitless silence and that it should not be transmitted in writing for the knowledge of those who come afterward.

Therefore, we who want to write his biography implore God's mercy unceasingly. And we beg *the one who made the tongues of babes learned and loosened the tongues of mutes into speech* (Wisd. 10:21) and gave the power of human speech to the humble ass of the foolish prophet so as to overcome his folly (cf. Num. 22:21–33) to grant us an abundance of words, so that what the mind has conceived, the tongue will be able to bring forth, once it has been set in order by my truthful pen. For God, whose nature cannot be swayed from its goodness and who always seeks opportunities through which He may confer a benefit, never ceases to devote the free-flowing abundance of His goodness to men. Let those who are invited to enjoy His benefits be ashamed to be subject to the tyranny of the devil and ashamed to fail to give thanks to such a giver!

And so it is that He conferred the gift of His grace upon this man of whom we have decided to speak. Through Vitalis's life-giving teaching, he gave healthful medicine to the souls of those poisoned by the corrosive venom of the ancient serpent, and when he had healed their wounds, he showed them the path to salvation. So it was that he spent the talent entrusted to him by the Father (cf. Matt. 25:14ff.), for the benefit of many people through his life and words. And he did not hide his burning lamp under the bushel of fear (cf. Matt. 5:15), but disdained men's threats.

But let us put these things aside and persist in carrying out the proposed work. Let us offer this notice for the glory of God and the use of the reader, seeking to please that One alone and asking the reward for works from Him from whom the secrets of hearts are not hidden, for Whom the mute speak, and to Whom all silent things answer.[2]

Here ends the Prologue.

Here begins the life of St. Vitalis, the first abbot of Savigny [Book 1][3]

1. In the province of Bayeux, one may find a certain village that the inhabitants call Tierceville. A man named Renfred lived in this town; he was married to a woman named Rohaid.[4] They strove hard and diligently to serve God; they did

---

2 Sauvage, 358n1, suggests that this is a reference to 2 Pet. 2:16, which discusses Balaam and his ass.
3 This is the beginning of Book 1, although the text does not say so.
4 Reigfredus and Rohardem (Rohardis in the subject case). The mortuary roll entries give different forms for the names.

not turn a deaf ear to his commands, but devoutly carried them out (cf. Mic. 7:16; Ps. 37:14). Indeed, they were vigilant in supporting the poor and needy and they gave them alms, for as it is written, *Give alms and lo all things will be clean for you* (Luke 11:41). They also sheltered them at night, which is not the least of the works of mercy. The apostle [St. Paul] says about this action that *they have pleased God through this, for they have taken angels into their dwelling* (cf. Heb. 13:2). They worshipped God very eagerly, making the payments sanctioned by canon law [that is, tithes] without any pretext or delay, and they carried on living through their righteous labors. While they were persisting in these things and in these sorts of holy works, they had a son, at whose birth they had much reason for joy, and they quite properly took the most attentive care in raising him. When he was washed in the holy font of baptism this baby was named Vitalis.

Oh, a name notable for great grace! Oh, the inexpressible clemency of God! Oh, the inexplicable providence of the Creator! Oh, who would be sufficiently able to properly marvel at the heights of divine counsel?! Oh, who could penetrate its depths?! For divine power does through people what seems good to it – very often those things that are proper for salvation – even though they do not know. I believe indeed that divine counsel in its inscrutability did not want this child to be called by this kind of name without purpose. I think by this name it was already foretold that he would become a participant in heavenly life.[5]

I say that this man was rightly worthy to be called by such a name, this man who put perishable life behind him and panted after heavenly life with the pious covetousness of his soul and also was able to inspire many people by his words and example

Thus he rightly shone forth with such a name, this man who revealed the wiles of the devil through prudent explanation, who drew many people from the devil's corrupting mouth with salubrious advice, and who, once they returned to their earlier health, showed them the path of salvation. Rejoice, church of Savigny, and make merry that you have deserved to have such a great and so wise a founder! Rejoice, I say, all you who dwell at Savigny and exult, and know that what is said through the prophet Isaiah is fulfilled in you: *Strangers shall consume the deserts now turned into plenty* (Isa. 5:17). Where the resting places of the wild beast used to be located and the birds of heaven were accustomed to build their nests, praises to God now ring out in many people's voices, and where perhaps thieves lay in wait for the blood of the innocent, now the place is devoted to divine contemplation;

---

5 In Latin, the word for life is *vita*. So every time the text uses the word "life," the reader should be aware that a medieval reader encountering the text in Latin would hear an echo of Vitalis's name. There were many saints of that name after whom he might have been named.

FIGURE 4: *Hellmouth, carving detail. (Conques/Wikipedia/Peter Campbell.)*

"Thus he rightly shone forth with such a name, this man who revealed the wiles of the devil through prudent explanation, who drew many people from the devil's corrupting mouth with salubrious advice" (I: 1). While this phrasing may strike modern readers as a metaphor, medieval hearers would perhaps take this more literally. Many churches that featured sculpture had an image of souls being cast into the mouth of hell, often depicted as the maw of a monster. This sculpture from the early twelfth century is part of a depiction of the Last Judgment, when people were condemned to hell or accepted into Paradise for eternity. It is placed over the entry of the church of St. Foy at Conques, which was a major pilgrimage site. Traces of paint can still be seen; when the paint was fresh, pilgrims would be able to see the various figures very clearly, so they might contemplate which way they hoped to go and amend their evil ways. The knight being cast down into hell in the far right of the image is a reminder that many people were concerned about the problem of knightly violence in this period. Scholars think that this image drew on a well-known local miracle.

and the land which vipers and thorns and fruitless trees occupied is now watered with the tears and weeping of holy men.[6]

What more shall we add? The land that once lay uncultivated and uninhabitable responds to the hands of the cultivator and now provides food for the nurslings of Christ. The power of God is magnified, for He produced water from a stone in the desert for the children of Israel (Num. 20:8–11). His omnipotent mercy is glorified, for He turned a vast solitude into a support for His servants. But as I say this, I feel fire in the deepest depths of my heart. To confess the truth, I am filled with the most lofty joy. Who indeed, except a mentally deficient person, would not rejoice when he sees such a congregation of the servants of God devoutly giving praise to God and assiduously assisting in divine work? Oh, venerable man Vitalis, you were the beginning of all these things with the help of God, and you prepared this place for all these people through the wisdom given to you by God, as God wished, and you transmitted the example of your good memory to those who came after. Your memory is quite properly made manifest in people's mouths, you through whom God is known to have built a house of great religion for the praise of His name.

But now let this digression suffice; let the pen return to the project.

That when he had been set to learning his letters, he had grace in learning them

2. So when the child I mentioned above was old enough to be properly taught his letters, his parents set him to studying letters. Divine goodness endowed him with intelligence and sharpness of wit. By a sort of childish omen, those with whom he went to school already called him "the little abbot" at that time, and showed him as proper reverence as their ages would permit. Indeed, he was loved by everyone and he was dear to all.

But, Christ, I recognize Your works in all these things, You who magnify your saints, so that You even infuse some of them with the free-flowing dew of Your spirit from their cradles. And I know it is within Your authority to raise up whomever You wish. With reference to this man, however, divine clemency is said to

---

6 This is an entirely conventional version of the "foundation myth," the notion that a given landscape was entirely barren (except for the thieves) before the monks got there. On this point, see Noël James Menuge, "The Foundation Myth: Some Yorkshire Monasteries and the Landscape Agenda," *Landscapes* 1 (2000): 22–37. Menuge argues that these depictions of wilderness were not intended to be literal but rather to express the moral transformation that establishing a monastery caused in a particular place.

have performed a certain miracle when he was still a little boy that it would be most indecent to pass over in silence.

That when he was going swimming, a fish wished to drown him

3. It happened one day in summertime, that the students, his companions, went to the water to swim, and took the little boy with them for that purpose. When they had gone into the water and had begun to bathe themselves, look!, a fish clung to his back and wrapping itself around him, wanted to dive. When his companions saw this, they were seized by fear and leapt out as quickly as they could and left him alone wrestling with the fish in the water. But although they had left the water, lamenting and aghast, they filled the air with clamoring and great ululations, and called upon God and St. Mary with repeated cries. When they saw the boy in the water with the fish but by no means dared go to him, they mourned greatly, and they were rendered dumbfounded by the mischance of this event. Suddenly, they saw the boy leave the water, and the fish, which to that point had clung to his back, wished in no way to leave him.[7] When they see this, suddenly their great sorrow is turned to joy, and those who were compelled by grief to weep, rejoice wholeheartedly because they see the one they feared to lose rescued from danger.

Oh, how great is the malice of the ancient enemy! Oh, how his villainy is always eager to cause harm! For I believe the devil now also had a premonition that at some time in the future he should suffer the loss of many of those following him through Vitalis's teaching. For that reason, he strove to kill Vitalis if he could and take his life from their midst. But because it is written, *there is no wisdom, there is no learning, there is no counsel against the Lord* (Prov. 21:30) and because *the Lord guards all those who love him* (Ps. 144:20), the demon could not finish what he had begun, because the Lord powerfully rescued his servant from the devil's plots. Indeed, I conclude from this event that just as fishermen draw fish from the river, thus Vitalis would draw men from the world.[8]

Pay attention, reader, and diligently ponder and then let the words of the Truth be fulfilled: *The servant is not greater than his Lord* (John 13:16, 15:20)! For just as the devil wished to destroy the new-born Christ through his agents (John

---

7 As Sauvage suggests (361n1), this is probably an octopus. See above, p. 83, for a discussion of this passage.
8 There is probably an allusion here to the passages in the Gospels where Jesus tells his apostles they will become fishers of men (Matt. 4:19; Mark 1:17).

13:16) and he wanted to drown the Hebrew children in the water through Pharaoh (Exod. 1:22), in the same way, as I believe, he wanted to pull this boy under, lest he might profit anyone through his teaching.

That he left his country out of the love of wisdom

4. So that he could more freely devote himself to acquiring wisdom, he decided to leave his native soil out of love for it, and, now that he was a little more grown up, to go to the soil of other regions. He did not waste his time there but devoted himself with all his powers to studying wisdom. And as he did not receive it lazily nor listen with a deaf ear, he stowed it with his tenacious memory in the depths of his heart. And thus infused with no small learning, he set out for home, and his return gave no small joy to his parents and friends.

As he frequently devoted himself to meditating on divine law, he diligently gave his wealth to those having nothing. He was not unfamiliar with human law either. He was not ignorant of rhetorical color nor the elegance of Ciceronian eloquence. Because it is truly written, *hidden wisdom and an unseen treasure: what is the use of either?* (Sir. 41:17), he did not want to hide what goods he had, but he brought them forth in public for the utility of the many. And he did not wish to silence the truth, either because of fear or threats, but he denounced the evil deeds of the wicked in a loud voice. He took care always to keep to the company of good people; from a tender age he loved the holy life.

That the count made him his chaplain

5. Since Vitalis was endowed with such great wisdom and eloquent charm and since he was enriched with the best character, the count of Mortain, who truly knew these things about him, wanted to have this man with him and made him his chaplain. His wisdom reached the Normans and Bretons and came to the Gauls and Angevins and also crossed over to the English who dwell in places across the sea. And since he lived for a long time at that man's court, he strove to please him so that he should not displease God. For indeed he had read what had been written, *Return to Caesar those things belonging to Caesar, and those things that are God's, to God* (Matt. 22:21; Mark 12:17; Luke 20:25), and he rendered to the count the obedience he owed and he performed the worship he owed to God. Indeed, God granted him such grace that the count and countess showed him every honor and the whole household held his words in veneration and none presumed to contradict what he said, and all, hanging upon his mouth, reverently obeyed his words as a disciple obeys a master.

How he consoled the weeping countess

6. But we should not pass a matter over in silence that he told one of his disciples, because of that man's authority. One time, he found the countess weeping and troubled by great sobbing and sorrow. He quickly asked the reason for her sorrow and learned from her own mouth that the count did not respect her and had presumed to beat her. The venerable man was moved by her pain and said that he was angry that the count had presumed to do such things to her and that the bond between himself and the count would have to be broken, unless the count agreed to refrain from visiting such injuries upon the lady.

Of the count who submitted to a beating at his hands

7. So then it happened that Vitalis left Mortain and did not let the count know about his departure. But when it was announced to the count, the count followed him without delay and once the count had given him a pledge that he would make satisfaction [for his misdeed], the count got him to return. But the reason he left remained hidden and only those two knew it. When they returned and secretly entered the chapel, the count, who begged for compassion, began to implore the venerable man not to hesitate to whip him as much as he wished. The prince took off his clothes and stood nude before the reverend man who stood over him and struck him with bitter blows. But as the prince humbly begged Vitalis to have mercy on him, the venerable man chastised him as much as he wanted to with the descending switches.

Oh, he was a man endowed with the greatest liberty! Oh, he was a man outstanding for his great authority! The apostolic statement which says, *where the spirit of God is, there is liberty* (2 Cor. 3:17) is really true. He was truly free, this man to whom the countess did not fear to disclose her pain and at whose hands the count himself did not blush to humbly submit himself to be beaten!

We have recorded these things, which were written in French, in more publicly accessible writing, faithfully translating them into Latin speech. But we know about what we have written below from the narratives of faithful men. Still you ought to know that we have only described the man walking upon the earth to this point; now we undertake to describe him as if he were an eagle, hanging above the earth and intent upon the heights.

Concerning the petition made to build Savigny

8. Then when he decided to build the monastery of Savigny in the region of Normandy and Brittany, and he found a place appropriate for winning souls, he went

to ask Lord Ralph of Fougères, who possessed the place, so that he could build it. And with the help of Ralph's wife, he got the place and the wood lying next to it as Ralph's donation and as the donations of his two elder sons. But the younger one, named Henry, did not wish to grant what the others had granted Vitalis for either a prayer or a price.[9]

But all things [may be accomplished] by the power of God.[10] For truly it is written, *the Lord will fight for you and you will be silent*[11] (Exod. 14:14). What the man did not wish to do, God in his mercy carried out. For the holy man looked at him, indignant with spiritual zeal, and announced that this boy who did not want to consent to his request was not full of the good spirit. And then, when Vitalis was going home, the boy was seized by illness, and he was tormented with great pains as the illness grew worse. For this reason, he sent after the man of God, and at the urging of this great necessity, Vitalis was led back to him in haste. So now that he was afflicted with illness, the boy did not put off doing what he had earlier not wished to do when he was well. And so his pains subsided and he was returned to health. Afterward he left the world and took up the monastic life in this same house, and he died there on his last day in holy religion.

That he converted whores from their notorious business

9. Divine generosity gave him a great gift of grace in converting women dishonored by abominably filthy lust. For when he discovered women who were engaged in this ignominious work, he converted them from this shameful disgrace, drawing them to him with the sweet name of daughters and with gentle blandishments. And furthermore, when they converted, he married off those who promised marital continence. And he left these women legitimately married, whom he had found hunting the souls of men in this foul business and whom he had rescued from shameful depravity, and he left them rich by taking up a collection from people of faith, who helped these women because of his preaching.

Truly, we recognize the witness of the Gospel that *publicans and sinners were received by the Lord* (Luke 15:2), demoniacs were cured, those who were ill were freed from their misfortunes. And now we see that sinful women were plucked

---

9 The historical record shows that Ralph had five, not three, sons, but one died before Savigny was founded (Sauvage, 364n4).

10 The manuscript is defective here.

11 The manuscript reads *regnabit* (rule), the Latin of the Vulgate *pugnabit* (fight). It is not clear whether Stephen has altered the words here or the copyist has done so. However, the sense of what follows suggests that Stephen intended to follow the Vulgate wording.

out of the horrid whirlwind of evil deeds by the care of the servant of Christ and were returned by his warning and advice to conjugal modesty. But the One who once took care of these people in His own person now did these things through His servant. But just as scribes and Pharisees were scandalized when sinners were received, perhaps there will be someone who, when he hears these things, may condemn them with an ill-intentioned heart or will judge that Vitalis could not have done such things. But whoever this person may be, someone who is not afraid to gnaw upon Vitalis's deeds with a venomous tooth, let that person know that a poisoned tongue will not harm Vitalis. However, by saying such things, this person will only increase his burden of sin with an additional one.

But anyone can easily learn from the things written below how abundant a grace he had in restoring and re-establishing peace among the discordant.

Of the knights who did not wish to pardon their enemy

10. One day when he was preaching in public, a knight was present who had turned another man over for execution.[12] For this reason, the brothers of the dead man were trying to kill him, so that they might avenge their brother's blood. When the man of God had preached his sermon, the knight flung himself at Vitalis's feet. When the saint asked what was wrong, the man told him and so the situation was known. These other men were summoned right away. Vitalis, when he was approaching to make peace, addressed one of them and asked if he really hated that man so much. This man, however, replied that he felt such hatred toward that man that the magnitude of his hatred could not easily be expressed in words and that it was painful for him to see that man still alive. When the holy man responded to this and asked if it were possible for him to uproot the flame of hatred from his heart, the man is said to have answered in the following way:

"If I had one foot in paradise but the other in hell, I would gladly pull my foot back from paradise, if I could get the revenge I desire in hell!"

Oh, what a hard heart! Oh, a heart blinded by malice! Oh, diabolical anger! Oh, perverse anger! Oh, anger that cannot be satiated except by the death of another! It is written, *for the anger of man does not carry out God's justice* (James 1:20). How

---

12 This sentence is slightly ambiguous, but it is clear that the knight did not himself kill the man, and Stephen does not imply in any way that his actions were not legal. The logical assumption is that some sort of judicial process was involved. However, it is possible to read this to mean that the knight had passed the individual over to someone else, who killed him.

indeed could someone carry out God's justice, whose heart is infected with such evil that he rages after the death of another?

When the man of God heard this, he pronounced him to be full of an evil spirit, and at once ordered him to leave his sight. When the man had left but had not yet gone far, Vitalis ordered him to be called back again. When this had been done, Vitalis had the knight fall at the vengeful man's feet in the form of a cross and said, forcefully dropping the sword into the hands of the other man,

"Look you! Now avenge the blood of your brother, if you can! And do whatever you most desire, if God permits!"

What a marvelous thing [happened then]! When the man raised his sword hand to take vengeance, suddenly, the man's hand and whole body trembled. The sword sank down, and the now powerless man fell at Vitalis's feet. And the proud man, who earlier did not want to obey the words of the man of God, now lay before him with the neck of his pride broken. Now that God's power was known, he was stupefied by this event and carried out what he had previously disdained to do when admonished by prayer, freely sparing [the other man]. And so when peace was restored between these people whom he had found in discord, the man of God left them pacified by friendship's chain.

Of the man who did not wish to be reconciled with his adversary by Vitalis's warnings

11. At another time, discord broke out among men at London. Since a very rich man, who had been gravely wounded in that fight, had lost his hand, Vitalis went to him to make peace with his enemies. But that man disdained to lend his ear to Vitalis's words. Instead, when Vitalis entered his house, he tried to defend himself with weapons. The man of God, who was armed with spiritual weapons, urged him to make peace with the adversary who had harmed him. When he refused to do this, the man was seized with pain; he was horribly shaken, with spew boiling out of his mouth. And so through the mediation of the man of God, peace and concord were established between the man and his adversaries.

We describe true things, even if they are not things we have seen. We ask whether he would have been able to do these things, except through divine power. Why should the One who is known to have done much greater things, indeed all things, not be believed also to have done these things through His servant? In saying these things, let us protect ourselves with a battlement of caution, lest we stray from the truth. And let us commit the whole matter to God, to whom nothing is impossible. But instead, if we turn our attention in particular to what is most important, we know that because of his piety, he had power over unclean spirits. As indeed the sayings of the Fathers attest, when lust is cast out, when wrath is driven away and holy chastity is put on, and the spirit is adorned with the beauty of concord, the spirits of fornication are shut out. And assuredly this is much the greater miracle because the soul is more precious than the flesh.

That he predicted a most monstrous death for a man not wishing to listen to him

12. A certain armed man arrived; when another man who was present at the preaching saw him – indeed the man who had come was his enemy and unceasingly sought his death – he ran gripped by fear to the feet of the holy man. The holy man, recognizing the reason for this fear, ordered the man who had arrived to leave [his sword] outside of the church and thus he might be present with the others for the word of God, if he wished. Since the man frequently interrupted him and disdained to listen to him, Vitalis, this best sower of the Word, alight with the fire of zeal, stretched his hand toward the altar, and with the witness of the glorious Virgin Mary, announced that this man would not by any means die a good death.

The conclusion to the matter showed what he had said was true, *nor did any of his words fall to the ground* (1 Sam. 3:19), as it is written. For not much after that, that man was caught in the act in the woods with another man's wife by her husband, and died a horrible death and his body was devoured by dogs and even lacked human burial (cf. 2 Kings 9:10). Be warned by this that the words of holy men should not be held in contempt, for when they are irked by awareness of evil men's arrogance, the Holy Spirit, which dwells in them, is saddened, and the insult is punished for Its sake; to go against It cannot come out well. Lo indeed the ill-fated man who spurned the words of the holy man perished the worst of deaths. If he had wished to listen to his words piously and humbly, he would have lived so as to be saved, and by avoiding this shameful act, would not have incurred a terrible death.

That he detected the machinations of the devil

13. Then another time, when he was similarly occupied in preaching and the people were listening to his words very intently, he said these things while he was speaking:

"Beware and listen diligently and do not stop doing what you have begun, whatever you may hear. For the enemy of all good things is greatly enraged, because you so devoutly receive the word of God. For that reason, he does not cease to plot maliciously to distract you from what you are listening to."

After his warning, a great and noisy clamor was heard outside, and there was an outcry that fire was burning the town down. The people, however, because they were terrified by this noise, did not remember the words of the man of God well, and they at once went outside, but they saw none of the things they had heard about. And when they returned, confused, the servant of God spoke to them thus:

"Didn't I say to you that you shouldn't leave because of things you would hear? Look, the devil would gladly have done more, if he could have done more, but he got no advantage from this, because he could not harm you."

Alas, how great is the fragility of humankind! Alas, how small or nonexistent its stability is! Alas, how quickly humanity falls apart; how quickly it is distracted! Alas, it can be diverted from what it proposes to do by a simple impulse, when any reason appears! O how great is the devil's evil! O how full of deception his malice is! O how presumptuous is his boldness in always doing harm! For truly he is tormented, enraged, and stirred by the goads of envy when he knows somebody has been taken from him and has submitted to the sweet yoke of Christ.[13] This can be seen in the words of evil spirits, when in the Gospel they say to the Lord, "What have you to do with us, Christ, son of the living God? You have come before your time to torment us" (Mt 8:29). But oh, what an industrious man! Oh, a man full of wisdom! I should say – I ought to say – what I feel. I do not think that he lacked the spirit of prophecy, this man who could both predict the horrible death of a man and also detect the machinations of the devil.

That he thought little about taking care of his body

14. But how much he despised caring for his body, and how much concern he had for spending the talent of God's word that was entrusted to him (cf. Matt. 25:14–30), is clear from one of his deeds, which I put down here. One time, it was necessary for him to move from the place he was staying at to another. When he had taken to the road, he entered the woods, but because he lost track of the correct route, he wandered around through its byways and endured a three-day fast with his companions. At length on the fourth day, he emerged [from the woods]

---

13 The manuscripts say "something" (*aliquod*), but the reading "somebody" seems to make more sense in the context.

and entered a certain village, and putting hunger out of his mind, he became engaged in preaching. He drew out his sermon until nearly midday, when, because the monk who was with him was murmuring under his breath, the people knew how long he had been fasting. For indeed it is written, "Lo the eyes of the Lord are on those who fear him and in those who hope concerning his mercy that he may feed them in hunger" (Ps. 32:18–19). I judge that he was nourished by his internal sweetness of spirit, and therefore that he was little (or not at all) troubled about feeding the body.

What now, what ought one to say about the laziness of negligent pastors? What ought ruinous slothfulness to reply? They are quick to stuff their bellies with exquisite foods, but are late and slothful, should I say not only to preach, but also to pray. To these people, what scripture says is apt: "Woe to those shepherds who feed themselves" (Ezek. 34:2) and "dumb dogs not able to bark" (Isa. 56:10). For they are puffed up with the honor of their position and rarely or never preach a word to win souls. For while they care for fleeting things alone, they think rarely or not at all about the reason for their office. But indeed this man who strove by vigilant effort to sow the seeds of the word of God showed that he smacked of something very different.

That having spurned men's advice, he committed his case to the will of God

15. The short notice set down below shows how forceful he was in asserting truth and how much he loved it. For a controversy arose between him and the abbot of Caen because of a part of the town of Mortain and the court date was set. (He had accepted the property as a gift from the count and then he gave it back to that convent.)[14] When the day comes, he goes to the place for the hearing, and when he has been summonsed by his adversaries' words, he enters the church alone and prays for as long as he is there. He came back when he was done. He testified to the truth and committed his case to the will of God. But the abbot of Caen, perhaps thinking that it was God's will that Vitalis should receive what he asked for, agreed to his request, and left after putting an end to the litigation. Yes, indeed, it is clear from this that God litigated His servant's case, who, having spurned a "reedy staff" (2 Kings 18:21), namely the help of men, did not wish to put his hope in a man, but fled to Him when need loomed.

---

14 This is one of the events that can be corroborated by an outside source. In this case, the charter survived, and Stephen must have seen it. It is printed in *Vital*, 266–7.

O how good You are, Lord, to those who have hope in You! For You have said, "whatever you ask for believing, believe that you will receive" (Matt. 21:22; Mark 11:24), and You fulfilled this for this servant. What will those people say who have been conquered by monstrous covetousness? Who are blown about by the winds of avarice and who invade other people's property with lawsuits and violence? Truly, if perhaps they were touched to the heart in these matters, they would uproot this terrible vice and strive to be rescued from its sway.

However, so that my words may not bore the reader by their prolixity, let this first book end, so that the reader may grow strong and hasten the more devoutly to reading other things.

1. I had decided to put an end to this work with a few other things, but, since you who have learned about his life from his followers who are still alive force me [to write more], now that I have put aside certain things by which I was busied, I will be sure to note down a few more other things which may be known through this telling.

So we have described some of his virtues above, but now it remains to us to show what great patience and love he had toward his enemies. For truly, because there's no mistake in scripture, which says, "All who wish to live piously suffer persecution" (2 Tim. 3:12), and because there cannot be an Abel whom Cain's malice does not harass (cf. Gen. 4), that man had many enemies. However, he overcame them with patience.

That those who envied him wanted to kill him, because they were embittered by his proximity

2. When that place [Savigny] was first cultivated, some men who had earlier used the wood lying near that place for their own purposes were set on fire by the torches of malice.[15] Angry that he was nearby and thinking that they would no longer have the wood, they tried to kill him. One day, when he took to the road, men in cahoots with them were lying in ambush and greeted him with arrows. But through God's virtue, he remained unharmed and whole among the many showers of them. So when the arrows had been launched in vain, those men, who were stupefied by this event, came out of their hiding places to him and confessed their guilt; they acquired swift forgiveness from him.

What ought to be said of our pride? What ought our insolence to say in response? Certainly when we are angered by a frivolous word or even a sign, if we

---

15 Cf. above, 1: 1.

are not able to do anything, we permit a detestable rancor to exist in our hearts, nor can we look at those envious of us with true perception. If, however, at some time we can find a place, let us vomit out the pestilent infection we have hidden when we desire to avenge ourselves, for the Lord says, "Love your enemies" (Matt. 5:44).

That some men, obeying the orders of a certain knight, wanted to kill him

3. A certain knight was sorry that because of Vitalis's admonitions the offerings of the faithful were carried to Savigny, something he did not wish, so he attempted to have him murdered. When he heard that Vitalis was passing by, he sent sons of pestilence after him, evil men who were to carry out his orders against Vitalis. But when they came to a waterway that the man of God had already crossed, they were not able to cross, and they remained there, frustrated in their every effort, held there by the power of God. But then a certain man who was more evil than the rest and was more ready to do harm arrived riding a spirited horse. He began to berate them as slackers, because they had not finished what they had begun. Thus blinded by malice, he mounted the bridge with his horse, but prevented [from crossing] by the just judgment of God, he fell into the water. Although by God's judgment he himself escaped the danger with difficulty, the horse perished in the water.[16]

Then one of the others, who was dumbstruck by this miracle and was feeling remorse in his heart, began to pray and begged humbly that the Lord and the man of God would permit him to cross over. When he had received permission, he came to Vitalis and confessed that he was guilty. He at once received forgiveness, and Vitalis led him back to the others, who remained unable to cross. He similarly forgave them easily, saying that he did not flee from death, but it was his desire that when death came he would be able to come to his Lord. By these words he showed that he would willingly undergo martyrdom for the love of God, if it happened that someone dared to inflict it, and he was prepared to die for Christ, so that he might be crowned with the palm of martyrdom. We can therefore gather that although he did not suffer a bodily passion, he kept his mind ready to undergo it. This is recognized to be a sort of martyrdom, if the devout mind is held always ready to undergo it and the true way of life is always kept unblemished.

---

16 Many modern readers, of course, will feel sorry for the poor horse. For a medieval reader, the death of the horse in lieu of the man was an act of God's mercy. Just a reminder of the ways in which medieval people will have read this story differently.

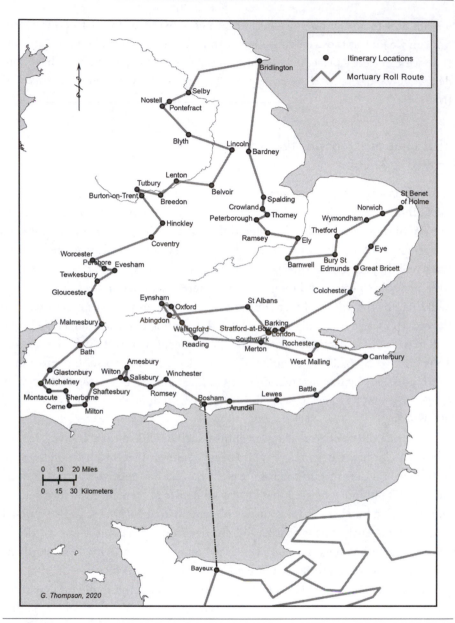

MAP 3: *The travels of St. Vitalis's Mortuary Roll in England. (Adapted from a map done by B.-M. Colland in Jean Dufour and Jean Favier,* Recueil des rouleaux des morts (VIIIe siècles–vers 1536), *vol. 1 (VIIIe siècle–1180) [Paris: Boccard, 2005]; map drawn by Gordie Thompson.)*

This map of the travels of Vitalis's mortuary roll in England is testimony to his connections in England (where in his lifetime one could travel easily in elite circles without speaking English) and to how widespread his reputation was there at the time of his death. Even though when Vitalis died, Savigny had no daughter-houses, a number of English daughter-houses were established in the decades after his death.

Of the plot against him by those who envied him

4. At some time a council where many churchmen came together was held in England.[17] Among them there were some who were said to have conspired in his death.
When this was announced to the man of God, he was not afraid to go there, because
he was prepared to die for the truth, and since he had confidence in the Lord, he
refused to avoid their malign machinations by hiding himself. So when he arrived
there, he climbed to one of the higher seats and began to sow the seed of God's
word. But he suffered a false accusation from one of this perverse party; when Vitalis
had uttered two pronouncements and each had been heard, this man rebuked his
words, disparaging him in the hearing of the whole council. But when the third one
was heard, that evil tongue restrained itself from reproof. And admiring the power
of Vitalis's word, he exalted with praises in everyone's hearing what he had earlier
condemned. He confessed himself to be guilty and asked for mercy, along with the
other conspirators, saying that Vitalis would not have been able to say such things,
were he not a dwelling of the Holy Spirit. And the Lord magnified His servant all
the more gloriously, in that He had him raised up by praises from people who had
impugned him. Indeed there is no more robust testimony than when that man who
had tried to incite a crime spoke praiseworthy things. Vitalis kindly forgave them;
his perfect victory over them was that God turned their perverse counsel to good
to the glory of His name. This indeed is the perfect victory of the saints over their
enemies, that is, when their enemies are converted to good, abandon their malice,
and become the proclaimers of the truth they had impugned. See here, we show the
power of his patience on one hand, but we are not silent on the loving heart directed
at his enemies. For it relates to patience that he bore persecution patiently, to love
that he most kindly forgave those who persecuted him.

But let Moses's memorable deed come to mind and consider something that
is the same in this one. Indeed, when Moses, by God's command, wished to lead
the children of Israel from Egypt and Pharaoh did not want to let his people go,
Moses was forced by the king's foolishness to afflict that land with plagues. When
he attacked him by turning the waters into blood and producing frogs, Pharaoh's
magicians did the same, but when the third plague, the plague of gnats, came forth
the magicians failed, and having lost all the power of their art, they said, "This is
the finger of God" (Exod. 8:19). And this is similar: once and a second time hostile
words were brought forth in reproof of the holy man, but the third time the man
was restrained from his bold malice and ascribed Vitalis's words to the Holy Spirit.

---

17 Moolenbroek and other scholars have identified this as the council of London of 1102 (*Vital*, 168–9;
Sauvage, 373n1).

That he freed some men who had been condemned to death

5. At one time, when the holy man went to England to preach and he poured out words of salvation upon the people, it happened that he met two men sentenced to be hanged as they were being led away. Having pity on them, he at once absolved them and sent them away in the presence of the bailiff, just like St. Nicholas, nor did the bailiff presume to go against his will.[18]

Of the man he brought back to renewed life

6. Let this worthy matter be remembered; it happens to come down to us through earlier people's telling. One time, some knights who were unwilling to agree to his words and who refused to be reconciled with their enemies went away. But on that trip they were struck by a serious blow. For one of them slipped from his horse, fell to the ground, and lay there like a dead man. When it was announced to Vitalis, he was brought to the place and a great crowd of people accompanied him as he went to see this spectacle. But when he came to the place, he urged [them] to kneel in prayer, so that God might deign to show His power to the glory of His name and the benefit of the watchers. They did so. When the prayer had been completed, he spoke to the man. At Vitalis's voice, the man revived as though waking from a deep sleep. Vitalis ordered him to tell in front of them all where he had been or what he knew had been done with him. That man answered that by his own deserts he had been sent to Hell, but that he had been restored to life by the merits of the holy man and by his prayer. He promised, truly, that he would completely renounce knighthood and then spend his life in holy religion. The holy man took care to send him to an abbey, where he might end his life in holy conversation. That man always strove to obey Vitalis's teachings, and he lived there faithfully for a long time in holy conversation.

No one should suspect that the stories we insert here are invented because of the novelty of this matter. For we describe not our own stories, but ones which are proven by the testimony of the faithful and handed down to us.

How he consumed a spider during the holy mystery

7. Then one day, when he was hidden from men's sight standing at the holy altar in the midst of the holy mysteries, perhaps to show his power, a spider fell into

---

18 "Bailiff" = *justicia* (justice). Sauvage notes that this is probably a jailor or bailiff in charge of taking the prisoners to be executed (375n1).

the holy chalice. He could not remove it; the human hand could not assist it. Thus armed with faith, he received it with the holy sacrament, nor did he suffer any evil from it. And why should one marvel? For he truly believed that he was receiving the body and blood of the Lord. He was not incorrect to believe that this great mystery could even overcome any venom. Indeed, according to the testimony of the Truth, "All things are possible to the believer" (Mark 9:22). And so He said to the disciples, "If you had faith even the size of a grain of mustard, you would say to this mountain, 'Move yourself into the sea' and it would be done" (Matt. 17:19). And so it is that Paul praised this same thing [faith] with such great praise, since through it, listing this man, that one, and the other one by one, he shows them to have pleased God (cf. Rom. 4).

I am about to say marvelous things and it may be that these things will be judged to be uncertain by some people because of their greatness, but I swear to God, whom I desire to serve with all my mind's focus, that these are not our inventions that we include here, but we know these things from the narrative of men of the faith living in holy religion.

One day, when the holy father was lingering among the people and sowing God's word, this same spider was said to have left his body by way of his foot. And indeed rightly, for it was quite proper that what he miraculously received, miraculously came forth. For truly, the One who could leave His mother and have the seal of her womb remain untouched and who wanted, contrary to what is usual, to bring water forth from a stone for His people could reveal this sort of miracle in His servant. Let the faithful man hear this, so that he may be made the more ardent and devout. Let the doubter hear this, so that he may be confirmed more robustly in faith. Let all hear this, so that the virtue and faith of this man may be known and the magnificence of the Lord may be glorified.

Of the woman who was warned by a dream to prepare food for him

8. There was a certain knight whose wife was said to be not very faithful to her marriage bed. However, when the holy man was at Coutances to recall wanderers of this sort to continence, as was his habit, he decided to receive hospitality at this woman's house, although it was a long way from that city. And when he was on the way, the sun went down and the day ended before he got there. Right then, the people at whose house he had decided to be entertained had gone to bed to be refreshed by sleep. But although that woman was now asleep, she was awakened by a loud voice in a vision, and this same voice commanded that she prepare food for the holy man. But when her husband's voice rebuked her, [saying] that she

had been woken by a dream, she went back to bed. Again the voice warned this woman that she should quickly prepare the things it had told her to, because it said that Vitalis would stay there the whole day. And when this had happened a third time, the advance messenger of the holy man arrived and said that the man of God was there. And thus it was proved by the conclusion of the business that the woman had not been aroused by a dream, but had seen true things in a vision. And she was quite properly warned to prepare necessities for him, because he came for this purpose: that he should bestow upon her the salvific teaching of life, and that she who was branded by the mark of a bad reputation should be brought back to the protection of discretion by his words.

That he made shepherds safe from robbers and also how the thieves were caught

9. At a time when war was raging in those places where certain shepherds of the holy man were feeding their beasts, the shepherds, who greatly feared an attack by robbers, said to him that they would move elsewhere, to prevent the animals they looked after from being carried off. The holy man gave them a guarantee and promised to make good to them whatever damage they should suffer from the robbers. When they had accepted his pledge, they remained there, and they suffered no harm from predators. Indeed, thieves came by night and entered the building where the flocks were kept, and they led many cows off, but they were unable to take the ones they had seized off the grange.[19] Indeed, they went around in circles all night, led by an erroneous spirit and exhausted by vain labor, and they accomplished nothing at all. Recognizing the power of God in a miracle of this type, and gesturing with their staffs and confessing their sin, they submitted themselves to the holy man, from whom they were favored to receive forgiveness.[20]

That the sick were restored to health by the hairs of his garment

10. Let us not leave out a story that a certain nun who lived in holy conversation was accustomed to tell. She said that one time one of her sisters extracted hairs from the clothing of the holy father; mixing them with water, she gave them to the

---

19 Grange = *curia*. However, *curia* can also mean courtyard, in which case one would have to imagine the thieves leading the animals around in circles unable to find the gate.
20 Several of the elements of this miracle are echoed in the miracle of the tunic in Stephen's life of St. Firmat. As Sauvage points out (378n1), the gesture with the staffs is an invitation to Vitalis to beat them if he wished.

sick and fevered to consume. When they had drunk this sort of potion, they were restored to their earlier health, as they themselves attested.

We read that the hemorrhaging woman was restored to her earlier health, when she touched the fringes of the Lord's garment (Matt. 9:20; Luke 8:43); we also read that the sick were placed in the open so that when Peter passed they might be restored to health by his shadow (Acts 5:15); but He who acted Himself or through the exalted chief of the apostles, was also able to perform marvels through His Vitalis by enriching him with virtues. Oh Lord, how marvelous You always are in Your saints! So that the very glorious power of the holy man might be known, You not only wanted to perform miracles by his presence, but also to help the needy through the smallest things that belonged to him, to demonstrate his power.

That when he was preaching in England, the people, although they did not understand French, understood his words

11. We also add another miracle, namely how, following the example of the earlier believers, by the merits of His servant, He made an unknown language intelligible in the hearts of his audience by a subtle infusion of the Spirit, no doubt by Its doing (cf. 1 Cor. 14). For when he was staying in England one time when he was by himself, it happened that he was placed in a church to preach a sermon to an innumerable multitude of people. But since there were many there who did not know French, God deigned to infuse the grace of His generosity into the minds of the audience, because as long as the sermon lasted, everyone understood the French he spoke, although, when the sermon was finished, by this same grace it did not persist in them. Therefore one should understand through this that right understanding was given for a time to those who heard him, so that they could understand the words of the Holy Spirit, which proceeded from his mouth; then, so that they would not waste that grace in idle chatter, they were deprived of it by the grace itself.

That he preached a sermon at the council of Reims at the order of the Lord Pope

12. This item should by no means be left out, that he was not only an object of reverence and fear to the kings, princes, and powers of this world because of the eminence of his sanctity, but also that this man followed the words of blessed Job and tore open their jaws and ripped the stolen goods and booty of the poor from their teeth with the powerful hand and extended arm of free authority (Job 29:17).

To show this (leaving out many other indications of the pope's mark of distinction toward the man of God), this example suffices: that when he was invited to the general council at Reims by the Lord Pope, he ordered Vitalis to give a sermon at the council meeting, and he gave Vitalis many gifts when he was going home after the council as a proxy for their bond and singular friendship, namely so that the blessed man might always be comforted by having been refreshed by the affection of such a father. Also the Lord Pope attested before many people about him that he had not found a single other person among all those on this side of the Alps who so condemned in strict and harsh speech all the things he found reprehensible in the apostolic bishop himself, not disguising it with appeasement or adulation, and who made it clear to him out loud.

Something else one ought not to be silent about happened in that council: he got the dignity of this privilege for the church of Savigny from the Lord Pope, that if the whole diocese of Avranches, along with the bishop, was for any reason deprived of the mass and other offices, the church of Savigny might nonetheless do whatever is proper for the divine office, fully and in every detail, and that it would not deserve to be under interdict or prohibited from divine offices, except for its own fault and that of its chapter.[21]

Brief Epilogue

13. Now that we have given a somewhat brief account of these things that were treated in a somewhat more protracted way about the life of St. Vitalis, let us note down certain of his virtues that are included in the Roll that was written at his death, and then we shall come to his demise. So this father, as we have said above, was raised from childhood in liberal disciplines; when he came to manhood and was placed among an abundance of goods, he began to love poverty, and as though he were holding this Gospel phrase before his eyes: "He who does not renounce what he has cannot be my disciple" (Luke 14:25), just as it is said of blessed Benedict, "he disdained the world with its flower as though it were a desert."[22]

Therefore, rescued from the ruins of this fleeting world by the hand of divine mercy, he led the hermit's life in the place which is called Dompierre for

---

21 This was a fairly standard exemption given to the Cistercian order and then requested by other houses. Andres had a similar indulgence (William of Andres, *Chronicle*, 283).

22 Gregory the Great, *Dialogues*, introduction to Book 2, p. 55, gives this passage as "he saw how barren it was with its attractions and turned from it without regret," but Stephen is quoting the Latin exactly. This should remind you to be aware that translators may translate, as King Alfred said in his translation of Gregory's *Pastoral Care*, word for word, sentence for sentence, or thought for thought.

seventeen years, frequently visited by the proven and honest people of his time, namely Lord Robert of Arbrissel, who built the monastery called Fontevrault, and Lord Bernard of Tiron, and also other very illustrious persons of this same profession. They held extremely frequent meetings in this same place of Dompierre, just like the holy fathers, and they discussed the state of the Holy Church and things useful for souls. These friendly and frequent meetings with these people mentioned above showed in how holy a manner he lived in this profession, how much he disdained the world and loved poverty, how parsimonious he was to himself, how generous to the needy, and how intent he was on fasting and vigils, prayers and other holy works, saying with the prophet "You will be a holy man with the holy" (Ps. 17:26).

That he untiringly sowed the seed of God

14. How untiring and faithful a dispenser of the divine word he truly was is proven by the way the brothers who accompanied him broke down from the work and because of that work, for although they themselves were sitting and following each other in obedience to him, they never saw him sit during preaching, and although the hearers were often exhausted, they never saw him grow weary. If anyone wants to understand in words how many people's plots he tolerated, how much hardship in thirst and hunger, how much heat and other intemperateness of the weather he bore in carrying out this duty, that person would give up, worn out by the effort. For he, seeking nothing earthly, did not seek his own things, but things belonging to Jesus Christ (Phil. 2:21), laboring hard to this end: that he might restore peace among the discordant, that he might provide food and clothing to the needy, hospitality to the wanderers, forgiveness to the guilty, legitimate marriages to the whores, and homes for the leprous and other necessities. God conferred such grace on him that, although he undertook difficult or impossible things, he never failed to accomplish them with God's help.

While he carried out these things and works of this kind of sanctity for seventeen years, at length, he was forced by the prayers of the brothers, a multitude of whom had flowed to him not least because of his sanctity, to become the father of more than 140 people of both sexes, chiefly, following Gregory, deciding to be of use to many rather than to live for himself alone.[23] But when he was placed in rule he did not desert his earlier poverty; he nevertheless occupied himself in

---

23 Gregory the Great, *The Book of Pastoral Rule*, trans. George E. Demacopoulos (Crestwood, NY: St. Vladimir's Seminary Press, 2007), 36–8 (I: 5).

preaching. He was a great founder of churches, a most constant defender of the poor, the sharpest reprover of tyrants, the righteous and modest pastor and most pious provider for the flock entrusted to him.

I shall add a certain miracle below lest it be passed over in silence by our negligence.

Of his brother, who fell from a high place but was not hurt at all

15. Once when carpenters were busy building the structures of the monastery of Savigny, a piece of wood fell from high up. The holy man's brother according to the flesh [that is, his sibling] fell to the ground with it, but the holy man raised his eyes and hands and his brother sustained no wound from that collapse. Those who were present marvelled at the outcome of the event and were stirred to praise of God.[24]

Now that these few things have been laid out at length, let us turn the pen from his virtues to his death.

Of his death

16. At the time that had been ordained for him to receive the fruit of his labor and for God to reward him, he went to Dompierre on an urgent matter, when suddenly he began to be troubled by pain in his body. But the servant of God strove not to give in to the pain of the illness nor in any way to stop his accustomed prayers. Indeed, the night he died, in the year of the Incarnation of the Lord 1122, on the 16th Kalends of October [September 16, Monday], he rose early for Matins, rang the signal for the brothers to rise, sang regular Matins, and began the matins of St. Mary, but did not finish them. For when the monk who was doing the reading asked him for a blessing, he said this blessing to him: "May the intercession of the Holy Virgin Mary join us to the college of angels." When he had finished this, he sent his spirit forth. On the Sunday, he had offered the holy sacrifice to the Lord [i.e., the Eucharist], after which, on the second night, a victor forever, as we believe, his spirit ascended to the Lord. When he was dying, it is said, a bright cloud appeared there, and a sweet smell fully filled the house in which these things happened. And rightly indeed a sweet odor appeared at his death, as his preaching infused the smell of eternal life in the world, so that it might be said, "We are the good odor of Christ in every place" (2 Cor. 2:15). So

---

24 This also echoes a miracle of St. Benedict; Gregory the Great, *Dialogues*, 76–7.

when the holy man left the world, the people came from various places to the place where he died.

That the people of Le Teilleul wanted to take his body and couldn't

17. But the people of Le Teilleul wanted to keep his body when it was carried through their midst. But although many tried to do this, they were frustrated in their every effort. Instead, they were completely unable to move the bier from where it had been placed, although they tried three times, and when they had failed completely, two monks who were coming along picked it up easily and rejoicing carried it on their own shoulders to his own abbey, and they kept the body unburied for three days out of reverence for the holy Father with psalms and prayers. By this very evident miracle, I believe, God made it known that he did not want to deprive the church of Savigny of its own pastor. But how properly and modestly he treated those subject to him may be gauged from those who, with the eyes of pious love, clung to him even when he was dead and could scarcely bear to be parted from him.

Of his soul's assumption

18. On the same day on which the blessed man went to the Lord, with God's permission, Vitalis deigned to reveal his glorious assumption to the corporeal eyes of a monk who was a long way away from Savigny and wasn't even professed to that house.[25] This person was a man of great religion and very famous for holiness in all things. When he was sitting with some other brothers in a certain place, he suddenly leapt from his seat, raised his eyes and hands on high, and began to run around among them. Although the brothers who were present with him did not see this without great amazement, they did not dare to correct and reprehend him at once because they knew him to be a man of great holiness and reverence, so they decided instead to await the end of the business. But when the venerable man after the short space of an hour sat down, once again taking his usual seriousness and humility upon himself, he began to think more attentively about the vision he

---

25 Moolenbroek suggests that this story was intended to point to St. Bernard of Clairvaux, without actually saying his name (*Vital*, 73). If he is correct (and the supposition is reasonable), this is another way in which the later history of Savigny and Stephen's positionality have affected the shape of the biography, since there was no affiliation with Clairvaux at the time Vitalis died. Moolenbroek points out that there are a number of parallels between this biography and that of St. Bernard (*Vital*, 65–6).

had seen. The brothers began to press him vehemently to explain to them what had befallen him without delay. He answered them,

"At the time you saw me joyous and exulting, the blessed abbot Vitalis was freed from the prison of the flesh and was assumed into heaven with inexpressible glory, to the singing of angelic choirs, and I had to rejoice in his glory with every effort of my body and sentiment of my mind."

That a sick person received his health under his bier

19. So in the meantime, while his corpse was being kept around, God glorified His servant with miracles even when he was dead, this man who He had adorned with virtues when he was alive. For a man who was badly impaired by a sickness of his ears or hands got permission through many prayers to lie under his bier and when he got his health back there, he went off happy.

That a person who offered a mass for him smelled a good odor

20. To multiply His great works, the Lord added this event at the body of His servant, so that the faith of the auditors and watchers would rejoice and their spirit be consoled. For when a person who was serving at his funeral offered the holy sacrifice to the Lord for him, he smelled a very sweet fragrance as he assisted at the holy altar. It came from the side where the still unburied body lay and spread sweetly. And thus the Lord filled the place where these things happened with the smell of sweetness when Vitalis's soul, freed from the prison of the body, returned to the fatherland, as we believe; and thus in order to demonstrate his merits, the miraculous fragrance would delight them when the servant of God was being given over to burial. And rightly indeed did his body smell sweet in this way, this man who was armed with the adornment of chastity. He spurned the stink of the vices, and relied upon the virtues and so avoided the filth of sins. He was a hundred times better off – better off! – embalmed by the virtues than protected from worms by being smeared with myrrh and aloe. For the virtues protect and shut out the poison of the venomous serpent [i.e., the devil], but myrrh and aloe, even if they protect the body from corruption, do not free the soul from punishment. For what difference does it make to this man now when his soul rests in the heavens, this man who at another time went through various regions barefoot sowing the word of God, with calluses on his feet hardened by harsh labor, who tamed his body with the roughness of haircloth? Or rather, how much the more gloriously he exults, how much more difficult things he would have endured for the love of

God, for when the work grows, the reward for the work also grows. O what a good bargain, to buy the blessed realm forever by labor in the world!

Concerning the tomb where his body was placed

21. It would seem ridiculous to leave out without marveling at it what is said about the sarcophagus his body was put in. For, as many of the inhabitants of the place testify, when the sarcophagus was put in the parish church of St. Mary of Savigny and many of their ancestors tried to move it, their effort met with no success. When the holy man was told about this by some people, he answered thus, full of the spirit of prophecy,

"Let it be," he said. "Let it be, because God will keep this for me."

Then, at the ceremony of his burial, it was taken from the church with the greatest ease and was as easily carried to the place of his burial as if it weighed nothing at all. It has been carried to burial in the oratory of the same church he founded, in the northern part, where even after his burial because of his merit, the Lord is known to have shown miracles. I include a few of these below and thus put an end to this work.

That a lay brother was freed from a fever at his tomb

22. A daily fever vexed a certain lay brother of the house, nor could any remedy be found by any means against this trouble. One night, he went to keep vigil at the tomb of this father in order to get his health back, and while he was there, he fell asleep. When he was asleep, he saw this sort of vision. It seemed indeed that half of the cover of the sarcophagus was opened to him, and a voice came down from on high and told him to leave. It seemed to him that he answered it saying that he wouldn't go at all until he merited to receive his health from the holy father. When this same voice had twice ordered him to go and he had answered saying the same things, the third time this same voice commanded him to go, speaking a little more harshly, and it said when he answered in a similar way that he would be healed. He left there comforted and ate some food, and as the fever was now gone and his health restored, he got better.

Of the brother cured of a lesion on his shin through blessed Vitalis

23. One of the brothers developed a very serious lesion on his shin, one that ate into and consumed his shin nearly entirely. Since no application of corporeal

medicine helped or aided him in any way, he spurned the administrations of corporeal medicine, turned his whole hope to Christ, and placed the acquisition of his health before blessed Vitalis. When he had slept overnight at the tomb three times, he attained the fruit of his hope through the rapid acquisition of his health, with the assent of God and the assistance of blessed Vitalis.

That a certain brother was freed from bodily illness at the tomb

24. Another lay brother, who held the position of gardener, labored under a grave bodily infirmity. Then when he stayed awake during one midday siesta at the tomb of the blessed father, he suddenly was made whole.

Of the raving brother who was freed from insanity by blessed Vitalis

25. So that it should be even clearer how great the power and virtue of the blessed man was, which he possessed from God, against the tyranny of the devil, it can be very easily recognized by the chapter below. A brother wearing the habit of religion in the house of Savigny was given to Satan by the secret judgment of God to the ruin of his body. With his senses all in a whirl, he became frenetic, in such delirium and horrible insanity of mind that I might say he could not be subdued and held by men's strength, but only barely by the strongest and most confining of chains. Indeed, he foamed at the mouth, promising horrible things in the hearing of those standing around, and spitting saliva in their faces. Horrible in appearance, he turned his head to the point of dizziness and declared by the most certain of signs the malice of the one possessing him.[26] But because he had made living arrangements with two men, they were wounded by that charity which knows how to weep with those who weep and to be ill with those who are ill, and to be troubled by those who are troubled. Just as he did not know the end of his suffering, in the same way they did not know the limits of their lamentation and mercy. And when they had begged God with many prayers for no small time for the recovery of his health, still they were not heard; indeed, the Lord reserved the glory of this man's health for His confessor Vitalis.[27]

---

26 This image of possession has been remarkably persistent (if you've ever seen *The Exorcist*, you'll be familiar with it)!

27 Echo of a miracle told in the life of Benedict, *Dialogues*, 81–2. However, in the Benedict life, the monk reverts when he sees other junior monks ordained (the saint has made him promise not to seek ordination) and when he presents himself, the devil immediately seizes him again.

In the meantime, this vision was shown to a religious monk from this same church. For he saw St. Vitalis on the edge of his sarcophagus, dressed in white vestments and saying to him,

"Come and quickly bring me that man who has left the service of the Lord," repeating this three times.

When he had pondered in silent mental ruminations whether perhaps it was that man who was suffering, blessed Vitalis, answering his thought, said, "It is that one; it is that one."

And when they told this to the abbot, then by the order of the abbot the man was led to the tomb of the blessed father, where he stayed for some nights, along with certain brothers who kept guard on him. Now from that time he was restored to wholeness and returned to health and the desired soundness by the prayers and merits of the holy father.

That a certain foolish monk was cured at his tomb

26. There was a certain monk who had gone out of his mind, left the monastic life, and made a spectacle for the world; the wretch wandered here and there like a simpleton.[28] Coming to this place [i.e., Savigny] one time, he spoke with the sacrist of the place. This man led him to prayer and advised him to pray at the tomb of the holy man. When the sacrist said anything verbally to him, the man, prompted by his stupidity, repeated the same things back to him. At length, when he was left there alone, he fell asleep, and upon waking, he felt himself to be troubled by a great illness. But as it appeared, this pain was the remedy for his pain, for when he poured out his error by weeping, his senses returned to him. And when he was whole, he sought the monastic life again and lived in it free from such indisposition from then on. He was accustomed to visit this abbey every year and because of the memory of his cure he wished to have something from it. But in all these things the only thing being shown is that, as it is written, "the death of his saints is precious in the eyes of God" (Ps. 115:15).

So look, we have taken care to commit these things to memory, falling into common speech, concerning the virtues of the blessed man, at your demanding insistence; we give thanks to God, Who allowed us to understand and deigned

---

28 "Wandered" = *girabat*. A monastic reader would make a connection between this passage and the part of the rule of St. Benedict where Benedict condemns the *gyrovagi*, the monks who wander around (the worst sort in Benedict's view). *Sancti Benedicti regula monasteriorum*, 19.

to give us some speech to explain them. Therefore at the end let us ask for mercy from omnipotent God, so that the One who carried His servant, as we believe, to the celestial realms may forgive us our faults through the intercessionary merits of that man. And giving us His grace, may He allow us to live in so holy a fashion that we may be worthy to be among those He recognizes when He chooses the good,[29] and cleansed by the complete purification of our vices, that we may be given to the company of the holy angels, where we shall be able to see Him face to face (cf. 1 Cor. 13:12) and never sated by seeing him, praise him without end. May He deign to fulfill this, Who lives and reigns, the true and only God for ever and ever. Amen.

Here ends the life of St. Vitalis

29 A reference to the Last Judgment, when the good will be separated from the evil. Figure 4 shows a detail of the portal at Conques showing the fate of the damned, but that church, and many others, also depicted the joy of the blessed in their judgment portals.

APPENDIX 2

✠

The Life of St. Firmat

About the translation

I've translated this biography from the Latin version published by Émile-Aubert Pigeon at the end of the nineteenth century.[1] Pigeon also provided a French translation for those who read French, and while I've looked at it, my translation derives directly from the Latin. I have also consulted the version of the life published in the *Acta sanctorum*.[2] Although the version in the *Acta sanctorum* was printed earlier than Pigeon's version, the Pigeon is full of what appear to be copying errors, and I wanted to check the two Latin versions against each other, as they were copied independently. I have not consulted the manuscript, which Pigeon found in the cartulary of the collegiate church of Mortain; it may no longer even be extant, given the fate of so many of the manuscripts from this region.[3] Errors might be made by the author (all authors do make errors in writing!), by the medieval copyist, by the modern transcriber(s), or by the typesetter when preparing a text for printing; this is yet another reminder of the complicated path by which medieval texts may reach us. Pigeon does not include any subdivisions of the four long sections but seems to have created paragraphs as he saw fit and added the headings (so heads up! the headings are modern). These paragraphs do not line up with the numbered paragraphs contained in the *Acta sanctorum* version, which seem to have been created by the editors, following typical editing practices for Latin texts.

---

1 Pigeon (1) and Pigeon (2).
2 *De s. Guilielmo*, 334–41.
3 Pigeon (1), 57.

As you read this biography, you will find it quite different in some ways from the life of St. Vitalis. These differences were great enough that many scholars have doubted that this biography was Stephen's work. One objection – the one voiced by the editors of the version printed in the *Acta sanctorum* – has been that as a highly educated man, Stephen should have known of the utter unlikelihood of a western cleric being drafted as the patriarch of Constantinople, given that the eastern and western churches were at odds with each other. They suggest it was an interpolation.[4]

However, we have no other life of Firmat and Robert of Torigni says that Stephen wrote one. Furthermore, there is a thirteenth-century copy of the Latin biography in a collection of saints' lives written at Mont Saint-Michel, where Robert was the abbot. (I am grateful to Sara McDougall for bringing this manuscript to my attention; it may have been the text the *Acta sanctorum* editors transcribed.)[5] The existence of this manuscript has persuaded me that the biography is Stephen's work. To the objections of the *Acta sanctorum* editors, I would respond that Stephen's sense of his job in writing this biography was almost surely not our sense of what he ought to have done. We might want to insist that he be historically accurate, as we would define it. But as Charles Jones pointed out in a famous article about Bede, the "true law of history" that Bede refers to is to report what people have said.[6] I also see in the biography of Firmat some themes and concerns shared with the life of Vitalis. It *is* different, but writers often produce very different texts for different audiences.

The format of the life is also different: four long chapters rather than chapters divided for reading. This raises some further questions about the purpose that this biography might have been written for and what earlier form it might have had, if any. Were the four chapters originally four books, with subdivisions? Perhaps. The version Pigeon read was not recorded in the liturgical books but rather the cartulary, and so it may not have been the main version used by the canons. The manuscript version is divided into sections, although of uneven lengths, suggesting that it was intended for private reading rather than liturgical use.

One further note is necessary. Although both Pigeon and the *Acta sanctorum* call the saint William Firmat, the biography itself refers only to Firmat, as Pigeon points out.[7] The name William was attached to the saint and, interestingly

---

4 *De s. Guilielmo*, 338–9. The whole episode is printed at the end of the chapter as an endnote for that reason.

5 Avranches, Bibliothèque municipale, ms. 167, ff. 125r–130v.

6 As reported by Roger Ray, "Bede's *Vera lex historiae*," *Speculum* 55, no. 1 (1980): 1–2.

7 Pigeon (1), 60.

enough, the name William Firmat appears in the witness list of a charter issued by Stephen in his capacity as bishop of Rennes.[8] While this is obviously not our saint, the man might be named after the saint; if so, it is a token of his popularity. The *Acta sanctorum* editors note that the saint was called William in their day (the late seventeenth century).[9]

So what might you do with this other saint's life? In medicine they often say, "Watch one, do one, teach one." You've watched me do one. So here is one for you to do. You have a lot of information about the author and the times in which he lived (even if you conclude that Stephen was *not* the author, the dating is approximately right), and I've also offered a few comments about this biography in the course of the book you've just read. In addition, I've translated Pigeon's notes into English where they appear helpful and also supplied some from the *Acta sanctorum* version where useful. But to make sense of this narrative, you'll need more information (more context!) than I'm supplying here. What questions do you need to ask? What passages require deeper analysis? What can you make of this biography?

The text

Prologue[10]

Paternal piety's generous affection toward its children demands that generous children should demonstrate pious affection by imitating the habits of their pious father. In regard to this, however, Divine Paternity's loving and effective kindness has chosen some earlier guides, enlightened the ones it has chosen and, once they have been enlightened, put them in front of us to imitate so as to direct our feet upon the road of peace in the journey of this life. Marvelous God, so that God's great wonders may be made more magnificent, has performed marvelous things in His saints through miracles and virtues.[11] The Christian[12] custom has come about of passing on their characters and deeds in writing, in praise of Christ and for the education of Christians so that those who come after will remember.

---

8 *Cartulaire de Saint-Melaine*, 91.

9 *De s. Guilielmo*, 334.

10 Because the chapter divisions appear in both transcriptions, they must be in the manuscript, although since the manuscript itself is a copy, they were not necessarily in the original.

11 Although this passage reads quite redundantly in English, the redundancy comes directly from the Latin. This sentence contains the words *mira, magnificentur, magnalia, mirabilis, miraculis*, and *mirabiles*, and God is twice named.

12 Pigeon (2), 41, reads *mos christianae religiones*, but I follow the version in *AASS*, 334, in reading *mos christianae religionis*.

Among these saints, we have taken up Christ's confessor Firmat, a man of worthy memory, who won not the smallest amount of glory in his holiness. As I take up his deeds that are worth remembering out of the love of charity, I beg that his intervention might obtain from the piety of heavenly graciousness that the things I say may, with the assistance of divine favor, bring about[13] praise for the highest King, honor for the exalted soldier [of Christ], and salvation for us sinners.

Chapter I

The first acts of St. William, his retreat to his hermitage, his pilgrimage to the East[14]

So the Lord's outstanding confessor, Firmat, was born in the city of Tours, the nobler son of nobles; instead he ennobled his kin. From the first moments that this remarkable boy entered childhood, he was educated in liberal disciplines. For already the spark of divine kindling was lit in his boyish mind, which consequently set the two-fold light of knowledge burning.[15] Thus a bright and easy wit, a subtle intellectual ability, and a tenacious and fixed memory were all strong in him. But when he became a youth, I can by no means express in words how powerfully the strength of his soul emerged, how much the elegance of his character. His speech was sweetly affable, his response pleasantly sweet, his words customarily modest, his actions characterized by careful temperance. He taught the path of reason in his words, the road of truth in his actions. He was an upright fighter for justice, a straightforward advocate for prudence, a moderate teacher of temperance, and an outstanding champion of fortitude.[16]

Enriched with the dowry of these virtues, he became a canon in the church of St. Venantius[17] at the request and with the consent of the canons. He showed himself to be faithful to them in the things entrusted to him, truthful in the promises he made, and dutiful in carrying out their business. He was gracious to those beneath him, respectful toward the powerful, obedient to the best. There was in

---

13 Pigeon (2), 41, gives *pervenio*; *AASS*, 334, gives *provenio*. One of the two misread an abbreviation, but which? My guess is that Pigeon is incorrect here, and I've translated accordingly.

14 This, and the other headings, were composed by Pigeon.

15 This is a little obscure, but Stephen seems to mean that he learned both sacred and secular knowledge.

16 Justice, prudence, temperance, and fortitude are the four cardinal virtues.

17 Pigeon (1), 57, identifies this as St. Vincent's, but the text quite clearly says St. Venantius, and there was a chapter of canons of St. Venantius in Tours, which the compilers of the Tours volume of *Gallia christiana* (14: 187–8) mention as being famous for St. Firmat.

him no cause of discord, no seed of conflict. In this man who was ruled by out-standingly charitable good will, there truly was no gnawing worm of envy.

Then when a little time had passed, he was embroiled in the cares of the earthly army. And so he carried out the duty of that army, while he did not put aside the project of the canonical one. Apart from these things, the grace of celestial knowl-edge, which foresaw that he would be a vessel of election for it, so endowed the man of God with progress in the art of medicine that the innumerable sick people who flowed to him returned with joy to their homes when they had recovered their earlier health. And thus he was adorned with the three-fold gift of book learning, military arms, and principles of medicine.

When he had gathered innumerable riches, however, a little avarice began to tickle his mind, prompted by the wiliness of the devil. But God's kindly mercy un-dermined the evil enemy's malice; God deigned to expose the hidden plots of the secret plotter to the holy man. For one night, when care for his personal business compelled him to leave Matins more quickly than usual, he found a devil, looking like an ape, sitting on the chest in which a lot of money had been stored. When the man of God demanded to know who was sitting on his property, the devil said, "I'm not watching over your property, but mine."

Now cautioned by the clever seducer's warning, therefore, Firmat fortified him-self with the sign of the cross and remembering his weakness, he took refuge in the assistance of prayer. And for all the rest of that night (and from the beginning he accused himself of having buried the wealth of the poor in his own garden), he re-membered that he had read, "Unless someone gives up all that he has, he cannot be my disciple" (Luke 14:33); and elsewhere, "Sell what you have and give alms" (Luke 12:33); and again, "Go and sell what you have and give it to the poor, and then come follow me" (Matt. 19:21; Mark 10:21; Luke 18:22). While he was reflecting in careful meditation, he discovered salvific advice and he determined voluntarily to give to the poor of Christ what he had gathered against the will of Christ.

Now when day returned to the earth, that extraordinarily mild man addressed his mother, whom he looked after with a son's care (for his father had already died), with sweet speech. He said,

"You see, mother, that this world's form is breaking down. Like a fragile reed it pierces the hand of anyone who relies on it, if anyone relies upon it.[18] But God made man in the image of God, so that man might share in divinity

---

18 A possible reference to a letter of St. Jerome in response to Algasia (letter 121), in which he gives a number of interpretations. The Latin here reads "cui si quis innititur, velut calamus fragilis perfo-rat manum innitentis." Jerome's Latin reads "calamus fractus: cui qui inniti voluerit, pertundetur manus ejus" (Jerome, *Epistola CXXI ad Algasiam*, in PL 22: 1012).

by doing the things that belong to God. Since therefore, as long as we are in this world, we are sojourners absent from God and the time is short, let us give back to God the things that belong to God, exchanging eternal and heavenly things for earthly and perishable ones in a blessed bargain.[19] Take whatever portion you want of the goods that heavenly goodness has given us; but when we have given the rest to the poor, it will be given to the one who gives all good things. I am hoping to have your consent to my taking up the religious habit."

His mother, drenched with the pious dew of tears, said to him with maternal love,

"Why, my son? Why do you think about deserting your mother? Who will be my sweet consolation when I have been deserted? Who will alleviate my widowhood? Who will be the staff of my old age? If you wish to fight for your King, know that I will fight at your side. If you seek the solitary life, you will have only me, the one who was your devoted nurse, as a humble servant, so that she who served you when you entered onto the road of corruptible life may serve as you enter upon the road of celestial life. Concerning your property, my son, let foresight provide what it knows will be useful."

When his mother had discussed these things with her son, the son rejoiced in his mother's plan, and the mother in her son's company. They therefore sold everything they owned and when these things had been given to the poor, they turned the treasure which the devil had claimed as his own into heavenly treasures in the hands of the poor. And when they had done these things, they left the city of Tours seeking the city that was to be [that is, the heavenly city], the mother with her son. And sent by divine will to the place called "Seven Brothers," they built a hut in a solitary retreat, where the mother provided the son with food for the body and the son served a spiritual meal to his mother.[20]

Since, however, he was very frequently visited by his fellow citizens, because they were related to him or rather because of his holiness, and a great influx of

---

19 Bargain = *commercio*; this is the language of the marketplace. However, the whole phrase "exchanging eternal and heavenly things for earthly and perishable ones in a blessed bargain" comes from plainsong. The Cantus database lists examples as early as the 1100s, but the text is associated with the feast of St. Vincent of Saragossa, which may explain why Pigeon assigned Firmat to the church of St. Vincent ("Cantus: A Database for Latin Ecclesiastical Chant," University of Waterloo, accessed at http://cantus.uwaterloo.ca/id/006785a). It appeared in mortuary rolls and grants to churches and many other places.

20 *De S. Guilelmi*, 336nb, comments that the editors could find no place called Sept-Frères. They posited that it may have been a reference to the "Seven Sleepers" and perhaps that it was a place called "Les Hermites" (the Hermits), a little north of the city of Tours. This village still exists; it is about 37 km from Tours by modern roads.

lots of people came to see him, he deprived his native land of his presence when his mother died in peace (the only reason he was living in the Touraine). Warned against the breeze of popular favor by vigilant caution,[21] he wanted to achieve the treasure of a good conscience. So he went away from there to Laval, and in the wood called "Concise," he entered a solitary hermitage.[22] But when he was there, and he was not focused on taking care of himself (that shaggy priest sang the mass with uncut hair), he was, as a result, troubled by various annoyances. I judge that I ought not to be silent concerning this one, as it was the reason he left.

Some pernicious youths of damnable mind secretly led a prostitute, an accomplice in their iniquity, to his hut and when they had given the impudent woman some money, they persuaded her to do this audacious thing: that she should exercise a woman's worthless wiles any way she could to entice God's confessor into committing fornication. When they had hidden in the woods, as it was now just beginning to be dusk, she knocked on the saint's door and begged with tearful cries,

"Most holy priest, I ask will you open the door? Will you open up right away for this wretched woman? So that savage cruelty will not devour this unarmed woman alone or bestial ferocity will not tear her to pieces or ghostly horror drive the life from her?"

This perfectly pious man received her and showed her the pious graciousness of hospitality such as he could and should have done. He lit a fire and offered her bread to eat. But she, who had not forgotten her evil plot, flourished such enticements at the man of God as she was able to. The holy athlete recognized the plots of the deceitful devil, and he was not surprised that an impudent woman, if she played the whore, would wage the usual conflict alongside the devil. And the one who fought against the saint with the fire of lust was conquered by material fire. For the holy man put his naked arm on the burning firebrand and of his own free will inflicted a harsh punishment on his flesh, so that the fleshly temptation of arousal would not harm him: In the future the burn scar would be a sign as long as he lived of his earlier suffering.[23]

---

21 "Breeze of popular favor" = *popularis aura favoris*, which echoes a Roman phrase (*popularis aura*) found in Cicero, Horace, Virgil, and Livy.

22 Laval in Mayenne. Concise lay between Laval and Saint-Berthevin (Léon Maître, *Dictionnaire topographique du département de la Mayenne* [Paris: Imprimerie Nationale, 1878], 90). This location put him in the same general region as Robert, Vitalis, and Bernard, although before their time.

23 This story resembles two told about St. Benedict. In the first, there is no actual woman. Benedict is simply overcome by the memory of a woman, but he throws himself into a patch of thorns and nettles. As in this story, physical pain drives away desire (Gregory the Great, *Dialogues*, 60). In the second story, a priest who envies him sends seven women to dance in the monastery garden in hopes of tempting some of his monks. Benedict, thanks to his earlier romp in the nettles, is immune to desire, but he fears for his monks and so leaves (71–2).

When the woman saw this, she let out a sobbing cry. She fell at the feet of the saint and with tearful groans she begged mercy for her insanity. She said,

> "Have mercy, most holy priest, have mercy on this most miserable of sinners, since she was sent to you by the worst advice, fraudulently to stain your holy innocence."

But when those evil-doers saw her, they were led to repent. They broke in through a back door, beating on their breasts, tearing their hair, and also begging mercy with groans on high for their boldness. But this outstandingly gentle man, giving thanks for their repentance, sent them away with her absolved. They went back and they did not cease to preach everywhere about what had happened. The people ran together, set alight with marvelous love, to accost such a great man.[24] But the servant of God, fearing to be driven by the breeze of popular renown, secretly left that place.

Crucifying the world for himself and himself for the world,[25] remembering in his frequent meditation what great things the Lord suffered on the cross for his sake, he took up his cross to visit the holy places of Jerusalem and began to follow in the tracks of the Lord. But because after the inhabitants had expelled men of the Christian religion, they ruled Jerusalem with pagan rites and their unchecked power extended all around, so when he came to Outremer[26] he left the direct route and with many companions entered certain byways.

When they came to the dry wastes of the deserts, what with the heat of the summer and the sweat of their labor and the dryness of the region, they developed an immense thirst. Their guts were tormented inside and the dry pathway of their arteries caused their life-giving breath to falter. The thirsty explorer races all around through the valleys and thick woods, wherever any sort of scanty little spring might gush out or where a marsh might exude at least some sort of meager liquid. No rivulet of spring water, no marsh seeping anything but gravel is discovered, only that when they seek to treat the illness, the search to find a remedy makes the illness worse.

When they had been abandoned by human aid, the sentiment took root more strongly that they should beg for divine help with the man of God[27] mediating for them. This immensely kind man had compassion on their wretchedness and with

---

24 Pigeon's text reads *tantam*, where the *Acta sanctorum* version reads *tantum*, modifying "man."
25 There are echoes here of Gregory the Great's commentary on the Song of Songs, without there being any exact quotation.
26 Outremer = *cismarinum regionem*. I've translated the Latin into the contemporary French name for the crusader kingdoms (which did not yet exist in Firmat's day).
27 Pigeon: *Dei vivo mediante*; AASS: *Dei viro mediante*.

his knees on the earth but his mind open to the heavens, drenched with the dew of tears, out of his sorrow he poured out this suit.[28]

> "Omnipotent God, Creator of the elements, Whose most clement will every created thing miraculously obeys, Who produced water from a stone for Your people making their way through the deserts to the Promised Land (Exod. 17), manifest the amazing power of Your virtue through Your mercy toward this group of people, who are worn out by burning thirst. Open a vein of living water for us, so that this people, freed from thirst and refreshed by Your sustenance, may preach Your great deeds everywhere."

When he had said these things, the most holy confessor Firmat, seizing hold of the Holy Spirit with his entire mind, understood that his prayers had been heard. When he had made the sign of the Lord's cross on the ground, he fixed the staff he carried to support him on the road to the dry crest of the mountain. When it was pulled out, a spring of clear water, smelling very sweet and tasting very healthful, bubbled abundantly forth and began to irrigate the sloping valleys. And thus marveling, the people came together from all around, and when they had gratefully cooled their thirsty heat at the fountain's new sweetness, bedewed with joyful tears, they extolled the power of God with the prayers they owed Him. They embraced Firmat's feet and called him the author of their salvation. They were joyful about their present health, but more that they were glorified by having such a great companion given to them, one who might put the present plague to flight and also make them more secure in their future well-being.

It happened on that same journey that the man of God left the known area of the paths with his companions and not knowing what road he was on, he wandered through long and circuitous ways. And when in their usual manner, his companions sought his help, he sought the help of the Lord. And lo! a raven that he had raised in his little dwelling and that he had not seen for a long time cried out with a loud call, beckoning with its wagging tail and flitting about with a swooping feather. And it began to show them the path through the byways, going in front like a leader. The man of God understood that divine help was before him, and that the One who fed Elijah by the river Cherith (1 Kings 17:1–7) through the service of a raven led Firmat, who was climbing through the desert, a raven leading him. The raven, however, ate human provisions and directing the steps of men,

---

28 Suit = *quaerimoniam* (*querimoniam*). Because the word can have strong legal implications, I have translated it as suit, as in lawsuit. One might expect that instead of sorrow (*compunctio*), which can also mean remorse, the text would read *compassio* (compassion), but the two transcriptions agree here.

it tamely took food from the human hand offering it. And whenever the route was unknown, the raven always went in front of the voyagers.

However, just as the Lord tests his chosen ones in the furnace [cf. Wisd. 3.6], Firmat was cooked in the fire of tribulation in just this way.[29] In case any unpurged small and rusty stain should perhaps have clung to the man of God, God permitted him to be captured by his enemies in the land of Jerusalem, to be bound, beaten, and in the end to be delivered into prison. At various times he was forced to go on all fours with heavy weights put on his back, which dug into his back with their attached spines. But Firmat, this most powerful athlete of God, patiently endured it, undergoing all these torments with a joyful face, and although the death as a martyr that he desired did not follow, there was no lack of the torment or cause of martyrdom. But God's kindly disposition delivered him from this prison when and as He wished. And because he had suffered so many and such torments for Christ in prison, the Lord granted him through His Grace afterward that while Firmat was alive and after that, when many people in prison shackles called upon Firmat's name, they would be released from their prisons by divine aid. A few of these miracles will be told individually in what follows.

Chapter II

When he returned to Gaul, William lived the holy life, primarily at Mantilly. He shone with miracles and prophecies.

Now that he had completed the pilgrimage he had proposed to undertake, he entered holy Jerusalem and the human mind is not able to describe in every detail the tears of compunction and joy he shed when he was visiting the holy places. And after he had stayed there for a few days, he decided to return via Constantinople. He longed with a sweet desire to visit the bounds of the apostles, whose bodies were buried there with marvelous honor.[30] However, when he came to Constantinople, directed there by the will of God, the bishop of the church of that city had died and the neighboring fellow bishops had come together to choose another bishop.[31] They begged the Lord with tears and prayers for a worthy pastor,

---

29 In addition to its appearance in the Bible, this passage also appears in the liturgy of masses for martyrs and all saints. See the "Cantus" site.

30 Pigeon (2) offers the information that the tomb of St. Andrew was there, and that there were also relics of St. James the Lesser (46n1). At this point, the *Acta sanctorum* version skips to his arrival in Brittany. The text is given, however, at 338na.

31 The text, which is clearly faulty in some places, has *coepiscopi*. It isn't clear, however, whether *chorepiscopi* wasn't intended. This would be *suffragans* (the bishops under the authority of an archbishop). I have gone with what the Latin actually says here, however.

ordaining a three-day fast. And when they sat in that church on the appointed election day awaiting a single sign from God, they did not dare to elect anyone. And lo! Firmat entered that church to pray. Then informed by a divine revelation, the bishops laid hands on him and ordained him the bishop with praises and canticles and without delay, while he refused and cried out that he was unworthy. Therefore, now that he had been made a bishop, it is not possible to say with what vigilant guardianship the careful pastor kept watch over his flock. And when the proclamation of his holiness was made public in brief, the greatest honor was paid to him. But because he had always abhorred public reputation and he had been forced to receive the burden of this honor, and because he judged the solitary life was a quicker route to the joys of [eternal] life, he thought to return to Gaul, if an appropriate moment should arise for him to do so.

Therefore, one day when a solemn feast was imminent, the noblemen of his church came to him. They said,

> "Father Firmat, tomorrow we are supposed to go in procession and when we cross in front of the palace of the prince, upon whose alms our church depends, we have to make a processional halt in reverence for our prince and in his honor.[32] The observance of this halt in the customary manner has always been demanded of us as an obligation whenever this solemn day rolls around. We have taken care to explain this to you, so that in consenting to our custom, you may not presume to offend our prince."[33]

Firmat said, "By no means! By no means is the honor owed to the creator to be given to any created thing! I know who said, 'You should adore your Lord and serve him alone' [Matt. 4:10, Luke 4:8]. Therefore, while I should be pleased to serve the King, I judge it is of no import to displease an earthly king or prince."

Saying these things, he would not agree to their persuasions. And when he was following the procession the next day, when he passed by the palace of this prince (whose mind was unstable), while the others were making their obeisance, the prince who was standing there and seeing that he was deprived of the honor of his

---

32 Processional halt = *statio*. While this can mean just a stop, it is also the name given to halts for prayers in religious processions in Rome. While the word is obviously related to the "stations" of the Cross, these are much later in origin.

33 What is being described here is rather obscure. First the custom is described as a *superstitio*, or observance marked by fear or false belief. It is not clear what goes on during the halt, but the implication is that the members of the procession were perhaps expected to prostrate themselves, rather than simply show respect or say prayers for the prince. It was custom to perform *proskynesis* (prostration) before the emperor, so this story may reflect tensions between westerners and eastern Romans in the twelfth century.

obeisance, threatens the bishop with death, the clergy with exile, and the church with destruction. Afterward, the clergy urged him to make peace with the prince, giving consent to the custom.

Firmat said, "Look for, I ask you to look for, a bishop for your church. For of my own free will I now put down the burden I was forced to pick up. May the Lord be with you and may God arrange my paths well."

Saying this, he put down his pastoral staff in their presence. The clergy guessed that he had done this in anger and they thought that on the morrow they might soften his rage, but Firmat, in the silence of the dead of night, wishing to devote himself to God alone, left the gates of the city secretly, solitary and alone, and took to the road, the raven again directing his steps, so that when they looked for him, he would not be found.

When the next day dawned and the bishop's departure became known, the clergy raised a huge outcry. A tearful tumult arose and many wailing folks ran to the house of the bishop. The city was stirred up; the people wept; the clergy lamented and they confessed that they had lost the bishop given to them by God on account of their sins. The prince repented and sent messengers all around, commanding them to seek out the bishop, and when they found him, to bring him back with the honor due him. Some of the clergy even followed his path as far as Gaul, where they asked him, with prayers and tears, to make his presence known. But God's confessor Firmat obtained his desire by the grace of God; while he was looked for by many people in many places, he did not wish to be discovered by any of those seeking him. Instead, with God's providence directing his steps until he came to Brittany, he stayed for a time in the region of Vitré, where in the parish of Dourdain,[34] he opened the earth with his staff and poured in the water he had taken with him from the Jordan river and called upon the name of Christ. A perpetual spring of clear liquid then emanated from it. In memory of this miracle, it is called the spring of St. Firmat by the inhabitants of this little place.

When, as a result, he was given the worthy reverence for this new miracle, he avoided being honored by men and went alone to the place that is called Fontaine-Géhard and from there to Savigny.[35] He established two little dwellings in

---

34 Dourdan in Breton. This is a place in Brittany, but again, close to the places where the other holy men lived. Dourdain is 25 km from Fougères by modern roads.

35 The *AASS* suggests that this place, Fons-Gihardi, might be Gahard in Brittany, which is about 15 km as the crow flies from Dourdain (339nd). However, there was a Fontaine-Géhard, where there was a priory of Marmoutiers, near Mayenne, in the canton of Châtillon-sur-Colmont (Maître, *Dictionnaire topographique*, 128). It is about 38 km to Savigny from Châtillon-sur-Colmont.

these places. He didn't stay there for a long time but from there went to Mantilly. Finding there the best habitation and the one most suitable for himself, it pleased him to stay there for a while.

So then he made himself a little dwelling pleasing to himself, where he entered a marvelous battle with the devil, engaged in amazing abstinence, fasting, vigils, and prayers. His virtue grew with the desire for such parsimony that many times when evening came he broke his fast with roots. His little bed, covered with a small strewing of twigs, was encircled by four trunks connected in a square. In the middle of this squared off place was a three-footed stool, upon which Firmat sat and sang hymns at night and when sometimes he swayed, forced to do so by sleep, the stool, made in this fashion, fell down and dumped the man sitting on it. Thus wakening from sleep at once, Firmat sang psalms and hymns and fought against drowsiness to the degree that human frailty permits. When at last he succumbed to the sleep where the blow of the falling stool sent him, he took a brief nap and thus never did he take off his clothing, belt, or footwear at night.

The devil, that enemy of holiness, envied him and miserably attacked him many nights, appearing to the sight as a loathsome and horrible sort of creature. But that man was of unconquered strength, that athlete was of wondrous patience, that minister was of kindly humility, that man was wounded by love.[36] For so much had God's charity wounded his heart with such ardor that from the day on which he gave his property to the poor, he had not received a penny. Whether he was a bishop or a hermit and he sang a mass, if anyone offered him silver or placed gold on the altar, he hated the sight of any coins; he accepted bread and honey and other foods to eat. But whatever was offered to him, whether during the mass or in his cell, if someone was there asking for alms, he gave it all to the one begging and kept nothing for himself. He didn't care what he ate or drank. Many times he even forgot that he had not eaten any food and he sought his evening couch fasting.

One day a builder built his little dwelling for the love of God and the prayers of the blessed bishop, and because the laborer is worthy of his food [Matt. 10:10],[37] the builder had provided no food for himself, believing that he would be properly

---

36 There are echoes here of commentaries on the Song of Songs, 2 and 4, where the term is not *caritas*, but *amor*, but the notion of love being a wound that opens the heart is present.

37 The *Acta sanctorum* version omits the word *operarius* (workman). It appears in the original biblical passage, however. Later in this story, Stephen will draw on the other version of the phrase in Luke 10:7, where the worker is said to be worthy of his reward.

fed by this man of such great charity. When midday came, his servant Aubert came to him. He said,

> "May your charity provide me, my lord, with food for your worker, since your generosity has left no food in your little hut."

The holy hermit answered, "God will provide victuals for his servants, my son."

Now when the sun was declining toward evening, lo! a boy came bearing four loaves of bread, which a matron who was well known to him had sent, and he gave them to the man of God. When he had accepted these loaves with thanks, along came a poor little man asking for alms. The holy priest gave him the four loaves of bread and he sent the man away from his little hut happy. Aubert was outraged at this and rebuked God's saint with these words:

> "Your workman put up with both burden and heat until the eleventh hour of the day[38] and lo, he is fasting and thirsty, and you sent someone unconnected to you away loaded down with bread, and you didn't hold back one scrap for your workman. What should we do for him, because I don't have anything to put before him?! You are accustomed to preach what is written. The reward for your worker should not wait until tomorrow on your part. What reward will follow if the builder is sent away, melting in the heat, worn out with the work and fasting, and broken down by hunger?"

The saint said to him, "O man of little faith,[39] God does not desert those who hope in him, as he said, 'Do not worry, saying what shall we eat or what shall we drink? For your father knows what you need' [Matt. 6:31–2]. Go, set the table and call the workman. If you are just, God will not trouble the soul of the just man with hunger."

When he had set the table, although they had nothing to put on it, the sound of knocking was heard at the door of the hut. Aubert came out in his usual way to announce to his lord who it was. And lo, there was a serene youth with a shining face, smelling of ethereal perfume, resplendent with white robes, carrying three loaves in a pristine cape.

Aubert admired his beauty and ran to announce this to the lord.

"Go and take what the young man has brought," said the holy priest. "The one who brought it has already gone."

---

38 There's an echo of Matt. 20:9, Christ's parable of the vineyard, in the reference to the eleventh hour.
39 Cf. Matt. 6:30, 8:26, 14:31, 16:8.

The good servant went and found three loaves. He found no trace of the youth and rejoicing, he carried in the loaves for himself and the workman. From the first taste, they were restored with such pure fullness that it was evident to all that these were angelic loaves. But the blessed priest and bishop of God Firmat, alone in his chamber as was his custom and removed from them all, took a small piece of the bread to feast upon with tears and gave appropriate thanks to God.

Arthur of Champeaux, who had been appointed the warden of the woods, was joined in sweet friendship with the holy man.[40] He was accustomed to come alone often to visit blessed Firmat. It happened one day that Arthur, to hasten his journey to the holy man, took a path through the deserted part of the wood unarmed and on foot, but because he was sweating with the heat of the summer and of his labor, he took off the tunic that he was wearing and hung it on a stick and rested the stick on his neck. And lo, a little thief, lurking secretly in the hidey-holes of the woods, seized the tunic and took off running with rapid steps toward his lair. But Arthur, who was rushing along a shortcut toward God's saint, thought that the small delay needed to get his tunic back would be a very great loss: he thought that this had happened because of the wiliness of the devil, who wanted to prevent him from talking to the holy man. So continuing the journey he had begun, he found blessed Firmat reading in his hut. The saint said to him, smiling,[41]

"My friend, you have lost your tunic coming to us, but the tricks of the wily seducer will be of no profit, for he will return your garment to you."

Arthur said, "I think nothing of a trivial loss of this kind, when I am hastening to be refreshed by speaking with you."

So Arthur sat down and spent that day speaking about many things. Then suddenly the little thief [appeared and] fell at Firmat's feet, denuded of his own clothes and holding the tunic in his left hand and smith's tongs in the right. He said,

"Take these, Father, and inflict a proper punishment on the sinner who committed a nefarious theft against your friend."

---

40 Pigeon (1), 78, simply identifies this place (Campellis) as Champeaux. There was a Champeaux in Mayenne, in the canton of Évron, so perhaps this is the place. It is also possible that it was Campeaux in Calvados (*Orbis latinus: Lexikon lateinischer geographischer Namen des Mittelalters und der Neuzeit*, 3 vols. [Braunschweig, Germany: Klinkhardt & Biermann, 1972], 1: 399), which is not much further from Mantilly.

41 Pigeon has *subsidens* (sitting down or sinking down); the *Acta sanctorum* version *subridens* (smiling).

The saint said, "You have suffered enough torment up to now; may the Lord have mercy on you in the future. Give his tunic back to this man here and put your own tunic back on."

When the little thief was dressed in his own clothing, he confessed to the saint that when he was carrying off the other man's clothing, he was not able to go very far, and he returned many times to the saint's cell, and how even when he threw away the tunic he had taken wrongly, he did not get permission to go, but only to come to the saint for mercy. Firmat blessed the Lord and sent both of them away, the little thief happy about the mercy he had received, Arthur about the miracle.

A certain little woman gave the man of God three eggs and put them on the altar in his presence. When the saint saw this, he quietly murmured with a sweet whisper in the woman's ear,

> "Daughter, take this present that you have offered us improperly, because these eggs don't belong to me or you."

The woman, believing that the man of God did not know what he knew, said, "I have offered this little gift, whatever I am able in my poverty to give to your holiness."

The saint said, "Take it and place it on the ground."

When she had done that, two of them turned into little frogs. And the One who made a staff into a serpent to refute Pharaoh's incredulity [Exod. 7:8–10] made the eggs into little frogs to show the woman's untruthfulness. The woman was frightened, fell at the feet of the holy bishop, and confessed what she had done.

"Go," said the saint, "and give your neighbor back what is hers."

The woman left and returned the eggs, now restored to their earlier nature, as she had been commanded.

At that time Grimoard of Landivy,[42] who was very rich and was the provost of the region of Landivy, had a wife named Delice,[43] who was of the most savage inhumanity. Because she was the wife of an extremely merciful man, she seemed, to the holy bishop, to be a worthy person for him to rebuke, chiding and admonishing her. He went to her house to win her soul for Christ, and when he had been received with the honor due to him, he said this to her,

> "Why, daughter, do you run after transitory things? Why do you try to hang onto things that will fly away? The sheen of gold rusts; the clarity of gems

---

42 In northern Mayenne, about 20 km by modern roads from Mantilly and about 6 km from Savigny.

43 Delice = *Delicata*. While this is clearly a name, it is also clearly a description. The word *delicatus* can mean "refined," but also "soft" or "pampered." The sense of "pampered" seems to be meant here.

becomes clouded; the whiteness of clothing becomes darkened. So it is no wonder if the things destined for the body should perish when the beauty of the body itself perishes.[44] Tender youth passes and bent old age follows. But you, now rich in wealth, who scorn to relieve the miseries of the poor and turn a deaf ear to wretched people, in the course of your life will come to slim pickings. But rejoice, because in this way God will inflict severity on you in this world, so that he does not have to inflict a just and eternal revenge."

The woman was terrified by the prophecy, but although she was remorseful, she rejoiced in the promise. From that day forward and from then on she showed such great charity to the man of God that she wanted to serve him daily with food. So she sent a boy to the holy priest, entrusting some fish to him to be brought to St. Firmat with diligence. The boy, through a snare of the deceitful enemy, hid the two fish that seemed to him to be better in the hollow of a tree; he brought the others to be given to the man of God.

"I shall not accept those, my son, for myself," said Firmat. "I won't accept part of the devil's leavings. Take them, take them with you, I ask, and also those that you hid at the malicious prompting of the devil."

The boy, seeing that the saint knew both his action and its intention through the revelation of the holy spirit, fell to his feet and explained what he had done and offered many of his companions the fish he had hidden in the hollow trunk.

A certain priest was awake in his chamber when night had fallen, thinking in an admiring way about the life and miracles of St. Firmat, when lo! a voice came to him saying, "Rise up and seek fish and take the ones you have found to Bishop Firmat."

The priest rose up joyfully and looked for fish for the entire night. He found what he looked for and when he had found them, the joyful man purchased them and when he had purchased them, he brought them very joyfully [to the saint]. When he received them the next day, the holy father, smiling with holy laughter, said, "I do not thank you, but the one who spoke to you, who told you that you should bring these alms!" The priests rejoiced together, and each one commended the other to his prayers, kissing each other with a holy kiss.

Because a boy of damnable avarice had heard of Firmat's perfect charity, he went to the holy man to seek alms, but he collected a lot of bread in the meantime,

---

44 Pigeon reads *pereat corpori debita*; the *Acta sanctorum* version reads *pereant corpori debita*, which makes more grammatical sense. Pigeon may have ignored an abbreviation sign over the "a" in *pereat*, which would indicate an omitted "m" or "n," but it is worth remembering that he was reading the manuscript long after the *Acta* scholars were and that the writing may well have faded.

as was his habit. But when he drew near to the holy man's cell, he became afraid that nothing would be given to someone who had anything, so he hid the satchel, swollen with bread, in the dense bushes. Then standing before the saint, he asked for alms for God's charity.

"Go, my son," said the saint, "go, and eat the bread you have hidden and hasten to give the remainder to the needy, and when you will have done so, you can properly be a needy person and ask those who have a lot for alms."

Since he saw that what he had done was not hidden from the man of God, he went running to get the sack and falling at the feet of the saint, he asked for forgiveness.

Chapter III

His stay on the Rhône. His return to Mantilly and his death.

Arthur of Champeaux and William Espechellus, a man from that neighborhood who was very well known for his goodness and wealth, went one day to St. Firmat.

"Father," they said, "permit us to make a little pool for the beauty and utility of this place and the people who live here."

The saint said, "No construction is needed here for those seeking the future city. Rather the little stream of my spring by itself suffices for me."

These barons judged that the man of God would be pleased by something other than what he said, and when they had gathered their men, they began raise a pile [of dirt] in a well-packed heap. And when one day the workmen were doing the work they had begun, Aubert, the saint's servant, began to work with a tool he had picked up. Then one of the workmen, whose tool it was, unwisely grabbed the tool with a shove, and threw Aubert to the ground while Firmat was watching. The saint was sad that this injury had been inflicted on his servant and on the following night, he secretly left. And hastening his path through Gaul, he came to the place called Yenne on the Rhône.[45] There on an island that was washed on both sides by the Rhône, he found a little hut pleasing to him on one bank, and he stayed there for quite a while. This renowned man, an old man with venerable white hair, went to Jerusalem again, clad in a heavy breastplate but barefoot; he got there and then came back to this same place.

But from the day he left Mantilly, Arthur of Champeaux and William Espechellus spent their life sobbing and in tears and they insisted that war and continual

---

45 Eona (see *Orbis latinus*, 2: 23). There is actually a small island in the Rhône at Yenne (which is located in Savoy).

famine would occur in those parts after Firmat's departure and because of his departure. So therefore when they had gotten good advice, they set out on pilgrimage, barefoot and dressed in linen, and they resolved not to return without bringing the saintly bishop back. In the meantime, everyone in the whole neighborhood of Mantilly kept praying and fasting. These two, as they made their journey, begged with tears and prayers for the location of the holy bishop to be revealed to them. The Lord found their devotion acceptable, and he led them in a prosperous voyage to the place where St. Firmat lived. When they had persisted in their prayers, going as far as the lower bank of the Rhone, lo! there was a fisherman there sent by God, who had pulled a little boat up on the bank, in which he brought the pilgrims who were inquiring after Blessed Firmat from where he lived to that place. When Arthur and William entered the little cell and saw the man they desired to see, they were filled with such joy that they fell to the ground, embraced his feet, and held them in ecstasy for a while. And when at length they could find voice for their intention, they made this complaint.

"Why, best of fathers, did you leave the sons who you consoled with paternal affection desolate by your absence? Why did you subject the people who you nourished by your aid to war, famine, death, and exile by your departure? We ask you, Father, look upon the affliction of your sons, and make haste to return so that you may give them the usual solace. As God is our witness,[46] we either will die of sorrow here or go back joyful in the certainty of your return."

This outstandingly gentle man could not restrain his tears and he raised them up for a kiss. He said, "Cease, my sons! Cease to scorch me with your reproaches. My departure from you was caused by God's will and it will be his will that I return to you. Go back and plant my little garden."

And when they set a day when he was supposed to return to them, the pilgrims started back to their country joyfully. When they had gotten back, they announced Firmat's coming everywhere. And lo, on the hour of the day appointed, Firmat came through the woods of Mantilly alone. The rejoicing people ran up and they received their holy father with filial honor. They rejoiced that they had gotten their pastor back and gloried that their sterility had been driven away.

It happened that a citizen of Tours, a woman related to the blessed man, had an only son who had been put in chains. Rushing to the man of God night and day, the pitiable woman sped along her way, asking that her son be returned by the

---

46 As God is our witness = *Vivit Dominus* (as God lives). This idiom appears frequently in the Vulgate.

prayers of Firmat. She was in no doubt. When she knocked at the door of his hut, the servant came out and announced that his relative had come.

"Go," said the holy man, "and tell her that Firmat says this: 'Go in certainty that you will get your son back released and exonerated.' But she will not see my face."

The servant went out and passed on what he had been ordered to say. The woman left sad because she had not seen the saint, but joyful about the promise. And when she neared Tours, lo! her son came to her carrying his chains and shackles and said that he had escaped from danger through the prayers of the saint.

In that time Delice of Landivy, whose husband Grimoard had died in peace, had come to be very poor, just as the saint had prophesied. When she knew of the return of her friend, she gratefully ran to him very quickly and speaking about her current fear and future blessedness, she shed a lot of tears for each. The saint spoke words of exhortation to her and invited her to celestial delights. When she was getting ready to leave, she said,

> "Is there anything, Father, that you wish your handmaid to bring you? And any food that you would take from my hand?"

"Bring honey," said the saint, "when you return."

Delice left and when she asked around the territories and byways, she did not find it. Finally, a farmer she did not know produced some honeycombs for sale. Since she did not have anything else to give, she sold the cow, which was the only thing she possessed to sustain life, to the honey seller for the honey. She put it in a very clean vessel and came to the man of God walking as quickly as possible. Firmat said, taking the honey with thanks,

> "You sold your cow, my daughter, for the honey. God will give you the honied sweetness of the celestial life for this honey."

> "How happy I am, Father," she said, "that you would take something to eat from my hands."

And lo, there was a leper nearby who was asking for alms. This perfectly charitable man gave him all of the honey with joy. Delice, taking this badly, said,

> "Why, Father, did you not even keep the tiniest part for yourself?"

The saint said, "I asked for the honied charity of your mind, and fed by this, I wanted to refresh the leper with your honey."

Afterward, the honey seller came back to Delice and said, "I sinned in taking the cow for a modest amount of honey. Take your beast, but I ask you to make me a co-donor of your alms."

So thus it happened that the honey benefited all four of them: Delice and the countryman had a sign of their charity; Firmat had the sweetness of charity; and the leper had food to satiate himself.

Firmat was a man of such kindliness that birds, which flee from the sight of men, accepted food from his offering hand and eased the winter cold hiding under his garments. When he sat on the bank of the little pool and scattered breadcrumbs, a multitude of fish raced to him and were taken from the water unmoving by this gentle man's hand, but the saint then put them back in the vortex unharmed.

One day Aubert came running to St. Firmat and said,

"Holy Father, a huge boar is digging with his hooked tusk in the garden and is digging up the planted stalks."

The saint came to the boar, gently seized his ears, and shut him, now rendered tame, in the cell. And commanding him to fast, he kept him shut up during the night. The next morning he let him go, having commanded him not to dig any more in his garden. Similarly he forced goats and hares to come to him and giving them a gentle swat, forbade them to go into the garden. But as he was horrified by the entry of other townsfolk, he often went to Mortain to pray.[47]

So as the Lord wished to reward his worn-out soldier, who was unceasingly engaged in heavy labor, He let him know the day of his death, when he would be perennially refreshed by celestial rest. Firmat told his servants and also predicted many things in the spirit of prophecy. And dying in his little bed, his mind alert, his face serene, his voice sweet, he said farewell to the brothers and travelled to the Lord – to whom belong honor and glory forever and ever – on the eighth Kalends of May [April 24].

Chapter IV

The story of his translation and miracles.

Joscelin and Hubert, two of the canons of St. Évroul,[48] heard about blessed Firmat's death when they were coming from Gorron,[49] and sped up their journey so

---

47 Mantilly is about 20 km from Mortain by modern roads.
48 The collegiate church at Mortain was dedicated to St. Évroul.
49 Pigeon (2), 36n1, reports that the canons had been given the tithes and property in this place by Count Robert.

they would be present at his funeral. And when they were rushing there impetuously, while Joscelin's horse was running flat out, he lost his maniple.[50] When they completed the journey they had begun, the canon, who was a man of good will, thought this loss was trivial. And when he had shown proper observance at the funeral for St. Firmat, he suddenly discovered his maniple under his feet, and joyful concerning the miracle that had occurred, he revealed the sign to the people standing around.

On the eleventh day, the people of Domfront gathered in their region and the army of Mayenne in theirs to carry the body of St. Firmat off to their strongholds. But blessed Évroul of Mortain was chosen as the more worthy church, which according to the holy man's prophecy, would be dedicated to his burial. For by the order of Count Robert of Mortain, the clergy gathered with innumerable people following the eleventh day after his death and they took the venerable body out of its coffin and carried it to Mortain with acclamations and hymns. When the people of Domfront and Mayenne came to Mantilly, they found the coffin empty, and they returned in tears following their vain journey.

So when people were deciding on a worthy receptacle for his burial, they said,

"There is a sarcophagus at Maisoncelles[51] that no man can move. Michael, the bishop of Avranches, wanted to be buried in it.[52] But then Viscount Gilbert died and they wanted to put his body in the sarcophagus, but it remained immovable. Perhaps Divine Providence has reserved it for St. Firmat!"

So four men went there and lifted the sarcophagus onto a wagon without difficulty, and drove it in an easy passage to Mortain. And when they asked where in the church they ought to put it, the people who were there said that when St. Firmat washed his hands upon entering the church and going to the Holy of Holies, he said that the place where water dripped from the hands of the priest was a suitable place for the burial of clerics. So the sarcophagus was put there and the body of the saint was put in it and such a great smell of the sweetest odor wafted over the people standing about that even though it happened thirteen days after the death of the saint, the glory of the holy confessor was evident. For after that at his burial, hearing came to the deaf, vision to the blind, free movement to the

---

50 A liturgical garment, a strip of cloth worn on the left arm.
51 This is a very common name in the region, but perhaps Maisoncelles-la-Jourdan, about 23 km by modern roads from Mortain and about 50 km from Avranches.
52 Michael I of Avranches died in 1094 (*GC* 11: 477).

lame, cure to those possessed by demons, health to the sick, and purification to the leprous, under his patronage. Many people were freed from dungeons and chains, by God's aid, when they invoked his name.

In those days, Baldwin, a man of great name, illustrious in character and arms, the future king of Jerusalem was present. He was imprisoned, shackled with chains and leg-irons, in a prison dungeon by Robert, the most noble count of Mortain.[53] Begging the aid of Blessed Firmat with tireless prayers, worn out by the care of his vigil, he gave his limbs over to a little sleep. And lo, a handsome man with a rosy face, a man worthy of reverence with venerable white hair, sweet-spoken with a honied voice, appeared to him and gave him this advice.

"Tomorrow, brother, when you have a mass celebrated in the church of Saint-Évroul for the soul of Firmat and the souls of all the faithful, call upon the assistance of God with your prayers."

Therefore, when he got permission on the following day to enter the church, Count Baldwin requested a mass next to the tomb of Blessed Firmat as he had been advised to do: and lo, in that sacred hour when the host is broken, the rivets of the shackles, broken, leapt out with a long clang. The clergy was delighted about the miracle and the visionary dream and the miracle of the breaking was told to Count Robert.

"If it is the case," said Count Robert, "that this breaking happened through divine power, what it shattered once, it can shatter again. For I do not wish such a redemption of such a man to be spoiled by a falsified prelude."

They brought heavier and tighter shackles and Count Baldwin returned to his prison, as he had promised. Therefore, while a great multitude of the clergy and people were weeping, Baldwin left the church, bound with the heaviest of chains. Then on the following night, this same man telling him the same things appeared and on the next day, in the same place and at the same hour, while the clergy, along with the count and people were awaiting the outcome and everyone was watching, the web of chains was broken with a clang. Count Robert, who was joyful at the miracle, sent Count Baldwin, who was also joyful, back to his own lands with

---

53 The context of these events isn't entirely clear, nor that Baldwin was ever a prisoner of Robert of Mortain. He did have Norman connections, as he was at the Tosny court in 1090 and he married a Tosny (Heather Tanner, *Families, Friends, and Allies: Boulogne and Politics in Northern France and England, c. 879–1160* [Leiden: Brill, 2003], 133). His family was allied with Robert of Mortain in the succession struggles following the death of William the Conqueror, in support of Robert Curthose, duke of Normandy, so there is some connection, but not one, as far as I can find, of enmity.

the greatest honor. The shackles to this day are kept in the church in honor of the miracle.

In those days a poor little woman was hastening on her journey to St. Michael with some companions,[54] and when she heard about the celebrity of St. Firmat, she was struck with a burning desire to visit his tomb. While her company went on ahead, she rushed with a trembling step and a stuttering heart to satisfy her wish. When she entered the church of Mortain, the doorkeeper who was appointed to take care of the tomb was nowhere to be found, although they looked for him. However, because she was impatient about the delay, she bent her knees, beat her breast, and raised her heart to heaven along with her hands, and begged with sighs and groans for the doors of the shrine to be opened for her. And lo, while many people were standing around, the latch with the bolts and bars melted and bent as though a hand had flung it and struck the wood that stood across from it. The doors opened by themselves and the woman entered, and left happy at her entry.

There was a certain very rich old man in Barneville,[55] but he had been troubled for a long time with stone. Since he did not dare to entrust his members to any doctors because of his feeble old age, he pleaded with prayers for divine medicine to come to him. So then one night he was admonished in his dreams to go to the tomb of St. Firmat and to ask for help there. He feared to believe the vision, because he was not yet of perfect faith, but reinforced by a second and third vision, considering how he might carry out what he had seen, he fell asleep. He was astonished then, when he found the stone, the cause of his illness, next to him and he was healthy. Therefore, the next day, putting aside all his business, he went to the tomb of the saint and giving thanks to God, he left the stone for the canons.

Two knights from the court of the count of Mortain went into the church of St. Évroul and prayed at each of the altars. Then one of them said to the other,

"Let's go to ask for help at the tomb of St. Firmat."

"By no means," said the other. "I won't invoke the patronage of Firmat any more than of any other dead man."

Then when the first man rebuked the other man and bent his knee before the tomb of the saint, the other was seized with a sudden paralysis and fell headlong to the earth. The first man ran out yelling, stirred by the outcry of the sick man, and carried the sick man in front of the tomb of Firmat. But God, the Holy of Holies,

---

54 Mont Saint-Michel.
55 Perhaps Barneville (now Barneville-la-Bertran) in Normandy.

having shown the holiness of His saint, restored the sick man to his earlier health through the prayers of Firmat.

A deacon in the city of Bayeux had been afflicted by a grave weakness for seven years and had paid all his possessions to the doctors in vain, until he promised that he would visit the tomb of Firmat. And so he could carry out the vow, he had a cart prepared for himself. And he who had kept to his bed for seven years, in a brief moment was made whole. He went on foot to the tomb of the saint in the company of both his parents and a great multitude of relatives.

A fishbone was lodged in the throat of a good family man at Caen. He daily strove to expel it, as it caused him the most serious pain, and when he could not do this for many days, at length he fled to the aid of blessed Firmat, pleading that he should help him. At once, the bone was expelled and the healthy man went without delay to Mortain and gave thanks to the author of his health at the tomb of the saint.

A certain matron put a candle on the altar upon which the saint had many times celebrated the divine office. It did not cease to shine, as no one put it out, and it burned all night on the altar. The next day, however, when they discovered the embers and saw that the altar linen was not burned, the clerics gave thanks to God.

GLOSSARY OF TERMS AND CONCEPTS

✠

abbey: A **monastery** or **convent** headed by an abbot or abbess.

Acta sanctorum: A collection of **hagiographies**, organized according to the day of the year upon which the saint's cult was celebrated, created in the seventeenth and eighteenth centuries by Jesuit scholars attempting to put hagiography on a scientific footing.

against the grain: See **reading against the grain**.

ancient source: A source from the past that is not contemporary with the material it describes, but may be all that has survived. See also **primary source**.

archdeacon: The highest-ranked member of a cathedral **chapter** after the bishop. The archdeacon typically held a court and supervised business for the **diocese** in the Middle Ages.

Augustinians: Clergy who live in a community and follow the rule of St. Augustine, a rule for **canons** and canonesses. The Augustinians are regular canons.

Beguines: Women who lead a religious life, praying and doing good works, although they take no vows. Some medieval Beguines were organized into informal communities; some lived in association with established religious communities; and some simply lived on their own. Eventually, the Church would require all such women to live in communities; a few such communities still exist.

Benedictines: Monks and **nuns** who follow a rule composed by St. Benedict of Nursia in the sixth century. Although the Benedictines are sometimes spoken of as an order, Benedictine **abbeys** that were not affiliated with **Cluny** or with the **Cistercian order** were generally independent of each other.

bias in sources: What scholars mean by bias in sources is not willful distortion but rather the ways in which our sources can give us only a limited view of the past. That limitation may be caused by the kinds of sources a scholar looks at, by the patterns of survival of sources, or by the kinds of sources a period in the past produced in the first place.

calendar: The month-by-month lists of important church festivals and the days dedicated to the saints venerated by the Church at large, along with more local saints venerated by people in a particular institution.

Camaldoli: An order established at that location in Italy by St. Romuald that combined groups of **monks** and **hermits** (see **clergy**). The monks supported the hermits. There are still Camaldolensian communities today.

canon: This title might be given to the men serving as priests in a **collegiate church**, to priests who live in community and follow a rule for canons (regular canons), or for members of a cathedral **chapter**. This word also refers to an individual church law. A canon can also be a list: this is the "canon" in "**canonization**" (a person is being added to a list of official saints). Pay attention to the context when deciding which is meant!

canonization: The formal recognition of an individual as a saint. Early saints were not formally canonized but simply regarded as holy by their communities. In the twelfth century, a trio of bishops had the authority to formally recognize an individual as a saint, but in the thirteenth century, the power definitively to declare someone a saint became a monopoly of the papacy, as it is today.

canon law: The law of the Church, derived from the Bible, the writings of the Fathers of the Church (influential Christian writers writing up to the mid-seventh century), church councils and synods, and papal letters, called **decretal letters**, that set out legal opinions. Individual laws are also called **canons**. The legal theorists who developed canon law are called canonists.

cantor: The official who organizes the musical services of a church or **monastery**.

Carthusians: An order of **hermits**, founded by St. Bruno of Cologne, supported by **lay brothers** who interact with the outside world on their behalf. Their **monasteries** are generally referred to as charterhouses.

cartulary: A collection of the **charters** of an institution, copied into a book. These might be copied verbatim from the individual documents into the cartulary or they might be abbreviated or even "doctored" to make them more advantageous to the institution. Scholars sometimes also use the term to refer to all the charters of a given institution (whether gathered together or not), but that is not how I use the term in this book. Sometimes a writer would incorporate a **monastery**'s charters into the history of the institution. This would be a cartulary chronicle.

chancellor: The top official of a **chancery**.

chancery/chancellery: The office that produced official documents for the king of England or other powerful figures. The head of that office was a **chancellor**.

chaplain: A priest who serves in a private chapel or serves a specific individual or group. Royal chaplains served the king, holding services in his personal chapel and hearing his confession.

chapter: Various groups of **clergy** are called chapters. A cathedral chapter consists of the priests (called **canons**) who are appointed to serve in the cathedral. Like the canons of **collegiate churches**, they held **prebends** in the Middle Ages. Monastic chapters are gatherings of the **monks**, usually daily, to conduct monastic business, which they do in the chapter house of the **monastery**.

charter: A formal document created to record a transaction, such as a sale or donation of land, generally with some proof of authenticity such as a seal or a list of witnesses. Sometimes one or the other party in this kind of transaction would want to secure it further by getting a higher authority to confirm it in writing. That document would also be a charter.

chirograph: A special kind of **charter**, often recording an agreement, where two copies were made on the same sheet of parchment. The word *chirographum* would be written between the two copies and then the copies would be cut apart through the word using a zig-zagged line. Each side would sign and seal the other side's copy, so if there was a dispute the two documents could be matched up like pieces of a puzzle.

Christian apologists: Defenders of Christianity before Christianity was legalized in 313. Apology in this usage means "defense," not saying one is sorry for something (a **term of art**!).

Cistercian order: A monastic order founded in 1098 at Cîteaux, by monks seeking to follow the rule of St. Benedict as it had been originally written and intended. Unlike older **Benedictine** monasteries, the Cistercians had a centralized structure, with Cîteaux as the mother house. Four other houses – Clairvaux, Morimund, Pontigny, and La Ferté – were all founded directly from Cîteaux as daughter-houses, and all new **monasteries** in the order belonged to the "**filiation**" of one of these four houses (think of filiations as family trees). Relations among the houses were outlined in the *Charter of Love*, which supplemented the *Rule of St. Benedict*. Savigny, when it entered the Cistercian order, was assigned to the filiation of Clairvaux.

clergy: People who had entered some sort of religious orders, sometimes simply referred to as clerics. **Secular clergy** were all male and held either minor orders (which permitted them to marry) or major orders (subdeacon, deacon, priest) that from the high Middle Ages on barred them from marrying. They served outside of regular orders. **Regular clergy** were men and women who had joined a religious order that had a rule (**monks**, nuns, **canons**, and canonesses in this period). People in these orders lived together and did not marry.

Many rules required them to give up personal property as well. **Hermits** might live by themselves or in informal communities with individual huts, or they might belong to an order of hermits like **Camaldoli** or the **Carthusians**.

Cluny: A **monastery** founded in 910 to reinvigorate monastic life. It became extremely influential and **monks** from the monastery reformed many other monasteries and were asked to found others. It eventually became an order, although the Cluniacs followed the **Benedictine** rule and so are considered Benedictine monks.

collegiate church: A church served by a group of priests called secular **canons**, each of whom received an income, called a **prebend**, from a property endowment given to that church.

community of prayers: Monasteries and other churches routinely asked other religious institutions to pray for their members, offering prayers in return. These institutions were said to belong to a community of prayers.

context: See **historical context**.

convent: A **monastery** for nuns (female **monks**).

cult (of a saint): The veneration of a particular saint. Elements of the cult are the **liturgies** used in celebrating the saint and the altars and churches dedicated to that saint. This use of the word is quite different from the modern way in which the word "cult" is used to suggest a small and secretive religious group.

decretal letters: Papal letters providing a legal opinion on religious matters. While letters of early popes were incorporated into **canon law**, from the twelfth century on, papal rulings formed new canon law.

demesne: The land possessed by a lord that was directly cultivated for him or her, as opposed to lands farmed by peasants in exchange for providing rents and/or services.

diocese: the area over which a bishop has religious jurisdiction. An archbishop not only has a diocese of his own but also has authority over a group of other dioceses; that grouping is called a province.

documentary sources: Sources created to provide records for contemporary use. These would include **charters,** treaties, tax records, censuses, and the like.

Dominicans: The order founded in 1217 by St. Dominic to combat heresy through preaching (the official name is the "Order of Preachers"). Although different from the **Franciscans** in origin, the Dominicans became more similar to them in time and, together with the Franciscans, are often referred to as "friars" (brothers).

easement: The right to use a piece of property that a person does not own for a specific and limited purpose. Modern easements may include the right to cross someone's land if one does no harm. Medieval easements might include such things as the right to collect wood in a forest or fish in a marsh.

emotional regime: The conventions of how particular emotions are expressed in a given society. While human beings probably experience the same emotions whenever and wherever they live, different experiences trigger those emotions in different societies and people learn to express them differently. Thus men in the Middle Ages were free to weep publicly, while modern men in western cultures tend to refrain from it, although men in all cultures feel sorrow, pain, and pity.

exchequer: The English governmental financial office, where tax monies were collected and accounted for.

exemplum (**pl.** *exempla*): Moral stories, often found in collections intended to be used by preachers in their sermons. Saints' lives would be possible sources for these kinds of stories, but folk tales might be included if appropriate as well.

fabliau (**pl.** *fabliaux*): Short comic stories, often violent, produced in France from the thirteenth century onward.

figura: A way of reading the Bible in which texts from Jewish scripture were seen as foreshadowing the contents of Christian scripture. To give one example, the story of Abraham taking Isaac to the mountain to sacrifice him on God's command was taken by Christians to foreshadow God's sacrifice of Jesus.

filiation: The connection between mother and daughter-houses in the **Cistercian** order. Every male Cistercian house was assigned to a filiation (a kind of lineage) leading back to Cîteaux through one of the four great daughter-houses (Clairvaux, La Ferté, Morimund, or Pontigny).

formulary: A collection of models for producing documents of particular kinds. There were formularies for letter writing (such as a letter from a student to a parent asking for money), for **charters** of different types, or for poems one might drop into a **mortuary roll**.

Franciscans: The order founded by St. Francis in 1210 to preach repentance and moral reform. The Franciscans were wandering preachers, initially laymen as well as priests, and Francis envisioned an order that owned no property at all. Later, however, the order came to be dominated by priests and to have established houses. With the **Dominicans**, the Franciscans came to be known as the "friars" (brothers).

genre: A literary term referring to the type of writing a particular text belongs to. When a work shares characteristics with other works, it is said to share **generic** features. Modern examples of this might be "mysteries" or "romance novels" or "thrillers."

hagiography: Biographical accounts of people believed to be saints. These accounts may cover only a portion of the saint's life or may narrate the whole life, including any miracles worked by the saint after his or her death (posthumous miracles). The adjective to describe these accounts is **hagiographic**. A person who writes a hagiography is a **hagiographer**.

hermit: A person living a theoretically solitary life isolated from the secular world. In practice, many hermits lived in informal communities and there were monastic orders of hermits as well, like the **Carthusians**.

historical context: The set of historical circumstances that produce particular historical events, ideas, actions, or texts. This concept is particularly important, because it counteracts simplistic ideas about historical causality. Since we don't live in the past and therefore don't share experiences with past people, historians have to reconstruct the worlds of past people. Therefore, they often speak of "weaving" context, because they have to bring so many strands of past experience together.

honor: A term meaning both a person's good reputation and the property held by a noble person.

horizon of expectations: A literary term coined by Hans Robert Jauss to describe the relationships among works in a literary **genre**. All works belonging to the genre together define what kinds of things might be expected of a work of that genre (the horizon of expectations) without ruling out innovations, which may gradually change what is expected within the genre.

internal evidence: Evidence within a piece of writing that indicates the date it was written. For instance, if Lodge is correct that the St. Thomas in the **litany** of the *Book of Conduct* is Thomas Becket, the litany could not have been written before Becket was **canonized**.

laity: See **lay people**.

lay brothers/sisters: Starting in the late eleventh century, many monastic orders had lesser **monks** and nuns called lay brothers or sisters. These were people of lower social status who did not bring property to the **monastery** when they entered. They did most of the manual labor of the monasteries and often carried out many of the interactions with the world outside the monasteries. They were often illiterate. **Cistercian** churches had a separate place for lay brothers during services. Not to be confused with **lay people**.

lay people: Men and women who hold no ecclesiastical orders. Lay people may also be referred to as the **laity**. Not to be confused with **lay brothers** and **sisters**.

litany: A prayer naming God and a series of saints and imploring each in turn to pray for the one(s) praying.

liturgy: A set form of worship and prayer for a particular religious purpose. That might be the form of a general mass, for instance, or particular forms for particular occasions, such as a specific mass in honor of a saint or for the dead (a requiem mass) or a set of prayers and readings for a saint's day.

monastery: An institution where **monks** or nuns live following a monastic rule. Monasteries for women are usually called **convents** in English. Because many monasteries were (and are) governed by abbots or abbesses, they are sometimes also called **abbeys**. Monasteries that are not independent of a mother house might be ruled by priors or prioresses; if so, they are called **priories**.

monastic order: The group of monasteries at least nominally following the same rule. In some cases (such as the **Benedictines**), each of the monasteries was independent of the others, although all followed some version of the *Rule of St. Benedict*. Other orders, such as the **Cistercians**, had centralized direction.

monks: One type of **regular clergy**.

mortuary roll: A document created when an important person died. A brief account of the dead person was written, and messengers would take it to various churches requesting prayers for the dead. At these churches, local clergy would add an inscription to the roll and often request prayers in return. Additional pieces of parchment would be glued at the end of the roll for additional inscriptions. Most of the rolls that have survived are for **clergy**.

motivated reasoning: A process of reasoning which is powerfully shaped by the views the thinker holds. While not irrational, it tends to support prior beliefs and to explain away inconvenient facts. People find it very difficult to break away from views they've held strongly, even when there is considerable evidence against those views.

narrative sources: Sources written to tell a story. Historical narratives and **hagiographies** would both be examples of such sources. While narrative sources were often written to serve a perceived need, they were generally not created to record information that had a specific purpose.

obituary: A list of people connected with a religious institution, for whom the **clergy** would pray on a regular basis, usually on the anniversary of the person's death. Members of the institution would be automatically added, while others might be added because they were respected or because they had made a donation to the institution to secure these prayers or because they came from institutions with which the first institution was in a **community of prayers**. An obituary is also an individual death notice.

Order of Savigny: After Vitalis's death in 1122, a number of **monasteries** were founded in England and France that followed the rule of Savigny, while a few other existing houses took Savigny as their mother house. The order came to an end when Savigny joined the **Cistercian order** around 1147, over the objections of many of the daughter-houses.

ordinary gloss: A gloss was a commentary on a text, usually provided in the margins of the text. Many important texts had what was called an "ordinary" gloss, that is, a set of comments that were typically read alongside that text when students were studying it.

papal legates: Men commissioned by the pope to carry out particular tasks on the pope's behalf. Their authority overrode that of local **clergy**, because they brought with them the delegated authority of the papacy.

Peace of God: This movement, which began in the tenth century, attempted to limit violence to recognized combatants, protecting women, **clergy**, and merchants from attack. Church authorities were central to the movement, although rulers and nobles often worked with them or endorsed their regulations. The **Truce of God** designated Thursday, Friday, Saturday, and Sunday as military time-outs, when unauthorized violence was not to take place. In neither case was the purpose to limit the "authorized" use of violence by rulers; the target was "private warfare."

perspective taking: Figuring out how a particular event, idea, or practice was seen by participants and contemporaries. While this is sometimes referred to as empathy, many scholars prefer the term "perspective taking," because it is not easily confused with "having sympathy for" and because the term "perspective taking" makes it clearer that this is an intellectual, not an emotional, process. Historians sometimes take the perspectives of repugnant actors, with whom they have no sympathy whatsoever.

positionality: The way in which an author or reader has been shaped by belonging to a particular culture and having certain experiences, and so certain understandings of how the world works, what is important, and what things mean. This refers to modern authors as well as medieval ones, and to readers as well as writers.

prebend: A regular salary given to a secular **canon** or a cathedral canon. See also **chapter, collegiate church**.

Premonstratensian order: An order of regular **canons**, founded by St. Norbert of Xanten.

primary source: A source contemporary to the time period under consideration. Primary sources may be **documentary sources,** created for contemporary purposes, not particularly to tell us anything. They may be **narrative sources,** stories about the past. They may also be material sources, objects or bodies surviving from the past or pictorial sources, images, or sculpture. Sometimes, however, the earliest source we have comes from a later period than the time we are considering. In that case, we may prefer to call them **ancient sources.**

priory: A **monastery** led by a prior or prioress.

reading against the grain: Reading to find out things that a specific author did not consciously intend or that a record was not created to report. For instance, a medieval budget that records how much money the young men of the household were given to gamble with was not intended to tell us about the place of gambling in medieval society, but it can allow us to draw conclusions about how gambling was viewed.

regular clergy: Men and women who have joined a religious order for clergy and vowed to follow its rule. See also **clergy.**

relic: An object connected with a saint. That might be a part of the saint's body, such as a tooth or finger, or a "contact relic," something which had been in contact with the saint, such as an item of clothing.

reliquary: A container made to hold a relic. Reliquaries might be boxes, as in the casket in Figure 3, or when the relic was a body part might be in the shape of that body part. Small relics might also be incorporated into jewelry to be worn to protect the wearer or into crosses to be carried in processions.

sacrament: The essential rituals of the western medieval Church. There were eventually seven sacraments (baptism, confirmation, marriage, clerical orders, the eucharist [taking communion], penance [confession and absolution], and anointing of the sick), but marriage became one of them only in the twelfth century.

secular clergy: Men who have taken clerical vows but not joined a religious order. See also **clergy.**

seneschal: In France, the chief agent of a particular lord or the king in a given county or region.

social capital: The qualities or traits that allow a member of a group or network to gain benefits, such as positions or advancement, by creating relationships and a sense of mutual interest. (This term comes from the social sciences.)

sourcing heuristic: A heuristic is a rule of thumb, a set of procedures that falls short of being a set of requirements. Sourcing is the term historians use to refer to the questions they ask that establish where, when, why, how, and by whom a **primary source** was created. This comes so automatically to professional historians that they often don't even realize they are doing it.

terms of art: Words used within a field or discipline that have precise meanings but may not be common language terms or may be common terms used differently within that discipline. For example, historians speak of **primary sources** to mean sources from the time period being studied, while in common language the word "primary" may mean "most important" or "main" or "first."

tithes: Annual taxes on what was essentially income (grain grown or animals born), which in theory went to a church. In practice, many **lay people** collected tithes and kept them. This was a practice that church officials were attempting to rub out in the twelfth century. In most cases, people who gave up their tithes gave them to **monasteries**.

titulus (**pl.** *tituli*): An entry into a **mortuary roll** made by one of the churches visited by the clerics collecting prayers. See the example from the mortuary roll of Vitalis from Grestain that appears in this book (Figure 1).

toponym: The identification of an individual by the place he or she came from or was strongly associated with, as in Vitalis of Savigny or Stephen of Fougères.

translation: The moving of the body of a saint from one place to another. This often produced a second day upon which the saint might be celebrated, the day of his or her death and the day when he or she was moved to a new resting place.

transubstantiation: The doctrine that when a priest blesses the communion wine and bread they become the actual flesh and blood of Christ, even though they continue to look like bread and wine. This became doctrine in the eleventh century.

Truce of God: See **Peace of God**.

vernacular: The term used to describe the local languages people spoke, such as English or French, as opposed to Latin.

worked example: A case or problem that is given to illustrate a process, where the demonstrator makes explicit reference to the thinking and steps used to solve the problem.

BIBLIOGRAPHY

✠

Primary sources

Anselm of Canterbury. *Basic Writings*. 2nd edition. Translated by S.N. Deane. La Salle, IL: Open Court, 1962.

Atto. *S. Joanis Gualberti vita* [*The Life of St. John Gualbert*]. PL 146: 667–706.

Benedict, St. *Sancti Benedicti regula monasteriorum* [*The Rule of St. Benedict*]. Edited by Benno Linderbauer. Bonn: Peter Hanstein, 1928.

Bernard of Angers. *The Book of Sainte Foy*. Translated by Pamela Sheingorn. Philadelphia: University of Pennsylvania Press, 1995.

Bernard of Clairvaux. *In Praise of the New Knighthood*. Translated by M. Conrad Greenia. Trappist, KY: Cistercian Publications, 2000.

Bernard of La Chaise-Dieu. *The Tripartite Life of Robert, Abbot of Chaise-Dieu*. In *The Lives of the Monastic Reformers, 1: Robert of La Chaise-Dieu and Stephen of Obazine*, translated by Hugh Feiss, Maureen M. O'Brien, and Ronald Pepin. Collegeville, MN: Cistercian Publications, 2010.

Carta Caritatis [*Charter of Love*]. In "Order of Cistercians of the Strict Observance." https://www.ocso.org/wp-content/uploads/2016/05/EN-Carta-Caritatis.pdf.

Cartulaire de Saint-Melaine de Rennes suivi de 51 chartes originales. Rennes: Presses Universitaires de Rennes et Société d'Histoire et d'Archéologie de Bretagne, 2015.

Chrétien de Troyes. *Erec and Enide*. In *Arthurian Romances*, translated by Carleton W. Carroll, 37–122. Harmondsworth: Penguin, 1991.

Chronique de Saint-Maixent. Edited and translated by Jean Verdon. Paris: "Les Belles Lettres," 1979.

Delisle, Léopold. *Recueil des actes de Henri II, roi d'Angleterre et de Normandie concernant les provinces françaises et les affaires de France*. 3 vols. Edited by Élie Berger. Paris: Imprimerie Nationale, 1916–1927.

———. *Rouleau mortuaire du B. Vital, abbé de Savigni*. Paris: Berthaud Frères (photographs); Renouard (text), 1909.

———. *Rouleaux de morts du XIe au XVe siècles*. Paris: Renouard, 1866.

De s. Guilielmi Firmati, Moritonii in Normannia. In *AASS April III*, 334–41.

Dufour, Jean, and Favier, Jean. *Recueil des rouleaux des morts (VIIIe siècle–vers 1536)*, vol. 1 (VIIIe siècle–1180). Paris: Bocard, 2005.

Etienne de Fougères. See Stephen of Fougères.

Galbert of Bruges. *The Murder, Betrayal, and Slaughter of the Glorious Charles, Count of Flanders*. Translated by Jeff Rider. New Haven, CT: Yale University Press, 2013.

Geoffrey Grossus. *The Life of Blessed Bernard of Tiron*. Translated by Ruth Harwood Cline. Washington, DC: Catholic University of America Press, 2005.

Gregory of Tours. *De miraculis santi Martini episcopi* [*Miracles of the bishop St. Martin*]. In PL 71: 913–1008.

———. *Life of the Fathers*. Translated by Edward James. Liverpool: Liverpool University Press, 1986.

Gregory the Great. *The Book of Pastoral Rule*. Translated by George E. Demacopoulos. Crestwood, NY: St. Vladimir's Seminary Press, 2007.

———. *Dialogues*. Translated by Odo John Zimmerman. New York: The Fathers of the Church, 1959.

———. *Morales sur Job, Livres xxx–xxxii*. Edited by Marc Adriaen and translated by the nuns of Wisques. Paris: Cerf, 2009.

Guibert of Nogent. Monodies *and* On the Relics of Saints*: The Autobiography and a Manifesto of a French Monk from the Time of the Crusades*. Translated by Joseph McAlhany and Jay Rubenstein. New York: Penguin, 2011.

Jacques de Vitry and Thomas of Cantimpré. *Two Lives of Marie of Oignies*. Translated by Margot H. King and Hugh Feiss. Toronto: Peregrina Publishing, 1993.

Jean de Joinville. *The Life of St. Louis*. In *Chronicles of the Crusades*, translated by M.R.B. Shaw, 161–353. Harmondsworth: Penguin, 1963.

Jocelyn of Brakelond. *Chronicle of the Abbey of Bury St. Edmunds*. Translated by Diana Greenway and Jane Sayers. Oxford: Oxford University Press, 1989.

Lambert of Ardres. *History of the Counts of Guines and Lords of Ardres*. Translated by Leah Shopkow. Philadelphia: University of Pennsylvania Press, 2001.

Leclercq, Jean. "L'Exhortation de Guillaume Firmat." In *Analecta monastica*, 2nd series, 28–44. Rome: Herder, 1953.

The Lives of the Monastic Reformers, 2: Abbot Vitalis of Savigny, Abbot Godfrey of Savigny, Peter of Avranches, Blessed Hamo. Translated by Hugh Feiss, Maureen M. O'Brien, and Ronald Pepin. Collegeville, MN: Liturgical Press for Cistercian Publications, 2014.

Map, Walter. *De nugis curialium: Courtiers' Trifles*. Edited and translated by M.R. James, revised by C.N.L. Brooke and R.A.B. Mynors. Oxford: Clarendon, 1983.

Marbode of Rennes. *Epistola IV*. PL 171: 1474–5.

The Nibelungenlied. Translated by A.T. Hatto. Harmondsworth: Penguin, 1969.

Notker Balbulus [Notker the Stammerer]. *The Deeds of Charlemagne*. In *Two Lives of Charlemagne*, translated by David Ganz, 47–116. Harmondsworth: Penguin, 2008.

Orderic Vitalis. *The Ecclesiastical History of Orderic Vitalis*. 6 vols. Edited and translated by Marjorie Chibnall. Oxford: Clarendon, 1969–80.

Patrologia cursus completus, Series latina. 221 vols in 222. Edited by J.-P. Migne. Paris, 1844–1904.

Peter Tudebode. *Historia de Hierosolymitano itinere*. Translated by John Hugh Hill and Laurita L. Hill. Philadelphia: The American Philosophical Society, 1974.

Pigeon, Émile-Aubert. "Vie de Saint Firmat, patron de Mortain." *Mémoirs de la Société Académique du Cotentin* 13 (1897): 57–80.

——. "Vie de Saint Firmat, patron de Mortain (suite)." *Mémoirs de la Société Académique du Cotentin* 14 (1898): 32–59.

Raoul de Cambrai. Translated by Jessie Crosland. London: Chatto and Windus, 1926.

Robert of Torigni. *Le chronique de Robert de Torigni, abbé de Mont Saint-Michel.* 2 vols. Edited by Léopold Delisle. Rouen: A. Le Brument, 1872–3.

"The Saint Alban's Psalter." Project directed by Jane Geddes. University of Aberdeen. https://www.abdn.ac.uk/stalbanspsalter/.

Sauvage, Hippolyte, ed. *Vitae BB. Vitalis et Gaufridi primi et secundi abbatum Saviniacensium in Normannia. Analecta Bollandiana* 1 (1882): 354–410.

Skeat, Walter, ed. *The Wars of Alexander.* London: Trübner, 1886.

Stephen of Fougères. *Le livre des manières.* Edited by R. Anthony Lodge. Geneva: Droz, 1979.

——. *Testament.* In *Mémoires pour servir á preuves á l'histoire écclesiastique et civil de Bretagne*, vol. 1, edited by Hyacinthe Morice, 672–3. Paris: Éditions du Palais Royal, 1974.

——. *Vita sancti Vitalis.* See Sauvage.

Suetonius. *The Twelve Caesars.* Translated by Robert Graves and revised by Michael Grant. Harmondsworth: Penguin, 1979.

Talbot, C.H. *The Life of Christina of Markyate.* Translation revised by Samuel Fanous and Henrietta Leyser. Oxford: Oxford University Press, 2010.

Thomas, Jacques T.E., ed. and trans. *Le Livre des manières.* Paris-Louvain: Peeters, 2013.

Venarde, Bruce L. *Robert of Arbrissel: A Medieval Religious Life.* Washington, DC: Catholic University of America Press, 2003.

Vita Chounradi episcopi Constantiensis [*The Life of Conrad, bishop of Constance*]. PL 170: 863–76.

Vita Norberti archepiscopi Magdebergensis [*The Life of Norbert, Archbishop of Magdeburg*]. In *Monumenta Germaniae historica, Scriptores* 12, 663–706. Edited by Georg Heinrich Pertz. Hannover: Hahn, 1856.

Vita sancti Firmati [The Life of St. Firmat]. Avranches, Bibliothèque municipale, Ms. 167, ff. 125r–130v.

William of Andres. *Chronicle of Andres.* Translated by Leah Shopkow. Washington, DC: Catholic University of America Press, 2017.

Secondary sources

Auerbach, Erich. *Scenes from the Drama of European Literature.* Minneapolis: Minnesota Archival Editions, 1984.

Auvray, Claude. *Histoire de la congrégation de Savigny.* 3 vols. Edited by Auguste Laveille. Rouen and Paris: A. Lestringant & A. Picard, 1896–8.

Barlow, Frank. "Becket, Thomas [St Thomas of Canterbury, Thomas of London]." *ODNB.* https://doi.org./10.1093/ref:odnb/27201.

Bartlett, Robert. *The Hanged Man: A Story of Miracle, Memory, and Colonialism in the Middle Ages.* Princeton, NJ: Princeton University Press, 2006.

——. *Why Can the Dead Do Such Great Things?: Saints and Worshippers from the Martyrs to the Reformation.* Princeton, NJ: Princeton University Press, 2013.

Bates, David. "Odo, Earl of Kent." *ODNB*. https://doi-org.proxyiub.uits.iu.edu/10.1093/ref :odnb/20543.

Bates, David, and Véronique Gazeau. "L'abbaye de Grestain et la famille d'Herluin de Conteville." *Annales de Normandie* 40, no. 1 (1990): 5–30.

Bayliss, Martha. *Parody in the Middle Ages: The Latin Tradition*. Ann Arbor: University of Michigan Press, 1996.

Bertaux, Jean-Jacques. "Contribution à l'étude de l'art roman en Normandie: L'architecture des églises paroissiales romanes de l'ancien doyenné de Creully." *Annales de Normandie* 16, no. 1 (1966): 3–32.

Bishop, T.A.M. "A Chancery Scribe: Stephen of Fougères." *Cambridge Historical Journal* 10, no. 1 (1950): 106–7.

———. Scriptores regis: *Facsimiles to Identify and Illustrate the Hands of Royal Scribes in Original Charters of Henry I, Stephen, and Henry II*. Oxford: Clarendon, 1961.

Bisson, Thomas N. *The Crisis of the Twelfth Century: Power, Lordship, and the Origins of European Government*. Princeton, NJ: Princeton University Press, 2009.

Blacker, Jean. "Wace." *ODNB*. https://doi.org/10.1093/ref:odnb/28365.

Broadhurst, Karen M. "Henry II of England and Eleanor of Aquitaine: Patrons of Literature in French?" *Viator* 27 (1996): 53–84.

———. "Map, Walter." *ODNB*. https://doi.org/10.1093/ref:odnb/18015.

Brown, Warren C. *Violence in Medieval Europe*. Harlow & New York: Longman, 2011.

Brundage, James A. "Domestic Violence in Classical Canon Law." In *Violence in Medieval Society*, edited by Richard W. Kaeuper, 183–95. Rochester, NY: Boydell, 2000.

———. *The Medieval Origins of the Legal Profession: Canonists, Civilians, and Courts*. Chicago: University of Chicago Press, 2008.

Buhot, Jacqueline. "L'Abbaye normande de Savigny: Chef d'ordre et fille de Cîteaux." *Moyen Age* 46 (1936): 1–19, 104–21, 178–90, 249–72.

Burkardt, Albrecht. *Les clients des saints: Maladie et quête du miracle à travers les procès de canonisation de la première moitié du XVIIe siècle en France*. Rome: École française de Rome, 2004.

Burkholder, Peter. "Connecting the Curricular Dots: Designing the World History Survey with Gen Ed in Mind." *133rd Annual Meeting of the American Historical Association*. Chicago, January 5, 2019.

Burton, Janet, and Julie Kerr. *The Cistercians in the Middle Ages*. Woodbridge: Boydell, 2011.

Butterfield, Herbert. *The Whig Interpretation of History*. London: G. Bell, 1931.

Carruthers, Mary. *The Book of Memory: A Study of Memory in Medieval Culture*. Cambridge: Cambridge University Press, 1990.

Carter, John Marshall. "'Fire and Brimstone' in Anglo-Norman Society: The Preaching Career of St. Vital of Mortain and Its Impact on the Abbey of Savigny." *American Benedictine Review* 34, no. 2 (June 1983): 166–87.

Cleaver, Laura. "The Monastic Library at Le Bec." In *A Companion to the Abbey of Le Bec in the Central Middle Ages (11th–13th Centuries)*, edited by Benjamin Pohl and Laura L. Gathagan, 171–205. Leiden: Brill, 2018.

Conyers, Patrick. "Changing Habits: The Norman Abbey of Savigny and Its Congregation, 1105–1175." PhD Dissertation. University of Iowa, 2001.

Crachiolo, Beth. "Seeing the Gendering of Violence: Female and Male Martyrs in the *South English Legendary*." In *A Great Effusion of Blood?: Interpreting Medieval Violence*, edited by Mark Meyerson and Daniel Thiery, 147–63. Toronto: University of Toronto Press, 2004.

Crouch, David. *The Birth of Nobility: Constructing Aristocracy in England and France 900– 1300*. Harlow, England: Pearson-Longman, 2005.

——. "Roger, earl of Hereford." *ODNB*. https://doi-org.proxyiub.uits.iu.edu/10.1093/ref: odnb/47203.

Davey, Graham C.L. "The 'Disgusting' Spider: The Role of Disease and Illness in the Perpetuation of Fear of Spiders." *Society and Animals* 1, no. 2 (1990): 17–25.

David, Charles Wendell. *Robert Curthose, Duke of Normandy*. Cambridge, MA: Harvard University Press, 1920.

Davis, O.L., Jr., Elizabeth Anne Yeager, and Stuart J. Foster, eds. *Historical Empathy and Perspective Taking in the Social Studies*. Lanham, MD: Rowman & Littlefield, 2001.

Delehaye, Hippolyte. *The Work of the Bollandists Through Three Centuries, 1615–1915*. Princeton, NJ: Princeton University Press, 1922.

Donohue, Charles. "The Dating of Alexander the Third's Marriage Decretals: Dauvillier Revisited after Fifty Years." *Zeitschrift der Savigny-Stiftung für Rechtsgeschichte: Kanonistische Abteilung* 68 (1982): 70–124.

Duffin, Jacalyn. "The Doctor Was Surprised; or How to Diagnose a Miracle." *Bulletin of the History of Medicine* 81, no. 4 (Winter 2007): 699–729.

Duggan, A.J. "Ridel, Geoffrey." *ODNB*. https://doi-org./10.1093/ref:odnb/23618.

Elias, Norbert. *The Civilizing Process: Sociogenetic and Psychogenetic Investigations*. Revised edition. Translated by Edmund Jephcott, with revisions by the author. Oxford: Blackwell, 2000.

Evans, Gillian R. "Berengar, Roscelin, and Peter Damian." In *The Medieval Theologians*, edited by Gillian R. Evans, 85–93. Oxford: Blackwells, 2000.

Everard, Judith. *Brittany and the Angevins: Province and Empire, 1158–1203*. Cambridge: Cambridge University Press, 2000.

Eyler, Joshua R., ed. *Disability in the Middle Ages: Reconsiderations and Reverberations*. Abingdon: Routledge, 2010.

Eyton, Robert William. *Court, Household, and Itinerary of Henry II*. London: Taylor and Co., 1878.

Finn, Thomas M. "Sex and Marriage in the *Sentences* of Peter Lombard." *Theological Studies* 72 (2011): 41–69.

Gajano, Sofia Boesch. "The Use and Abuse of Miracles in Early Medieval Culture." In *Debating the Middle Ages: Issues and Readings*, edited by Lester K. Little and Barbara H. Rosenwein, 330–9. Oxford: Blackwell, 1998.

Galbraith, V.H. "Seven Charters of Henry II at Lincoln Cathedral." *The Antiquaries Journal* 12 (1932): 269–78.

Gallia christiana, in provincias ecclesiasticas distributa. 16 vols. 2nd ed. Paris: V. Palme, 1739–1880.

Geary, Patrick. *Furta sacra: Thefts of Relics in the Middle Ages*. Revised edition. Princeton, NJ: Princeton University Press, 1990.

Godding, Robert. "L'Oeuvre hagiographique d'Héribert Rosweyde." In *De Rosweyde aux Acta Sanctorum: La recherche hagiographique des Bollandistes à travers quatre siècles*, edited by Robert Godding, Bernard Joassart, Xavier Lequeux, and François de Vriendt, 35–62. Brussels: Society of Bollandists, 2009.

Golding, Brian. "The Religious Patronage of Robert and William of Mortain." In *Belief and Culture in the Middle Ages: Studies Presented to Henry Mayr-Harting*, edited by Richard Gameson, 211–30. Oxford: Oxford University Press, 2001.

———. "Robert, count of Mortain." *ODNB*. http://www.oxforddnb.com/view/article/19339.

Golinelli, Paolo. "*Sicut alter Alexis*: The Saint Alexis Model in Medieval Hagiography." In *Church and Belief in the Middle Ages: Popes, Saints, and Crusaders*, edited by Kirsi Salonen and Sari Katajala-Peltomaa, 141–52. Amsterdam: Amsterdam University Press, 2016.

Grant, Lindy. "Savigny and Its Saints." In *Perspectives for an Architecture of Solitude: Essays on Cistercians, Art and Architecture in Honour of Peter Fergusson*, edited by Terry N. Kinder, 109–14. Turnhout: Brepols, 2004.

Gravdal, Kathryn. *Ravishing Maidens: Writing Rape in Medieval French Literature and Law*. Philadelphia: University of Pennsylvania Press, 1991.

Hanska, Jussi. "The Hanging of William Cragh: The Anatomy of a Miracle." *Journal of Medieval History* 27 (2001): 121–38.

Hård af Segerstad, Kerstin. *Quelques commentaires sur la plus ancienne chanson d'états française, Le Livre des manières d'Étienne de Fougères*. Upsala, Sweden: Edv. Berling, 1906.

Jager, Eric. *The Last Duel: A True Story of Trial by Combat in Medieval France*. New York: Broadway Books, 2005.

Jauss, Hans Robert. *Towards an Aesthetic of Reception*. Translated by Timothy Bahti. Minneapolis: University of Minnesota Press, 1982.

Jeater, Diana. "'Theory' as the Practice of Asking Questions: Moving Second Year History Undergraduates from Knowledge Acquisition to Knowledge Construction in a UK University." In *Teaching History, Learning History, Promoting History: Papers from the Bielefeld Conference on Teaching History in Higher Education*, edited by Friedrike Neumann and Leah Shopkow, 77–93. Frankfurt: Wochenschau, 2018.

Justice, Steven. "Did the Middle Ages Believe in Their Miracles?" *Representations* 103, no. 1 (Summer 2008): 1–29.

Kaeuper, Richard W. *Chivalry and Violence in Medieval Europe*. Oxford: Oxford University Press, 1999.

———. *Medieval Chivalry*. Cambridge: Cambridge University Press, 2016.

Karn, Nicholas. "Nigel, Bishop of Ely, and the Restoration of the Chancery after the 'Anarchy' of Stephen's Reign." *Historical Research* 80, no. 209 (2007): 299–314.

Keefe, Thomas K. "William, earl of Surrey." *ODNB*. http://www.oxforddnb.com/view/article/46707.

Kelly, Henry Ansgar. "'Rule of Thumb' and the Folklaw of the Husband's Stick." *Journal of Legal Education* 44, no. 3 (1994): 341–65.

Kestnbaum, Ellyn. *Culture on Ice: Figure Skating & Cultural Meaning*. Middletown, CT: Wesleyan University Press, 2003.

Kieckhefer, Richard. "The Specific Rationality of Medieval Magic." *American Historical Review* 99, no. 3 (1994): 813–36.

Kleinburg, Aviad. *Prophets in Their Own Country: Living Saints and the Making of Sainthood in the Later Middle Ages*. Revised edition. Chicago: University of Chicago Press, 1997.

Knowles, David. *Great Historical Enterprises: Problems in Monastic History*. London and New York: Nelson, 1963.

Koziol, Geoffrey. "Monks, Feuds, and the Making of Peace in Eleventh-Century Flanders." *Historical Reflections/Réflexions historiques* 14, no. 3 (Fall 1987): 531–49.

Krötzl, Christian. "Miracula post mortem: On Function, Content, and Typological Changes." In *Miracles in Medieval Canonization*, edited by Sari Katajala-Peltomaa and Christian Krötzl, 157–75. Turnhout: Brepols, 2018.

Lambert, Tom. *Law and Order in Anglo-Saxon England*. Oxford: Clarendon, 2017.

Lawrence, C.H. *Medieval Monasticism*. 3rd ed. Harlow, England: Longman, 2001.

Leach, Jessica. "A Network of Holy Women: Early Thirteenth-Century Women in the Low Countries." PhD Dissertation. Indiana University, 2017.

Le Goff, Jacques. *In Search of Sacred Time: Jacobus de Voragine and* The Golden Legend. Translated by Lydia G. Cochrane. Princeton, NJ: Princeton University Press, 2014.

Little, Lester. *Religious Poverty and the Profit Economy in Medieval Europe*. Ithaca, NY: Cornell University Press, 1978.

Lodge, Anthony. "The Literary Interest of the 'Livre des manières' of Étienne de Fougères." *Romania* 93 (1972): 479–97.

Luscombe, David. "Salisbury, John of." *ODNB*. https://doi.org/10.1093/ref:odnb/14849.

Makdisi, George. "The Scholastic Method in Medieval Education: An Inquiry into Its Origins in Law and Theology." *Speculum* 49, no. 4 (1974): 640–71.

Martindale, Jane. "Eleanor [Eleanor of Aquitaine], suo jure duchess of Aquitaine (c. 1122–1204), queen of France, consort of Louis VII, and queen of England, consort of Henry II." *ODNB*. https://doi.org/10.1093/ref:odnb/8618.

Mattke, Christiane. "Verges et disciplines dans l'iconographie de l'enseignement." *Médiévales* 27 (Autumn 1994): 107–20.

Menuge, Noël James. "The Foundation Myth: Some Yorkshire Monasteries and the Landscape Agenda." *Landscapes* 1 (2000): 22–37.

Merck Manual of Diagnosis and Therapy. 17th ed. Whitehouse Station, NJ: Merck Research Laboratories, 1999.

Metzler, Irina. *Disability in Medieval Europe: Thinking about Physical Impairment in the High Middle Ages, c.1100–c.1400*. Abingdon: Routledge, 2006.

———. *A Social History of Disability in the Middle Ages: Cultural Considerations of Physical Impairment*. Abingdon: Routledge, 2013.

Mitchell, Piers D. "Retrospective Diagnosis and the Use of Historical Texts for Investigating Disease in the Past." *International Journal of Paleopathology* 1, no. 2 (2011): 81–8.

Moolenbroek, Jaap van. *Vital l'ermite, prédicateur itinérant, fondateur de l'abbaye normande de Savigny*. Translated by Anne-Marie Nambot. Assen/Maastricht, Netherlands: Van Gorcum, 1990.

Morin, D.G. "Un traité inédit de S. Guillaume Firmat sur l'amour du cloître et les saintes lectures." *Revue bénédictine* 31 (1914–19): 244–7.

Muessig, Carolyn. "Signs of Salvation: The Evolution of Stigmatic Spirituality before Francis of Assisi." *Church History* 82, no. 1 (March 2013): 40–68.

Musson, Anthony. "Crossing Boundaries: Attitudes to Rape in Late Medieval England." In *Boundaries of the Law: Geography, Gender and Jurisdiction in Medieval and Early Modern Europe*, 84–101. Aldershot: Ashgate, 2005.

Orbis latinus: Lexikon lateinischer geographischer Namen des Mittelalters und der Neuzeit. 3 vols. Braunschweig, Germany: Klinkhardt & Biermann, 1972.

Partner, Nancy F. *Serious Entertainments: The Writing of History in Twelfth-Century England*. Chicago: University of Chicago Press, 1977.

Peterson, Janine Larmon. *Suspect Saints and Holy Heretics: Disputed Sanctity and Communal Identity in Late Medieval Italy*. Ithaca, NY: Cornell University Press, 2019.

Pigeon, Hippolyte. "Étienne de Fougères et les Cisterciens." *Cîteaux: Commentarii cistercienses* 31 (1980): 181–91.

Pocquet du Haut-Jussé, B.-A. "Étienne de Fougères." In *Dictionnaire d'histoire et géographie écclesiastique*, vol. 15, edited by R. Aubert and É. van Cauwenbergh, 1224–6. Paris: Letouzey et Ané, 1963.

Poulle, Béatrice. "Les sources de l'histoire de l'abbaye cistercienne de Savigny au diocèse d'Avranches." *Revue Mabillon* 68 (1996): 105–25.

Raison, Abbé, and R. Niderst. "Le mouvement érémitique dans l'ouest de la France à la fin du XIe siècle et au début du XIIe siècle." *Annales de Bretagne* 55, no. 1 (1948): 1–46.

Ray, Roger. "Bede's *Vera lex historiae*." *Speculum* 55, no. 1 (1980): 1–21.

Reddy, William M. *The Navigation of Feeling: A Framework for the History of Emotions*. Cambridge: Cambridge University Press, 2001.

Rees, W.J., and J.R. Lumby. "The Abundance of Octopus in the English Channel." *Journal of the Marine Biology Association in the United Kingdom* 33 (1954): 515–36.

Richter, Michael. "Kommunikationsprobleme im lateinischen Mittelalter." *Historische Zeitschrift* 222, no. 1 (February 1976): 43–80.

Roguet, Yves. "La violence comique des fabliaux." In *La violence dans le monde médiéval*, *Senefiance* 36 (1994): 457–68.

Rose, E.M. *The Murder of William of Norwich: The Origins of the Blood Libel in Medieval Europe*. Oxford: Oxford University Press, 2015.

Rubin, Miri. *Corpus Christi: The Eucharist in Late Medieval Culture*. Cambridge: Cambridge University Press, 1991.

Russell, Jean Fogo. "Tarantism." *Medical History* 23 (1979): 404–25.

Sadler, Gregory B. "*Non modo verbis sed et verberibus*: Saint Anselm on Punishment, Coercion, and Violence." *Cistercian Studies Quarterly* 45, no. 1 (2010): 35–61.

Sheehan, Michael. *Marriage, Family, and Law in Medieval Europe: Collected Studies*. Toronto: University of Toronto Press, 1996.

Sinclair, Keith V. "L'inspiration liturgique du *Livre des manières* d'Etienne de Fougères." *Cahiers de civilisation médiévale* 40, no. 159 (July–September 1997): 261–6.

Skoda, Hannah. "Violent Discipline or Disciplining Violence? Experience and Reception of Domestic Violence in Late Thirteenth- and Early Fourteenth-Century Paris and Picardy." *Cultural and Social History* 6, no. 1 (2009): 9–27.

Southern, R.W. "Blois, Peter of." *ODNB*. https://doi-org/10.1093/ref:odnb/22012.

Stacey, Robert C. "From Ritual Crucifixion to Host Desecration: Jews and the Body of Christ." *Jewish History* 12, no. 1 (Spring 1998): 11–28.

Stark, Rodney. "Religious Competition and Roman Piety." *Interdisciplinary Journal of Research on Religion* 2 (2006): 2–30.

Swietek, Francis R. "King Henry II and Savigny." *Cîteaux: Commentarii cistercienses* 38, nos. 1–2 (1987): 14–23.

Takacs, David. "Positionality, Epistemology, and Social Justice in the Classroom." *Social Justice* 29, no. 4 (2002): 168–81.

Tanner, Heather. *Families, Friends, and Allies: Boulogne and Politics in Northern France and England, c. 879–1160*. Leiden: Brill, 2003.

van Engen, John. "The 'Crisis of Cenobitism' Reconsidered: Benedictine Monasticism in the Years 1050–1150." *Speculum* 61, no. 2 (1986): 268–304.

VanSledright, Bruce. "On the Importance of Historical Positionality to Thinking about and Teaching History." *International Journal of Social Education* 12, no. 2 (Fall/Winter 1997–8): 1–18.

Vauchez, André. *Sainthood in the Later Middle Ages*. Translated by Jean Birrell. Cambridge: Cambridge University Press, 1998.

Vincent, Nicholas. "The Court of Henry II." In *Henry II: New Interpretations*, edited by Christopher Harper-Bill and Nicholas Vincent, 278–334. Woodbridge: Boydell & Brewer, 2007.

Walker, Lorna E.M. "Hamo of Savigny and His Companions: Failed Saints?" *Journal of Medieval History* 30 (2004): 45–60.

Ward, Benedicta. *Miracles and the Medieval Mind: Theory, Record, and Event*. Philadelphia: University of Pennsylvania Press, 1982.

Ward, John O. "Ordericus Vitalis as Historian in the Europe of the Early Twelfth-Century Renaissance." *Parergon* 31, no. 1 (2014): 1–26.

Warr, Cordelia. "Visualizing Stigmata: Stigmatic Saints and Crises of Representation in Late Medieval and Early Modern Italy." *Studies in Church History* 47 (2011): 228–47.

Westhoff, Laura M. "Historiographic Mapping: Toward a Signature Pedagogy for the Methods Course." *Journal of American History* 98, no. 4 (March 2012): 1114–26.

Weston, Jenny. "Manuscripts and Book Production at Le Bec." In *A Companion to the Abbey of Le Bec in the Central Middle Ages (11th–13th Centuries)*, edited by Benjamin Pohl and Laura L. Gathagan, 144–70. Leiden: Brill, 2017.

Whetter, K.S. *Understanding Genre and Medieval Romance*. Aldershot: Ashgate, 2008.

White, Stephen D. *Custom, Kinship, and Gifts to Saints: The* laudatio parentum *in Western France, 1050–1150*. Chapel Hill: University of North Carolina Press, 1988.

———. "The Politics of Anger." In *Anger's Past: The Social Uses of an Emotion in the Middle Ages*, edited by Barbara H. Rosenwein, 127–52. Ithaca, NY: Cornell University Press, 1998.

Wineburg, Sam. *Historical Thinking and Other Unnatural Acts: Charting the Future of Teaching the Past*. Philadelphia: Temple University Press, 2001.

Wormald, Patrick. *The Making of English Law: King Alfred to the Twelfth Century*, vol. 1. Oxford: Blackwell, 1999.

INDEX

✠

Page numbers in *italic* refer to figures and maps. Numbers in **boldface** reference glossary definitions. This index does not cover the translated texts.